# THE SPURIOUS TEXTS
## OF
# PHILO OF ALEXANDRIA

# ARBEITEN ZUR LITERATUR UND GESCHICHTE DES HELLENISTISCHEN JUDENTUMS

HERAUSGEGEBEN VON

K.H. RENGSTORF

IN VERBINDUNG MIT
R.G. HAMERTON-KELLY, I. IRMSCHER, B. NOACK, OPPENHEIMER
H.M. ORLINSKY, H. RIESENFELD, J.R. ROYSE, H. SCHRECKENBERG,
A. WIKGREN, A.S. VAN DER WOUDE

## XXII

JAMES R. ROYSE

# THE SPURIOUS TEXTS OF PHILO OF ALEXANDRIA

# THE SPURIOUS TEXTS
# OF
# PHILO OF ALEXANDRIA

A STUDY OF
TEXTUAL TRANSMISSION AND CORRUPTION
WITH INDEXES TO
THE MAJOR COLLECTIONS OF GREEK FRAGMENTS

BY

JAMES R. ROYSE

J. BRILL
LEIDEN • NEW YORK • KØBENHAVN • KÖLN
1991

ISSN   0169-7390
ISBN   90 04 09511 X

*TO MY MOTHER*

# CONTENTS

# PREFACE

The work presented here has arisen from my study of the Greek fragments of Philo, and in particular from the attempt to identify as far as possible their correct locations within the Philonic corpus. During the course of these investigations, however, the number of the spurious fragments has continually increased, and the complexities of their textual transmission, mistaken identification, and eventual correct identification, are so involved, that it seemed advisable to devote separate attention to the discrimination of genuine and spurious within the Philonic tradition. It is hoped that such a study will serve to remove once and for all a number of texts which have cluttered studies of Philo's thought. At the same time we will be able to place correctly many genuine fragments, and also to shed some light on the intricate and in many ways still obscure processes by which we have received our evidence of ancient texts. What has been done here for Philo could doubtless be done for many authors, although the problems surrounding the text of Philo are particularly complex owing to the variety of sources which must be evaluated in recovering what we can of his original words.

This research could hardly have been undertaken without the use of the extensive resources of the Institut de Recherche et d'Histoire des Textes, Paris. I would like to express my deep appreciation to M. Joseph Paramelle for his kind and knowledgeable assistance during several of my visits to Paris. The particular manuscripts which I have studied by means of microfilms furnished by the Institut will be noted in the body of the work. For access to a number of printed books cited herein I am indebted to the resources of the British Library (London) and of the Bodleian Library (Oxford). Citations from several manuscripts were verified at the Bodleian, the Bibliothèque Nationale (Paris), and the Vatican Library. I have also frequently used the collections of the Graduate Theological Union (Berkeley, California) and the University of California, Berkeley. I am grateful to the staffs of each of these institutions for their courteous assistance, and in particular to Mr. Bruce C. Barker-Benfield at the Bodleian. The initial stages of my research were carried out at the Institutum Judaicum Delitzschianum, Münster (Westf.), and I would like to thank those associated with the Institutum for their many courtesies and helpful suggestions during my visits there, especially Dr. Heinz Schreckenberg (Münster), Dr. Harry Evert Faber van der Meulen (Dordrecht), and Dr. Jacques-Noël M. A. Pérès (Paris), the last of whom also provided invaluable assistance to me while I was in Paris. I am also grateful for many discussions concerning Philo which I have had with Professor G. D.

Kilpatrick (Oxford).  Professor Earle Hilgert (Chicago) has kindly read this work, and has made a number of helpful corrections and suggestions.  And I wish to thank Professor Theodore L. Brunner (Irvine) for his guidance in the use of the resources of the Thesaurus Linguae Graecae.

My work on Philo was initially undertaken at the suggestion of Professor Karl Heinrich Rengstorf (Münster), who made available to me Ludwig Früchtel's unfinished manuscript on the Greek fragments of Philo, and who has given steadfast aid and encouragement during my studies.  He has also most recently read two earlier versions of this work, thereby saving me from a number of errors.  I regret that there have been continual delays in the publishing of the results of these studies, delays which are entirely my responsibility, and which have occurred despite Professor Rengstorf's patient facilitation of my work in so many ways.  I hope that the present work will be a small tribute to the intellectual horizons opened to me by him, and to the many personal kindnesses which I have received from him.

James R. Royse

San Francisco State University
San Francisco, California
January 1990

# SIGLA

Abbreviations are, in general, taken from *Studia Philonica* 1 (1972): 92–96. The titles of Philo's works are cited as:

*Op, Leg All* 1–3, *Cher, Sacr, Quod Det, Post, Gig, Quod Deus, Agr, Plant, Ebr, Sobr, Conf, Migr, Heres, Congr, Fuga, Mut, Somn* 1–2, *Abr, Jos, Vita Mos* 1–2, *Dec, Spec Leg* 1–4, *Virt, Praem, Quod Omn, Vita Cont, Aet, Flacc, Gaium, Hyp (Apol), Quaes Gen* 1–4, *Quaes Ex* 1–2, *Provid, Anim, De Deo.*

The abbreviations used here for journals, series, and reference works are:

| | |
|---|---|
| *Aeg* | *Aegyptus.* |
| *BASP* | *Bulletin of the American Society of Papyrologists.* |
| *ByzZ* | *Byzantinische Zeitschrift.* |
| *CE* | *Chronique d'Égypte.* |
| *DBS* | *Dictionnaire de la Bible. Supplément.* Paris: Letouzey et Ané, 1928–. |
| *DSpir* | *Dictionnaire de Spiritualité.* Paris: Beauchesne, 1932–. |
| Fr. sp. | Fragmentum spurium (in chapter 4 below). |
| GCS | Die Griechischen Christlichen Schriftsteller. |
| *GRBS* | *Greek, Roman, and Byzantine Studies.* |
| *He* | *Hermes.* |
| *HTR* | *Harvard Theological Review.* |
| *JAOS* | *Journal of the American Oriental Society.* |
| *JQR* | *Jewish Quarterly Review.* |
| *JSJ* | *Journal for the Study of Judaism.* |
| *KP* | *Der kleine Pauly: Lexikon der Antike.* 5 vols. Munich: Alfred Druckenmüller, 1964–75. |
| LCL | Loeb Classical Library. Cambridge: Harvard University Press; and London: Heinemann. |
| *MGWJ* | *Monatsschrift für Geschichte und Wissenschaft des Judentums.* |
| *MPG* | *Patrologiae cursus completus. Series Graeca.* Ed. J. P. Migne. 162 vols. Paris, 1857–1912. |

| | |
|---|---|
| *Mus* | *Le Muséon.* |
| OCP | *Orientalia Christiana Periodica.* |
| PCW | *Philonis Alexandrini opera quae supersunt.* Ed. Leopold Cohn, Paul Wendland, and (for vol. 6) Siegfried Reiter. 6 vols. Berlin: Georg Reimer, 1896–1915. Reprinted: Berlin: Walter de Gruyter, 1962. |
| *Phlgs* | *Philologus.* |
| *PhWoch* | *Philologische Wochenschrift.* |
| *PLCL* | *Philo.* LCL. 12 vols. 1929–62. |
| *PM* | *Les oeuvres de Philon d'Alexandrie.* Ed. Roger Arnaldez, Jean Pouilloux, and Claude Mondésert. Paris: Éditions du Cerf, 1961–. |
| *PW* | *Real-Encyclopädie der classischen Altertumswissenschaft.* Ed. A. F. von Pauly and Georg Wissowa. Stuttgart: J. B. Metzler, 1894–. |
| *RAC* | *Reallexikon für Antike und Christentum.* Ed. Theodor Klauser, et al. Stuttgart: Anton Hiersemann, 1950–. |
| *RB* | *Revue Biblique.* |
| *REA* | *Revue des Études arméniennes.* |
| *REG* | *Revue des Études grecques.* |
| *RhMus* | *Rheinisches Museum für Philologie.* |
| SC | Sources Chrétiennes. Paris: Éditions du Cerf. |
| *SP* | *Studia Philonica.* |
| TLG | Thesaurus Linguae Graecae (see chapter 4 below). |
| *TLZ* | *Theologische Literaturzeitung.* |
| TU | Texte und Untersuchungen zur Geschichte der altchristlichen Literatur. |
| *TWNT* | *Theologisches Wörterbuch zum Neuen Testament.* Ed. Gerhard Kittel and Gerhard Friedrich. 9 vols. Stuttgart: W. Kohlhammer, 1933–73. |
| *VC* | *Vigiliae Christianae.* |
| WUNT | Wissenschaftliche Untersuchungen zum Neuen Testament. Tübingen: J. C. B. Mohr. |
| *WS* | *Wiener Studien.* |
| *ZAW* | *Zeitschrift für die alttestamentliche Wissenschaft.* |

In transliterating Armenian I have adopted the system of Rüdiger Schmitt, "Die Erforschung des Klassisch-Armenischen seit Meillet (1936)," *Kratylos* 17 (1972): 7. However, for technical reasons I have used "j̄" in place of the "j" with a haček above it. The sequence of letters thus is:

a b g d e z ê ə t' ž i l x c k h j ł č m y n š o č' p j̄ r̄ s v t r c' w p' k' ô f

Also, I am unable to print several of these letters in italics; consequently, I have placed the transliterated Armenian within quotation marks where one might expect italics, i.e., in titles of books and in citations of isolated words.

For the method used in citing editions of the fragments, see the Appendix.

References to manuscripts cited have been verified by the following methods: Through microfilms provided by the Institut de Recherche et d'Histoire des Textes (Paris): Ber. 46, Coisl. 276, Escur. Ω. III. 9, Marc. 138, Mon. 429, Ottob. 79, Vat. 1553, Vat. 1611, Vindob. suppl. 178. Through examination of the manuscripts at the Bodleian Library: Barocc. 51, Barocc. 143, Clark. 11, Digb. 6. Through examination of the manuscripts at the Bibliothèque Nationale: Coisl. 276, Par. 923. Through examination of the manuscript at the Vatican Library: Vat. 1553.

Also, references to manuscripts generally give the folio (and the column if needed), then in parentheses the line(s) of the lemma, and finally the line(s) of the text cited.

In general, the guidelines in *The Chicago Manual of Style* (13th edition, revised and expanded; Chicago and London: The University of Chicago Press, 1982) have been followed.

Finally, I should note that this volume was printed from camera-ready copy produced by use of the **Nota Bene** word-processing program.

1

# INTRODUCTION

The works of Philo of Alexandria have been a rich source of material for Christian thought, and it is within the Christian tradition that his words have been preserved.[1] In fact, the Christian utilization of Philo was so extensive that it was inconceivable to some that Philo had not actually become a Christian; and so we find stories of Philo's conversion to Christianity,[2] and occasional references in manuscripts to "the Bishop Philo."[3]

The importance which was accorded to Philo is evident from the considerable number of his works which have survived. These include the books preserved (more or less) intact in Greek, which were edited by Cohn, Wendland, and Reiter (in *PCW*). There are still others which are found in the ancient Armenian translation of Philo, dating from the late sixth century.[4]

---

[1]See Cohn, *PCW* 1:i–ii.

[2]See Emil Schürer, *Geschichte des jüdischen Volkes im Zeitalter Jesu Christi*, 4th ed., 3 vols. (Leipzig: J. C. Hinrichs, 1901–9), 3:636–37, and n. 8; idem, *The History of the Jewish People in the Age of Jesus Christ (175 B.C.— A.D. 135)*, a new English version, revised and edited by Geza Vermes, et al., 3 vols. (Edinburgh: T. & T. Clark, 1973–87), 3.2:816, and n. 17 (vol. 3, pt. 2, par. 34, pp. 809–89, "The Jewish Philosopher Philo," is by Jenny Morris). See further the study by J. Edgar Bruns, "Philo Christianus: The Debris of a Legend," *HTR* 66 (1973): 141–45. Both Bruns, 143, and Robert Devreesse, ed., *Les anciens commentateurs grecs de l'Octateuque et des Rois (fragments tirés des chaînes)* (Studi e testi, vol. 201; Vatican City: Biblioteca Apostolica Vaticana, 1959), vii, n. 2, refer to Anastasius Sinaita (*In Hexaemeron* 7 [*MPG* 89:961D7–11]), who says: Οἱ μὲν οὖν ἀρχαιότεροι τῶν ἐκκλησιῶν, λέγω δὴ Φίλων ὁ φιλόσοφος καὶ τῶν ἀποστόλων ὁμόχρονος κτλ. (Cohn also cites this text at *PCW* 1:cix.)

[3]See, e.g., the lemma Φίλωνος ἐπισκόπου found in two manuscripts for a fragment of *Quaes Gen* 1.55, as reported by Françoise Petit, ed., *Quaestiones in Genesim et in Exodum: Fragmenta Graeca* (*PM*, vol. 33; 1978), 54. See also note 50 below, and chapter 2, note 23, below.

[4]See Abraham Terian, ed. and trans., *Philonis Alexandrini de animalibus: The Armenian Text with an Introduction, Translation, and Commentary*

These include *Provid* and *Anim*, which were edited and translated into Latin by Aucher in 1822,[5] as well as *Quaes Gen*, *Quaes Ex*, and the fragment *De Deo*, which were edited and translated by Aucher in 1826.[6] Moreover, the Armenian translation of some of the works of Philo preserved in Greek[7] contains a brief fragment on the decad, which is now edited by Terian, who assigns it to Philo's lost Περὶ ἀριθμῶν.[8] There is also the less extensive ancient Latin version, which dates from the late fourth century. This includes a translation of the original book 6 of *Quaes Gen*,[9] which contains twelve sections not found in the Armenian.[10] However, it is clear that several works

---

(Studies in Hellenistic Judaism, Supplements to *SP*, vol. 1; Chico: Scholars Press, 1981), 6–9, who follows Sen Arevšatyan, "Platoni erkeri Hayeren t'arg-manowt'yan žamanakə" [On the Time of the Translation of Plato's Dialogues into Armenian], *Banber Matenadarani* 10 (1971): 7–20.

[5]Joannes Baptista Aucher, ed. and trans., *Philonis Judaei sermones tres hactenus inediti: I. et II. de providentia et III. de animalibus, ex Armena versione antiquissima ab ipso originali textu Graeco ad verbum stricte exequuta, nunc primum in Latium [sic] fideliter translati* (Venice: Typis coenobii PP. Armenorum in insula S. Lazari, 1822).

[6]Aucher, ed. and trans., *Philonis Judaei paralipomena Armena: libri videlicet quatuor [sic] in Genesin, libri duo in Exodum, sermo unus de Sampsone, alter de Jona, tertius de tribus angelis Abraamo apparentibus, opera hactenus inedita, ex Armena versione antiquissima ab ipso originali textu Graeco ad verbum stricte exequuta saeculo V. nunc primum in Latium [sic] fideliter translata* (Venice: Typis coenobii PP. Armenorum in insula S. Lazari, 1826). The *De Sampsone* and *De Jona* included in the latter edition are, of course, not by Philo (see chapter 5 below).

[7]See Terian, *Philonis Alexandrini de animalibus*, 3–4 (see 4 for the fragment on the decad).

[8]"A Philonic Fragment on the Decad," in *Nourished with Peace: Studies in Hellenistic Judaism in Memory of Samuel Sandmel*, ed. Frederick E. Greenspahn, Earle Hilgert, and Burton L. Mack (Chico: Scholars Press, 1984), 173–82. Incidentally, to Terian's references to Περὶ ἀριθμῶν (181–82) may be added (cf. Schürer, *History* 3.2:831, n. 55 [from p. 830]) the possible extracts in the Latin version: see note 10 below.

[9]See Petit, ed., *L'ancienne version latine des Questions sur la Genèse de Philon d'Alexandrie*, vol. 1: *Édition critique*, vol. 2: *Commentaire* (TU, vols. 113–14; Berlin: Akademie-Verlag, 1973). On the dating, see 1:8–13.

[10]These comment on Gen 26:19–35, and follow (the Armenian) *Quaes Gen* 4.195. (What earlier writers refer to as the eleven sections were seen by Petit to be twelve, since the old eighth section in fact consists of two sections;

of Philo have disappeared completely, and that others (including the *Quaestiones*) have lacunae of varying lengths.[11] Moreover, besides these direct sources, Philo is frequently cited in those medieval collections belonging to the two genres known as exegetical chains (or catenae) and florilegia, which had as their goal the preservation and ordering of valuable texts from the past.

Editors of Philo have drawn upon the printed editions—which are usually far from adequate—of these collections, and have also investigated the manuscripts themselves in the attempt to find new texts of Philo and to furnish new witnesses for previously known texts. Many, indeed the overwhelming majority, of the texts attributed to Philo in the chains and florilegia can be located within either his works preserved in Greek and edited in *PCW*,

---

see Petit, *L'ancienne version* 1:4, n. 2. Petit refers to these as 1\*–11\*, where 8\*\* is the former second part of the eighth, and in her *Quaestiones: Fragmenta Graeca*, 199–201, calls them IV.1\*–IV.11\*. I shall refer to these as *Quaes Gen* 4.195.1\*, etc.) These additional sections, along with some further sentences at the end of *Quaes Gen* 4.203 and 4.210, are edited and translated by Petit in Charles Mercier and Françoise Petit, eds. and trans., *Quaestiones et solutiones in Genesim III–IV–V–VI e versione Armeniaca, Complément de l'ancienne version latine* (*PM*, vol. 34B; 1984), 515–49. The Latin also contains some glosses, among which appear to be a few extracts from Philo's lost Περὶ ἀριθμῶν: glosses 5–7 to (the Latin version of) *Quaes Gen* 4.195.9\*. See ibid., 517 and 536–41, as well as Petit, *L'ancienne version* 1:71–72 (text), and 2:89–91 (commentary).

[11]See J. Rendel Harris, ed., *Fragments of Philo Judaeus* (Cambridge: University Press, 1886), 2–3; Schürer, *Geschichte* 3:686–87; idem, *History* 3.2:868. On the lacunae in the *Quaestiones* see my "The Original Structure of Philo's *Quaestiones*," *SP* 4 (1976–77): 41–78. The existence of lost works is further confirmed by the fact that the papyrus of Philonic books found at Oxyrhynchus contained at least one such work; see my "The Oxyrhynchus Papyrus of Philo," *BASP* 17 (1980): 155–65. As also noted there (161–62), Ludwig Früchtel, "Zum Oxyrhynchos-Papyrus des Philon (Ox.-Pap. XI 1356)," *PhWoch* 58 (1938): 1437–39, discovered that a fragment from the *Sacra parallela* edited by Hans Lewy ("Neue Philontexte in der Überarbeitung des Ambrosius, Mit einem Anhang: Neu gefundene griechische Philonfragmente," *Sitzungsberichte der Preussischen Akademie der Wissenschaften*, Philosophisch-historische Klasse [1932]: 82–83, no. 27) could be located in this papyrus.

or his works preserved in Armenian,[12] or, to a lesser extent, his works as they survive in Latin.[13]

Nevertheless, a considerable number of "Philo fragments" remain after such identifications have been made, and editors from Mangey on have devoted much effort to expanding and refining the set of such fragments.[14] Indeed, some texts which have been printed as "fragments" find their correct place in his Greek works, and their identification is now usually a straight-forward task thanks to Günter Mayer's *Index Philoneus*.[15] Once in a while, though, there may be some doubt concerning such localizations. Consider, as one example of potential problems, the brief text found in one manuscript of the *Sacra parallela*, Coislinianus 276, f. 160ᵛ (10–11) 11–12. This citation has the lemma: Φίλωνος ἐκ τοῦ περὶ μέθης β΄ λόγου, and reads: λόγου θείου ἡσυχία θάνατός ἐστιν ψυχῶν. Mangey referred this to *Conf* 37, where we read λόγου δὲ θάνατός ἐστιν ἡσυχία.[16] While the similarity is evident, it is

---

[12]The following gives a brief indication of the Greek fragments which have been located in the Armenian. *Quaes Gen* and *Quaes Ex*: see Petit, *Quaestiones: Fragmenta Graeca*; Joseph Paramelle, with the collaboration of Enzo Lucchesi, eds. and trans., *Philon d'Alexandrie, Questions sur la Genèse II 1–7* (Cahiers d'Orientalisme, vol. 3; Geneva: Patrick Cramer, 1984); and my "Further Greek Fragments of Philo's *Quaestiones*," in *Nourished with Peace*, ed. Greenspahn, Hilgert, and Mack, 143–53, to which some supplementary information may be found below in the Appendix on Petit's edition. *Provid*: see the extracts by Eusebius in Karl Mras, ed., *Eusebius Werke*, vol. 8: *Praeparatio Evangelica*, 2 pts. (GCS, vol. 43, pts. 1–2; Berlin: Akademie-Verlag, 1954–56); Harris, *Fragments*, 75–76; and Mireille Hadas-Lebel, ed. and trans., *De providentia I et II* (PM, vol. 35; 1973), 355–56. *Anim*: see Harris, *Fragments*, 11; and Terian, *Philonis Alexandrini de animalibus*, 263.

[13]Harris (*Fragments*, 42–43) located three Greek fragments within the twelve additional sections (see Petit, *Quaestiones: Fragmenta Graeca*, 199–201 [*Quaes Gen* 4.195.7*, 4.195.8*, 4.195.9*]).

[14]In general on these collections see Schürer, *Geschichte* 3:637–43; *History* 3.2:819–25. Many of these editions and sources will be discussed as we proceed.

[15]Berlin and New York: Walter de Gruyter, 1974.

[16]Thomas Mangey, ed. and trans., Φίλωνος τοῦ Ἰουδαίου τὰ εὑρισκόμενα ἅπαντα, *Philonis Judaei opera quae reperiri potuerunt omnia*, 2 vols. (London: William Bowyer, 1742), 1:410, n. z, says: "Nescio annon huc alludit Johannes ineditus tit. περὶ διδασκαλίας, ἐκ τοῦ περὶ μέθης β΄ λόγου· λόγου θεοῦ ἡσυχία, θάνατός ἐστι τῶν ψυχῶν. Ubi, ni fallor, redundat θεοῦ." Mangey's reference would seem to indicate another manuscript of

not exact, and Wendland said of Mangey's identification: "hoc an recte fecerit dubito."[17] Now, it seems to me very likely that the text in fact comes from *Ebr* 71, where we find λόγου γὰρ ἡσυχία θάνατος. This identification is supported by the lemma,[18] and we can suppose that the additions to Philo's words were made in order to clarify the meaning of the text. Such clarifications are often found in the excerpts, and are natural enough when a passage is lifted from its context.[19] However, in a brief extract such additions or modifications may, as in the case just examined, make its correct localization doubtful. The case just examined is extreme, since to the three words taken from *Ebr* 71 are added three other words, although the order is the same.[20] However, there are some other cases of considerable change. Consider, for example, *Heres* 21 where the Greek phrase οἱ σοφοὶ πάντες φίλοι θεοῦ becomes πᾶς σοφὸς θεοῦ φίλος.[21] Similarly, the phrase τὴν ἐξ ἔθους ἀργίαν καὶ σχολήν, πρᾶγμα ἐπίβουλον at *Flacc* 41 is transformed into ἡ ἐξ ἔθους καὶ σχολῆς ἀργία πρᾶγμα ἐπίβουλον.[22]

---

the *Sacra parallela*, Codex Rupefucaldinus (see chapter 3, note 8, below), which *PCW* cites as D^R. However, this brief citation does not occur in Codex Rupefucaldinus (cf. Wendland, *PCW* 2:xxvii, n. 1: "frustra autem in D^R hoc fragmentum quaesivi"), but is found in Coisl. 276, which Mangey confused with Codex Rupefucaldinus (see chapter 3, note 9, below). So I assume that Mangey's source here was Coisl. 276, despite the slight variation in lemma and text.

[17]*PCW* 2:xxvii, n. 1.

[18]Note, by the way, that the lemma ascribes this text to the *second* book περὶ μέθης. Thus, we have a further confirmation that our existing book was the second one, and that the first one is lost; see my "Oxyrhynchus Papyrus," 160–61, and the references in Schürer, *Geschichte* 3:655, *History* 3.2:836–37.

[19]Henry Chadwick, "Florilegium," trans. Josef Engemann, in *RAC* 7 (1969): 1132, comments: "Für Zitate in F. ist es charakteristisch, daß ihr Text unsicher ist u. die Zuschreibung an bestimmte Autoren schwankt. Die Ausdeutung führt natürlicherweise zu leichten Textänderungen." Reiter's discussion (*PCW* 6:xl–xlvi) of the texts from *Flacc* and *Gaium* found in the *Sacra parallela* is, I believe, the best treatment (for Philo at any rate) of the sorts of changes to which these excerpts are subject.

[20]Perhaps there was also some influence from a text of Basil, θεοῦ ἄγνοια θάνατός ἐστι ψυχῆς, cited from time to time in the florilegia (e.g., *MPG* 136:780B13).

[21]The Greek extract (Mangey 652.8; Harris 99.2) was located in *PCW*.

[22]The extract is found at *MPG* 136:1128C6–7 (Antonius), and is cited in *PCW* in the apparatus to *Mut* 170, but is not quoted at *Flacc* 41.

We find another difficult example in an unidentified fragment attributed to the *Quaestiones*, which begins: περιέχει τὰ πάντα, ὑπ᾽ οὐδενὸς περιεχόμενος. ὡς γὰρ ὁ τόπος κτλ.[23] In all the manuscripts this entire text is found as one undivided fragment, and has several parallels in Philo's writings.[24] Now in fact the first phrase (περιέχει — περιεχόμενος) is so close to *Sobr* 63 (περιέχει γὰρ τὰ πάντα πρὸς μηδενὸς περιεχόμενος) that Früchtel (in his manuscript which is discussed below) thought that this was the true source of the phrase, and included only the remainder of the text as a Philo fragment. But I believe that this action was too hasty. *Sobr* 63 differs slightly from the fragment's reading, and the manuscripts certainly provide no justification for a division[25] nor for the assignment to *Sobr*. Moreover, since Philo often uses similar phrases, it is likely that this entire text is simply one more such passage, and that accordingly it should be retained as a whole.

Our final example of difficulties is provided by the following text: οὐ θέμις τὰ ἱερὰ μυστήρια ἐκλαλεῖν ἀμυήτοις. This occurs as an isolated fragment,[26] and also as the first portion of a wider text,[27] which was assigned to *Quaes Gen* 4.8 by Bréhier,[28] and subsequently printed as a fragment of that section by Marcus.[29] Petit, though, correctly points out that only the latter part of the text actually corresponds to *Quaes Gen* 4.8, and prints the remainder, beginning with the line quoted above in brackets, as an unidentified fragment of *Quaes Gen*.[30] Moreover, Petit notes that this line is close to *Provid*

---

[23]This is Mangey 655.6 and Harris 73.5, and is most recently printed by Petit, *Quaestiones: Fragmenta Graeca*, 281, QE no. 1.

[24]Petit, ibid., refers to *Fuga* 75; *Sobr* 63; *Conf* 136; *Migr* 182, 192; and *Somn* 1.62–64; see also Folker Siegert, ed. and trans., *Philon von Alexandrien, Über die Gottesbezeichnung "wohltätig verzehrendes Feuer" ("De Deo"): Rückübersetzung des Fragments aus dem Armenischen, deutsche Übersetzung und Kommentar* (WUNT, vol. 46; 1988), 128, and n. 4.

[25]Naturally, the manuscripts can be in error on such a matter, but clearly their divisions between Philo texts are usually correct.

[26]Mangey 651.2.

[27]Mangey 658.4; Harris 69.4.

[28]Émile Bréhier, *Les idées philosophiques et religieuses de Philon d'Alexandrie* (Paris: Picard, 1908), vii, n. 2.

[29]Ralph Marcus, ed. and trans., *Philo, Supplement*, vol. 1: *Questions and Answers on Genesis*, vol. 2: *Questions and Answers on Exodus* (PLCL; 1953), 2:214.

[30]*Quaestiones: Fragmenta Graeca*, 147, n. b; 216, n. a. As Petit notes, the genuine fragment from *Quaes Gen* 4.8 in fact occurs as a separate text in Coisl. 276.

2.40,[31] and refers to Hadas-Lebel's edition where doubt is expressed whether this is really a fragment of that passage,[32] and the parallels at *Sacr* 60 and 62, *Cher* 48, *Fuga* 85, and *Quaes Gen* 4.8 are cited.

Now, it happens that Aucher had already printed this Greek text as a fragment of *Provid* 2.40. There his Latin translation of the Armenian reads "non licet apud illos, quorum capita minime sunt uncta, patefacere mysteria,"[33] while the Armenian itself reads "oč' ê aržan or oč' en iwłaglowxk', zxorhowrdn hanel 'i ver." And this phrase could, more or less reasonably, be seen as corresponding literally[34] to the Greek: οὐ θέμις ἀμυήτοις μυστήρια ἐκλαλεῖν.[35] Note, however, that at *Quaes Gen* 4.8 ἀμυήτοις is rendered by "anxorhrdic' ew anaržaneac'," a doublet which Aucher translates as "incon-

---

[31]Ibid., 147, n. b: "Il n'a pas été identifié mais on peut rapprocher sa première phrase de *Prov.* II.40." And at 216, n. a, she says that the words "correspondent d'assez près à *Prov.* II.40."

[32]Hadas-Lebel, *De providentia*, 270, n. 2: "Il n'est pas certain que le fragment relevé par Harris . . . corresponde à notre passage. Il n'est pas rare en effet de trouver sous la plume de Philon ce vocabulaire de l'initiation mystique . . . ."

[33]*Sermones tres*, 75. His note 2 on the word "uncta" reads:

Ut Mystici, mysteriorum ministri; vel teleturgi, initiati, etc. Verum ad praesentem locum potest referri illud, S. Jo. Damasceni dictum, quod notatur inter fragm. Philonis, Gr. Lat. Tom. II. p. 651 [i.e., Mangey 651.2], οὐ θέμις τὰ ἱερὰ μυστήρια ἐκλαλεῖν ἀμυήτοις.

[34]The chief sources of information concerning Armenian-Greek correspondences are Gabriêl Awetik'ean, Xač'atowr Siwrmêlean, and Mkrtič' Awgerean [Baptista Aucher], "Nor baṙgirk' Haykazean lezowi" [New Dictionary of the Armenian Language], 2 vols. (Venice: I tparani Srboyn Łazarow [Press of St. Lazarus], 1836–37), and Marcus, "An Armenian-Greek Index to Philo's *Quaestiones* and *De Vita Contemplativa*," *JAOS* 53 (1933): 251–82.

[35]For "oč'" = οὐ see "Nor baṙgirk'" 2:516A, and Marcus, "Index," 275. "Ê" is the copula. For "aržan" = θέμις see "Nor baṙgirk'" 1:355A, and Marcus, "Index," 257. "Or oč' en iwłaglowxk'" seems to correspond literally to τοῖς οὐκ ἀλειφομένοις, although "Nor baṙgirk'" 1:874B gives μεμυημένος, τετελεσμένος for "iwłaglowx." For "xorhowrd" = μυστήριον see "Nor baṙgirk'" 1:976B; Marcus, "Index," 266; and *Quaes Gen* 4.8 ("z" is the sign for the accusative, and "n" roughly corresponds to the definite article); the parallels, though, seem to indicate that the plural stood here in the Greek. For "hanel 'i ver" = ἐκλαλεῖν see *Quaes Gen* 4.8 and *Provid* 2.27.

sultis indignisque."[36] Thus, the Armenian does not have an equivalent of ἱερά, has the infinitive at the end, and may well not have an equivalent of ἀμυήτοις. While there is certainly some connection, it is not clear enough to justify viewing the Greek as an actual fragment of this text, especially since Philo makes similar points in similar words elsewhere. Nevertheless, it is also not clear that this is *not* a fragment of this passage, since the addition of ἱερά would be natural, as would the slight rearrangement of word order (in either the Greek excerpt or the Armenian version). Perhaps the reasonable position here is that the Greek *may* be a fragment of *Provid* 2.40.[37] Fortunately, most of the fragments with which we deal are more straightforward.

Other unidentified texts may yet be located by means of the Armenian version, although it is certain that most of these identifications have already been made.[38] And Philo's lost works may be the ultimate source of at least some of the fragments which remain, whose Philonic origin is occasionally confirmed by considerations of vocabulary, style, or thought. One may note, for example, that within the period from Homer to A.D. 600, apart from one occurrence in Aristotle,[39] only Philo uses μονωτικός:[40] the word occurs

---

[36]"Nor baṛgirkʻ" 1:162B cites ἀμύητος, ἄμυστος [*sic*] for "anxorhowrd."

[37]In his manuscript (discussed below) Früchtel included this Greek as a fragment of *Provid* 2.40. However, Früchtel could not examine the Armenian, and so was dependent entirely on Aucher's Latin. But there is another curious point. In his translation (from Aucher's Latin) of *Provid*, "Über die Vorsehung," in *Philon von Alexandria, Die Werke in deutscher Übersetzung*, vol. 7, ed. Willy Theiler (Berlin: Walter de Gruyter, 1964), 344, Früchtel does not make any comment on the passage discussed above. But on the final line of section 40, which he translates "denn es ist nicht gestattet, den Uneingeweihten die Geheimnisse zu verraten," he places a note (n. 3) which reads: "Der Schlußsatz ist in mehreren Catenen gr. erhalten." It is true that this final sentence is also a parallel to the Greek text, and contains the equivalent of μυστήρια (in the plural), as well as the same equivalent of ἐκλαλεῖν (again at the end). But in other respects it is even further removed from the Greek.

[38]On some of the problems involved in such identifications see my "Further Greek Fragments," 144–46.

[39]This passage was found through use of the TLG: Aristotle, *Politica* 2.6.1265ᵃ22: βίον πολιτικόν, μὴ μονωτικόν. Here the last two words are omitted in most manuscripts as well as in Bekker's edition, and preserved as above in two manuscripts only. Besides the occurrences in *PCW*, no other example of the word was in the TLG data bank (as of August 3, 1988).

[40]In fact, Liddell-Scott-Jones cites only Philo as using it, but Stephanus

seven times in *PCW*, and also in two unlocated fragments.[41] Note too that the juxtaposition of Num 23:19 and Deut 8:5 which occurs in one fragment[42] closely parallels similar comments in *Quod Deus* 53–54, *Somn* 1.237, and *Quaes Gen* 1.55. Thus, we have considerable confirmation that these three are genuine Philo fragments.

On the other hand, the evidence for Philonic authorship of many of the unidentified fragments rests mainly or even solely on the authority of lemmata in various manuscripts of the catenae and florilegia. Now, while these lemmata are generally correct, they are subject to loss, misplacement, and miscopying in the course of transmission,[43] and thus their attribution of a text to Philo may well be incorrect. And in fact quite a few of the fragments which have been printed under Philo's name can be identified with certainty as coming from other sources. It is with this aspect of Philo studies that the present work is chiefly concerned: the efforts which have gone into collecting the many texts which bear Philo's name must be balanced by an effort to remove from collections those texts which have no rightful claim to be by Philo, but have appeared within the literature on Philo because of the errors of medieval scribes or modern editors.

Indeed, various scholars have pointed out the spurious nature of particular fragments, but their identifications and discussions have appeared in scattered places, and seem not to be generally recognized within the literature on Philo. A more systematic effort to locate both genuine and spurious fragments of Philo was made by Ludwig Früchtel, who at his death in 1963 left a manuscript containing the results of his work on an updated collection (from previously printed sources) of the Greek fragments of Philo.[44] As one portion of his research Früchtel reported there his identifications of ten spurious texts (included in chapter 4 below), and also brought together the

---

informs us that it also occurs as a variant to μοναδικός in Aristotle, *Historia animalium* 1.1.488ª1.

[41]These are Harris 71.1 and 105.3.

[42]This is Harris 8.1.

[43]Wolfgang Speyer, *Die literarische Fälschung im heidnischen und christlichen Altertum: Ein Versuch ihrer Deutung* (Handbuch der Altertumswissenschaft, Erste Abteilung, Zweiter Teil; Munich: C. H. Beck, 1971), 41–42, comments under "Versehen der Abschreiber": "In Anthologien, Florilegien und Katenen sind sehr oft falsche Zuschreibungen durch Unachtsamkeit der Abschreiber entstanden." (See also his references at 42, n. 1.)

[44]This is entitled: "Philonis Alexandrini fragmenta Graece servata." See my comments on the Früchtel manuscript in "Original Structure," 65–66, n. 6.

identifications which had been made earlier by Harris and Wendland.[45] The present study continues Früchtel's line of inquiry, and provides as far as possible a general account of what has been discovered concerning those texts which have been spuriously assigned to Philo.

It will prove useful to examine the spurious fragments of Philo under two major headings corresponding to the sources of the texts which we have. First, there are the excerpts taken from Philo or assigned to Philo which appear in the chains on Genesis and Exodus or in the *Eclogae* of Procopius. As we shall see, these sources utilize over extensive areas only the *Quaestiones* among the works of Philo. This fact will enable us to discriminate confidently between genuine fragments from the *Quaestiones* and texts falsely attributed to Philo. A discussion of these sources and of various spurious texts found in them appears in chapter 2 below.

Secondly, there are the excerpts taken from Philo or assigned to Philo which are found in the florilegia, discussed in chapter 3 below, or within the catenae on books of the Bible other than Genesis and Exodus. The crucial point here is that these sources draw upon the entire range of Philo's works, including (as seems clear) some of those which have been lost completely. The sort of discrimination possible with the first type of material is thus impossible, since each Greek text found in these sources (whether attributed to Philo or not) could conceivably come from any work of Philo.[46] Hence, each text must be considered on its own merits, and a judgment made as to the likelihood of its being genuinely Philonic. As it happens, in quite a few cases it is certain that the text is not from Philo. In order to present these results perspicuously I have listed in chapter 4 below 61 separate "fragmenta spuria." These are all texts which have been printed or at least referred to[47] as

---

[45]In Früchtel's indexes he notes Harris's identifications of Fr. sp. 28 and 41 (but he ignores 20 and 27), as well as Wendland's identification of Fr. sp. 30. He refers to our Fr. sp. 40 as simply "Clem. Al. fr. spur. 72." See also chapter 3, notes 61–63, below.

[46]Of course, some such texts would be assigned to Philo only with great implausibility. If we found, for example, an excerpt from a later writer's work or a text with clearly Christian ideas, we would be reluctant to cite it as Philonic. Nevertheless, it is always possible that the later writer was simply quoting Philo at that point or that Philo in fact converted to Christianity. See, e.g., Mangey's comment on Fr. sp. 26, as cited below, his references for Fr. sp. 30 and 52, the reference of Combefis for Fr. sp. 51, and compare the remarks by Lequien on Fr. sp. 30.

[47]The only case where the text has not been printed as Philonic elsewhere or here is Fr. sp. 44, where 39 texts are collectively cited.

Philonic within the literature on Philo,[48] and which come from either the florilegia or the catenae on Biblical texts not covered by the *Quaestiones*.

Further, apart from errors of lemmata, there is also the possibility that a fragment attributed to "Philo" in fact derives from another of the many Philos of antiquity, from some of whom rather extensive texts have survived.[49] The likely confusion would seem to be with Philo of Carpasia, and several authors have even thought that the expanded lemma Φίλωνος ἐπισκόπου was used to indicate that Philo.[50] But, as noted in chapter 2 below,

---

[48]I include here the editions which are indexed in the Appendix, namely, the editions of the Greek fragments of Philo as well as of the *Sacra parallela* and of the florilegia of Antonius and Maximus, and also Howard L. Goodhart and Erwin R. Goodenough, *A General Bibliography of Philo Judaeus*, in *The Politics of Philo Judaeus: Practice and Theory*, by Erwin R. Goodenough (New Haven: Yale University Press, 1938), 124–321, 329–48 (indexes).

[49]We find, for instance, 61 Philos cited in *Paulys Real-Encyclopädie der classischen Altertumswissenschaft*, and 15 Philos cited in *Der kleine Pauly*. As far as I can tell, only modern scholars have actually assigned texts from another Philo to Philo of Alexandria. Note, though, that already Eusebius felt the need to warn his readers against confusing Philo Byblius with Philo of Alexandria (*Praep. ev.* 1.9.20 [Mras, *Eusebius* 1:39, ll. 12–13]): Φίλων δὲ τούτου πᾶσαν τὴν γραφὴν ὁ Βύβλιος, οὐχ ὁ Ἑβραῖος, μεταβαλὼν κτλ. In this connection, it may be interesting to note that a grave bearing the name Φίλων and from the Ptolemaic period (thus too early to be our author) has been discovered near Alexandria; see Jean-Baptiste Frey, ed., *Corpus Inscriptionum Iudaicarum*, vol. 2: *Asie–Afrique* (Vatican City: Pontificio Istituto di Archeologia Cristiana, 1952), 358, no. 1428 (the name Ἰώσηπ[ος] also is found: 357–58, no. 1427). On this ancient cemetery cf. Tassos Demetrios Néroutsos-Bey, *L'ancienne Alexandrie* (Paris: Ernest Leroux, 1884), 80–84; P. M. Fraser, *Ptolemaic Alexandria*, 3 vols. (Oxford, 1972), 1:57, and n. 165 (at 2:141); Schürer, *Geschichte* 3:41–42; and idem, *History* 3.1:47. Moreover, "Philo" is one of the Greek names which were especially common among Jews; see Victor A. Tcherikover, Alexander Fuks, and (for vol. 3) Menahem Stern, eds., (and vol. 3) with an epigraphical contribution by David M. Lewis, *Corpus papyrorum Judaicarum*, 3 vols. (Cambridge: Harvard University Press for the Magnes Press, Hebrew University, 1957–64), 1:xix; see also the indexes in these volumes for several Jewish Philos. (By the way, Lewis there, 3:139, re-edits the grave inscription cited above.)

[50]Mangey, *Philonis opera* 1:i: "Fuit etiam Philo alius Carpathius, saeculo post Dominum Nostrum quarto; cujus Fragmenta quaedam etiamnum extant in Catenis ineditis, quique vulgo appellatur, Ὁ ἐπίσκοπος, ut distin-

this lemma is regularly used for Philo of Alexandria.[51]  On the other hand, our Fr. sp. 44 actually consists of 39 texts from Philo of Carpasia (where the lemma is simply Φίλωνος) which Goodhart and Goodenough attributed to Philo of Alexandria.[52]  There is one further reported confusion of our Philo with Philo Mechanicus.[53]

---

guatur ab Hebraeo." Similarly, Ioannes Albertus Fabricius and Gottlieb Christophorus Harles, *Bibliotheca Graeca*, 12 vols. (Hamburg: Carolus Ernestus Bohn, 1790–1809), 10:479, say in connection with Philo of Carpasia: "Citatur etiam Philo episcopus aliquoties in Catena patrum ad Pentateuchum." Cf. also Jean-Baptiste Pitra, ed., *Analecta sacra spicilegio Solesmensi parata*, vol. 2: *Patres antenicaeni* (Typis Tusculanis, 1884), 310, n., as well as note 3 above, and chapter 2, note 23, below.

[51]See chapter 2, pages 14–15 and note 4, below.

[52]A less drastic version of this confusion occurs in the index to Marcel Richard, *Opera minora*, ed. E. Dekkers, et al., 3 vols. (Turnhout: Brepols, Leuven University Press, 1976–77), "Table onomastique," 3:xxvii. There we find under "Philon d'Alexandrie," among references to that Philo, the citation of "**10 536**," which refers to (the reprint in vol. 1 of) Richard, "Hippolyte de Rome (saint)," *DSpir* 7.1 (1969): 536. There Richard writes of some fragments first assigned to Hippolytus's commentary on the Song of Songs, but restored "plus tard à Philon." Richard is, of course, referring to Philo of Carpasia.

[53]Roberto Radice, *Filone di Alessandria: Bibliografia generale 1937–1982* (Elenchos, vol. 8; Naples: Bibliopolis, 1983), 121 (no. 369), cites A. Dain, "Le codex Hauniensis NKS 182," *REG* 71 (1958): 61–86, and then comments:

> L'autore descrive il codice *hauniensis* contenente, fra l'altro, estratti della *Mechanica Syntaxis*, attribuita a F. Per quanto Marouzeau, [*L'Année Philologique*] XXIX (1959), p. 138, citi questo testo alla voce *Philo Alexandrinus*, noi riteniamo, invece, che qui si faccia riferimento a Filone di Bisanzio. (Cfr. voce *Philon*, 48, in RE, XX, 1, pp. 53 sgg.). Citiamo, dunque, questo testo solo per correggere l'errore di Marouzeau.

Indeed, Dain refers to extracts of Philo of Byzantium's *Mechanica syntaxis*, and J. Marouzeau and Juliette Ernst, *L'Année Philologique* 29 (1959): 138, cite this under Philo of Alexandria, instead of under Philo Mechanicus. Moreover, they there refer to the longer notice on p. 291 under "Paléographie: Varia," where we find simply "Philon." In fact, this longer notice is clearly based on the author's résumé (presumably provided by Dain) which is

Sometimes the incorrect attribution of texts to Philo has extended to entire books. The decision in these cases is usually made on the basis of manuscript attestation, early citations, style, and philosophical or theological content, and these issues are generally fully treated in the relevant literature. However, the examples known are listed in chapter 5 for the sake of completeness.[54]

Finally, dealing with the fragments of Philo (genuine, spurious, and doubtful) is made difficult by the variety of sources containing them, and by the lack of adequate indexing or cross-references.[55] Accordingly, I have provided in the Appendix an Index locorum, which lists the major sources of Philonic fragments, along with the identifications, as far as they are known, of the fragments they contain. The material provided there also serves as an index to the discussions in this work of the fragments printed in these earlier sources.

---

printed at the end of the volume containing Dain's article (*REG* 71 [1958]: 511 [unnumbered]), where we also find merely "Philon" as one of the authors represented in the manuscript.

[54]On the general topic of false attributions, the article by Charles B. Schmitt, "Pseudo-Aristotle in the Latin Middle Ages," in *Pseudo-Aristotle in the Middle Ages: The "Theology" and other Texts*, ed. Jill Kraye, W. F. Ryan, and C. B. Schmitt (Warburg Institute Surveys and Texts, ed. W. F. Ryan and C. B. Schmitt, vol. 11; London: The Warburg Institute, University of London, 1986), 3–14, is of interest. Speyer, *Die literarische Fälschung*, will be cited from time to time. However, note that, except for the forgery of Nanni (discussed in chapter 5 below), the Philonic spuria all seem to have arisen through carelessness or misunderstanding.

[55]In his manuscript Früchtel provided indexes to the fragments in Mangey and Harris, and I have found these of great value in my own work. During the preparation of this volume, there appeared the work of Eric Junod, "Les fragments grecs transmis et édités sous le nom de Philon," in Jean Allenbach, et al., eds., *Biblia patristica, Supplément: Philon d'Alexandrie* (Paris: Éditions du Centre National de la Recherche Scientifique, 1982), 9–15. Junod's work treats the fragments in Harris, Wendland, Lewy, and *PCW*, but in a manner rather different from that adopted here, although I have of course checked my work against his. As did Früchtel, Junod found the true locations of Fr. sp. 21 and 22, as well as of a few other texts which can be found in *PCW*; but most of Junod's identifications were already made in *PCW* or other publications.

# 2

# THE CATENAE

The exegetical catenae (or chains) on books of the Bible consist of running commentaries on the Scriptural text by means of excerpts from Christian writers as well as from Philo and Josephus.[1] These elucidating texts, found in many Biblical manuscripts, are placed either in the margins to the appropriate Biblical passages, or within the Scriptural text itself so that a Biblical passage is followed by one or more exegetical comments.[2] Sometimes the catena expands in importance so that the Biblical text is mostly omitted.[3]

The comments are frequently accompanied by lemmata (with the name of the author in the genitive case), which provide the initial basis of assigning authorship. For Philo the usual ones are: Φίλωνος, Φίλωνος ἑβραίου, and

---

[1]A chief source of manuscript information is Georg Karo and Johannes Lietzmann, "Catenarum Graecarum catalogus," *Nachrichten von der Königlichen Gesellschaft der Wissenschaften zu Göttingen*, Philologisch-historische Klasse (1902): 1–66, 299–350, 559–620. The still standard survey of the catenae is that of Devreesse, "Chaînes exégétiques grecques," *DBS* 1 (1928): 1084–1233. For Philo in particular see Petit, *L'ancienne version* 1:18–23; *Quaestiones: Fragmenta Graeca*, 16–18; and *Catenae Graecae in Genesim et in Exodum*, vol. 1: *Catena Sinaitica* (Corpus Christianorum, Series Graeca, vol. 2; Turnhout: Brepols, Leuven University Press, 1977), xiii–xxxviii; as well as Devreesse, *Les anciens commentateurs*, 1–21. Also, there are remarks by Wendland, *PCW* 2:xv–xviii; Cohn, *PCW* 4:xxii–xxiv; Schürer, *Geschichte* 3:642, n. 31 (–643); and idem, *History* 3.2:825, n. 41. Goodhart and Goodenough, *Bibliography*, 157–64, and 166–71, supply some useful information, which must, however, be used with caution.

[2]Devreesse, "Chaînes," 1089–90.

[3]This is the case, for instance, with Londiniensis bibliothecae Britannicae Burneianus 34, a manuscript of inferior value used extensively by Harris. On the various forms in which texts with commentaries may appear, see Gerhardt Powitz, "Textus cum commento," *Codices manuscripti* 5 (1979): 80–89.

Φίλωνος ἐπισκόπου.[4] However, such lemmata are sometimes missing and, even when present, may well be incorrect. Indeed, they are subject to various types of errors within the transmission of the catenae. They can be misread and miscopied, especially when they are abbreviated. They can be misplaced, thus attaching themselves to an earlier or later text. They can be omitted, through oversight or because they were to be added later by a rubricator. And when they are lost there is the tendency for texts to coalesce, since the later text may simply be taken as a continuation of the previous text. In this way, several texts may come together under the name of the author of the first.[5]

Consequently, the presence of a lemma ascribing a text to Philo is no guarantee that we have there a text actually from Philo, and a genuine Philo text may appear anonymously or under someone else's name.[6] The lemmata do, of course, provide some evidence for ascription, and are often enough demonstrably correct that in the absence of other evidence one would certainly follow them. Happily, though, there is often other evidence, and it is to such further considerations that we now turn.

Philo's *Quaestiones*, being arranged in the sequence of the Biblical text, could readily be utilized by a compiler of a catena on Genesis and Exodus, and we in fact find in such catenae many texts which are ascribed to Philo and which correspond closely to the ancient Armenian version of the *Quaestiones*. In other cases texts which are either anonymous or assigned to other writers may be seen by comparison with the Armenian to be really from Philo.[7] Of course, there is often some difference between the Greek excerpt

---

[4]See Petit, *L'ancienne version* 1:20; *Quaestiones: Fragmenta Graeca*, 16; and *Catena Sinaitica*, xv; Devreesse, *Les anciens commentateurs*, 2.

[5]See Devreesse, "Chaînes," 1090–91, and 1097, speaking of early researchers: "Ce qui les a trompés, c'est de s'être fiés, sans plus du contrôle, aux lemmes de tous les manuscrits qui leur tombaient sous la main; . . . ." Some good examples (though not involving Philo) of problems with lemmata are cited by Michael Faulhaber, "Katenen und Katenenforschung," *ByzZ* 18 (1909): 391, and idem, *Hohelied-, Proverbien- und Prediger-Catenen* (Theologische Studien der Leo-Gesellschaft, vol. 4; Vienna: Mayer, 1902), 131–32. Cf. also the comment by Harris concerning the lemmata in the florilegia, cited in chapter 3, note 34, below.

[6]The need for care in dealing with the lemmata in catenae is well expressed by Albert Ehrhard in Karl Krumbacher, *Geschichte der byzantinischen Litteratur*, 2d ed. (Munich: C. H. Beck, 1897), 207.

[7]See, e.g., *Quaes Gen* 3.26 (Petit, *Quaestiones: Fragmenta Graeca*, 136–37); *Quaes Gen* 3.29 (ibid., 137–39); and *Quaes Gen* 4.203 (ibid., 206).

and the Armenian version, and this is only to be expected. The Greek may have been altered somewhat when the excerpt was made, or may have suffered within the textual transmission of the catenae.[8] Similarly, the Armenian translators may have misunderstood the Greek, or their version may have been corrupted during its transmission. And naturally the original Greek text of Philo may already have suffered some alteration by the time that Philonic manuscripts were used by the compilers of the catenae or the Armenian translators. Nevertheless, the agreement between the Philonic excerpts in the catenae and the Armenian version is usually quite close and often virtually perfect.[9]

Now, examination of the excerpts found in the chains on Genesis and Exodus leads to the finding that the compilers of these chains used only the *Quaestiones* and *Vita Mos* 1 from the Philonic corpus, and the limits of their use can be given precisely.[10] The chains on Genesis quote only from *Quaes Gen* among the works of Philo, beginning with *Quaes Gen* 1.55 on Gen 3:22 and ending with *Quaes Gen* 4.228 on Gen 27:35.[11] No other known citation

---

[8]The textual history of the catenae is itself very complex, and the manuscripts vary considerably in value; see the remarks by Petit, *Quaestiones: Fragmenta Graeca*, 17–18, as well as the more detailed information in her *Catena Sinaitica*, xxi–xxxvii. Unfortunately, earlier editors often used the manuscripts of lesser weight.

[9]See the remarks by Devreesse, *Les anciens commentateurs*, viii, on the general faithfulness of the excerpts in the catenae:

> Pour apprécier leur valeur, nous n'avons qu'une pierre de touche, mais elle est irrécusable: la concordance des extraits avec l'oeuvre de l'exégète d'où ils sont tirés,—quand cette oeuvre existe encore,—ou leur accord avec des citations indépendantes des caténistes. Or, il faut convenir que, depuis Philon jusqu'à Sévère, là où la confrontation est possible, elle se révèle exacte; nos collectionneurs retranchent, choisissent, mais ne trichent pas avec leurs sources. La raison en est simple: ils ne sont d'aucune école théologique et n'ont aucun souci de polémique; à Théodore de Mopsueste comme à Apollinaire, ils ont fait également bon accueil.

And on the characteristics of the Armenian version, see Terian, *Philonis Alexandrini de animalibus*, 9–14.

[10]Cf. Petit, *Quaestiones: Fragmenta Graeca*, 16, 18–19.

[11]See my "Original Structure," 53. As Petit notes (*Quaestiones: Fragmenta Graeca*, 42, n. a) there is an indirect citation of *Quaes Gen* 1.3 within a citation from Eusebius of Emesa.

from Philo occurs here, and the texts which are attributed to Philo in one manuscript or another but which cannot be referred to the Armenian text are often correctly assigned to some later Christian writer.

The chains on Exodus utilize *Vita Mos* 1 to a limited extent,[12] and also use one of the original books of *Quaes Ex* (perhaps the fourth), beginning with *Quaes Ex* 2.1 on Exod 20:25b and ending with *Quaes Ex* 2.49 on Exod 24:18.[13] Again, as far as we can tell, there is no use made by these chains of any other work of Philo.

Of course, it is conceivable that the chains quote texts from Philo which come from portions of his corpus now completely lost. But in the absence of any confirmation, such a view would be completely speculative. The evidence which we have indicates that the compilers of the chains on Genesis and Exodus used material from Philo's *Quaes Gen*, *Vita Mos* 1, and *Quaes Ex*, and nothing else.[14] And it is easily understandable why this should be so, since the compilers could thus simply follow along in these works of Philo as the chain proceeded.[15]

---

[12]Cohn (see *PCW* 4:xxii–xxiii) cites the catenae on Exodus for six passages from *Vita Mos* 1, but his sources are far from the best. (See his apparatus to *Vita Mos* 1.44–47, 93–94, 95, 96, 118, 140–42; and cf. Devreesse, *Les anciens commentateurs*, 21, n. 1.) Cohn also cites the catenae on Numbers for three passages from *Vita Mos* 2; see his apparatus to *Vita Mos* 2.218, 234–37, 238–42.

[13]See my "Original Structure," 56–57, 60–61; cf. Petit, *Quaestiones: Fragmenta Graeca*, 231, and 270, n. a.

[14]Cf. Petit, *Catena Sinaitica*, xv–xvii.

[15]It is not accidental that the *Quaestiones*, the books which were extensively used in the catenae, have been lost in Greek. Wendland, *Neu entdeckte Fragmente Philos: Nebst einer Untersuchung über die ursprüngliche Gestalt der Schrift De sacrificiis Abelis et Caini* (Berlin: Georg Reimer, 1891), 30, has the following perceptive remark:

> Es ist eine auf den ersten Blick befremdliche, aber wohl erklärliche Thatsache, dass gerade diese uns verlorenen Schriften in den Catenae fast ausschliesslich benutzt werden. Die Bibelkommentatoren, die die Aufgabe hatten, die Summe der vorangegangenen exegetischen Arbeit einem roheren Geschlechte zu vermitteln, konnten wohl mit wenig Mühe die für ihre Zwecke passenden Gedanken aus dem an den Faden des Bibeltextes angereihten Kommentare zusammenlesen; es fehlte ihnen aber die Belesenheit, und sie scheuten die Mühe, aus dem Zusammenhange der mehr sy-

Therefore, when we find a fragment in these chains with reference to Biblical passages where the Armenian version of the *Quaestiones* is extant, the agreement of the Greek with the Armenian is a reliable test of authenticity. If the fragment fits the Armenian, we can assign it to Philo and print it as a Greek fragment of the *Quaestiones*, whether it is assigned by a lemma to Philo, to someone else, or to no one. On the other hand, if the fragment has nothing to do with the Armenian, we can conclude (in the absence of other evidence) that the text does not come from Philo, even if a lemma somewhere or other does ascribe it to Philo.[16] A similar use can be made of the additional sections of the Latin version.

Using, then, this working hypothesis, we are able to discard several texts included by Harris or Wendland, and consequently by Marcus. These texts, which should really never have appeared among the fragments of Philo, are:

| | |
|---|---|
| *Quaes Gen* 1.77 | ἦν γνωσιμαχῶν Λάμεχ καθ' ἑαυτοῦ[17] |
| *Quaes Gen* 1.94 (a) | ἐκ τούτου — ἔκτισεν[18] |
| *Quaes Gen* 1.94 (b) | ὁ μὲν ἁπλούστερός φησι ὅτι κτλ.[19] |

---

stematisch angelegten Werke Philos auch zur Erläuterung anderer Stellen geeignete Citate beizubringen. Und nachdem nun das Brauchbare aus Philos Quaestiones in die Catenae übertragen war, konnte man sich der Mühe überhoben denken, dies Werk selbst zu lesen; man konnte es bei Seite werfen wie Clemens Alexandrinus' Ὑποτυπώσεις, Origenes' und Didymus' Kommentare.

Frederic C. Conybeare, in his review of Wendland's book, *The Academy* 40 (July–December 1891): 483, formulates this as:

no doubt, that Commentary [the *Quaestiones*] has been lost in the original Greek, just because, all the best bits of it having been copied into Catenae in the sixth and following centuries, it was not thought worth the while of scribes to continue to copy out so lengthy a work any more.

[16]Petit also utilizes this criterion on texts which have not been printed as Philo fragments, but are attributed to him in manuscripts; see *Catena Sinaitica*, 41–42 (G 35), 42–43 (G 36), 43 (G 37), and 178 (G 185).

[17]Mangey, 658.1b; Harris, *Fragments*, 17, already notes this as a gloss; Marcus, *Philo, Supplement* 2:190. See the apparatus in Petit, *Quaestiones: Fragmenta Graeca*, 72.

[18]Wendland, *Fragmente*, 47; Marcus, *Philo, Supplement* 2:191–92.

[19]Noted as a gloss by Harris, *Fragments*, 19.

| | |
|---|---|
| *Quaes Gen* 1.100 | δῆλον δὲ — ἡμάρτανου[20] |
| *Quaes Gen* 2.10 | ἰδοὺ τοῦτο — τούτοις[21] |
| *Quaes Gen* 2.15 | οὐκ ἐπειδὴ — προσαγορεύονται[22] |
| *Quaes Gen* 2.47 | ἐβδόμη — ἑορτάζειν[23] |
| *Quaes Gen* 2.64 | τόξον — ὑπερθήσομαι[24] |

---

[20]Noted as a gloss by Harris, ibid., 107.2, but edited by Wendland, *Fragmente*, 51–52. Cf. Petit, *Quaestiones: Fragmenta Graeca*, 81, n. c. Devreesse, *Les anciens commentateurs*, 17, prints this without comment.

[21]Noted as a gloss by Harris, *Fragments*, 107.3.

[22]Noted as a gloss by Harris, ibid., 21, and 106.3.

[23]Ibid., 106.4; Wendland, *Fragmente*, 49. Cf. Devreesse, *Les anciens commentateurs*, 18, n. 1; Petit, *Quaestiones: Fragmenta Graeca*, 104, n. b. Harris cites this from Burneianus 34 with the lemma Φίλωνος ἐπισκόπου, and adds (106):

> The passage need not be Philo Judaeus, and yet one becomes very sceptical as to the existence of another Philo, following closely on the lines of the former, and so often wrongly placed for him. Is it possible that Philo Episcopus is the name given to an expanded edition of the original writer, with perhaps a few Christian glosses?

It appears that there is no evidence which clearly supports this last suggestion; see Devreesse, "Chaînes," 1105; idem, *Les anciens commentateurs*, 2. However, Devreesse goes on (*Les anciens commentateurs*, 2 and n. 3) to note that some Christian supplements to Philonic excerpts may be explained by the reference to Φίλωνος ἐπισκόπου, and later (182, n. 1) even comments on Philo of Carpasia: "on serait tenté de l'identifier avec l' «évêque Philon» fréquemment nommé à côté ou à la place de son homonyme juif." Similarly, in his "Anciens commentateurs grecs de l'Octateuque," *RB* 45 (1936): 217, Devreesse says: "Il est fort possible qu'un bon nombre des fragments qu'on trouve dans les chaînes sous le lemme Φίλωνος ἐπισκόπου reviennent, en définitive, à l'évêque chypriote." See also chapter 1, notes 3 and 50, above.

[24]Harris, *Fragments*, 106.5, already suggests that this is not from Philo; cf. Devreesse, *Les anciens commentateurs*, 18, n. 2, and Petit, *Quaestiones: Fragmenta Graeca*, 117, n. c.

| *Quaes Gen* 2.71 | νεώτερον — Χάμ[25] |
| *Quaes Gen* 3.52 | οὐκ ἐπειδὴ — πληρουμένου[26] |
| *Quaes Gen* 4.195.7* | αὗται αἱ — μετῴκησαν[27] |
| *Quaes Gen* 4.195.8* | σωτηρίαν τὴν — ἔχοντες[28] |
| *Quaes Gen* 4.202 | ἐθάρρει μὲν — θεοῦ[29] |
| *Quaes Ex* 2.15 | διὰ τὸ — Λευιτῶν[30] |
| *Quaes Ex* 2.25 (a) | πρὸς τούτοις — ἐχθρῷ[31] |

---

[25]Harris, *Fragments*, 28, says that this "does not appear to be Philo."

[26]This "looks like an added gloss," according to Harris, ibid., 31. Cf. Mangey, 675.2b, Devreesse, *Les anciens commentateurs*, 19, and Petit, *Quaestiones: Fragmenta Graeca*, 145, n. e.

[27]Wendland, *Fragmente*, 86 ("Sicher erscheint mir der philonische Ursprung des Stückes nicht"). The text is printed from Parisinus 128 by Mangey, 676.1; and from Par. 128 (where the lemma is τοῦ αὐτοῦ [after *Quaes Gen* 4.195.7*]) and Barberinus 569 (no lemma) by Devreesse, *Les anciens commentateurs*, 20, n. 1. Cf. Petit, *L'ancienne version* 2:82, and *Quaestiones: Fragmenta Graeca*, 199, n. b, where she says that the fragment "ne répond à rien dans la version latine et n'est pas dans l'esprit de l'exégèse philonienne."

[28]Harris, *Fragments*, 42; Marcus, *Philo, Supplement* 2:272, n. c. Cf. Devreesse, *Les anciens commentateurs*, 20, and Petit, *L'ancienne version* 2:86, and *Quaestiones: Fragmenta Graeca*, 200, n. a.

[29]Mangey, 676.4b; Harris, *Fragments*, 44; Wendland, *Fragmente*, 86. Cf. Petit, ed., "Les fragments grecs du livre VI des Questions sur la Genèse de Philon d'Alexandrie," *Mus* 84 (1971): 120, and *Quaestiones: Fragmenta Graeca*, 204, n. a.

[30]Harris, *Fragments*, 53.

[31]Harris, ibid., 103.4, prints the text, noting that the final line is an allusion to Sir 12:10, and that Burneianus 34 adds part of Prov 26:25. Wendland, *Fragmente*, 100, gives another recension, saying that the text belongs "sicher" to *Quaes Ex*, and then (101, n. 2) cites the addition of Prov 26:25 in some manuscripts, referring to it as "Sirach 12, 10." Marcus, *Philo, Supplement* 2: 262–63, no. 23, prints the two recensions, and Devreesse, *Les anciens com-*

*Quaes Ex* 2.25 (b)      ταῦτα μὲν — Βηρσαβεέ[32]

Exod 24:11      τοὺς ἑβδομήκοντα — ἀπελείφθη[33]

On the other hand, this procedure will not be applicable when the text in question is from a section of the *Quaestiones* which is missing in the Armenian (and Latin). In particular, Fr. sp. 39 below relates to Gen 32:26, and the extant portions of *Quaes Gen* do not extend that far. Thus, one might think that the text could be from a missing section of *Quaes Gen* or even from Philo's lost work *De Iacobo*.[34] Fortunately, though, Devreesse discovered the true source of the text, and I have included the fragment among the fragmenta spuria because just the comparison with the Armenian (or Latin) would not be enough to show its spurious nature. This limitation applies as well, of course, to texts which come from catenae on books beyond Genesis and Exodus. For example, from a chain on Hebrews comes a text which is quite possibly from the lost section of the *Quaestiones* on Gen 14:20.[35]

---

*mentateurs*, 2, n. 3, suggests that the text is perhaps a Christian supplement. Petit, *Quaestiones: Fragmenta Graeca*, 259, n. a, correctly notes that this is "un texte étranger à Philon" (cf. also 279). By the way, the text is also found in Pitra, *Analecta sacra* 2:312, no. VI, where Pitra cites both the genuine fragment of *Quaes Ex* 2.25 and this spurious text as "Ex Pal. 203, f. 261 et Vatic. 1553, f. 129." Since the first part occurs in both manuscripts but the second part only in Pal. 203, this reference is misleading, and caused the confusion in Harris's and Marcus's references, although Petit blames Marcus alone.

[32]Wendland, *Fragmente*, 101, n. 2, refers to the text, printed in Mangey, 679.2.

[33]Mangey, 679.4; I have found no further reference to this. But there is no reason to think that anything is missing from *Quaes Ex* 2.38–39.

[34]It is conceivable that *Quaes Gen* originally went as far as Gen 32:26, but I believe that it is most likely that Philo ended *Quaes Gen* at Gen 28:8–9 with the extant section 4.245 (see "Original Structure," 52–53). That Philo wrote a *De Isaaco* and a *De Iacobo* is indicated by his comments in *Jos* 1 (see Schürer, *Geschichte* 3:665; *History* 3.2:846–47; L. Massebieau, "Le classement des oeuvres de Philon," *Bibliothèque de l'École des Hautes Études*, Section des Sciences religieuses 1 [1889]: 37; Cohn, "Einteilung und Chronologie der Schriften Philos," *Phlgs, Supplementband* 7 [1899]: 409).

[35]See my "Original Structure," 49, and notes 63–64; Petit, *Quaestiones: Fragmenta Graeca*, 227–28; and my remarks in "Further Greek Fragments," 145, n. 14. (The text is Harris 72.1.)

Furthermore, in some cases we may of course have additional evidence which suggests that a fragment is indeed from Philo even when it cannot be located within the Armenian (or Latin). An interesting case is a brief text printed by Harris from the *Catena Lipsiensis*:

> Διδύμους αὐτοὺς εἶναι ἀπὸ μιᾶς συλλήψεως, διό φησι πρόσκειται τῷ "ἔτεκε Κάϊν" "καὶ προσέθηκε τεκεῖν τὸν ἀδελφὸν αὐτοῦ."[36]

This fragment clearly relates to Gen 4:1–2, but there is nothing in the relevant sections of the *Quaestiones* (*Quaes Gen* 1.58–59) corresponding to this Greek, and there is no reason to suppose that the Armenian has a lacuna. One might thus conclude, as did Harris, that the text is falsely ascribed to Philo.

In this particular case, however, we have some further evidence. In the recently discovered papyrus of Didymus's commentary on Genesis, there is the following remark on Gen 4:2:

> Ὁ Φίλων μὲν οὖν βούλεται διδύμους αὐτοὺς εἶναι ἀπὸ μιᾶς συλλήμψεως· διό, φησίν, πρόσκειται τῷ "ἔτεκεν τὸν Κάϊν" τὸ "προσέθηκεν τεκεῖν τὸν ἀδελφὸν αὐτοῦ τὸν Ἀβέλ."[37]

It is thus evident that the catenae on Genesis have simply excerpted from Didymus his report of Philo's view,[38] and are not quoting the *Quaestiones*.

---

[36]Harris, *Fragments*, 107.1; there it is cited from the *Catena Lipsiensis*, i.e., Σειρὰ ἑνὸς καὶ πεντήκοντα ὑπομνηματιστῶν εἰς τὴν Ὀκτάτευχον καὶ τὰ τῶν Βασιλείων . . . , ed. Nicephorus Hieromonachos Theotokes, 2 vols. (Leipzig: Breitkopf, 1772–73), 1:105H3–106Γ5, with the lemma: ΦΙΛΩΝΟΣ ΕΠΙΣΚΟΠΟΥ. Harris remarks (*Fragments*, 107) about this and two other texts (107.2 and 107.3 [glosses on *Quaes Gen* 1.100 and 2.10]): "None of these passages seem to me to be Philo: they are ordinary glosses and nothing more." Wendland, *Fragmente*, 37, n. 1, notes that a text from Procopius is similar to Harris's Philo text. And Devreesse says (*Les anciens commentateurs*, 16, n. 6) of this text: "Sous le lemme Φίλωνος ἐπισκόπου, divers manuscrits donnent une glose de IV, 1–2 . . . ."

[37]Pierre Nautin with the collaboration of Louis Doutreleau, eds. and trans., *Didyme l'Aveugle, Sur la Genèse*, vol. 1 (SC, vol. 233; 1976), 276 and 278. The editors note that a few letters are missing in the papyrus, and they also use italics for the Biblical quotations.

[38]Note that the citation in the catenae of Philo's *Quaes Gen* 1.3 is similarly a citation via Eusebius of Emesa; see note 11 above.

Our judgment of authenticity then depends on the value of Didymus's testimony, and Didymus may well have been citing some work of Philo other than the *Quaestiones* here. In fact, such a citation in a later writer may conceivably come from any work of Philo, and so a comparison with the Armenian (or Latin) would be an inadequate test of genuineness. Here, therefore, we have simply an unidentified fragment which may well come from Philo.[39]

A related source of Philonic material is the *Eclogae* of Procopius, a summary of what may have been the original chain on the Octateuch.[40] Harris first noted that Procopius often quotes Philo verbatim, and in other places paraphrases him.[41] And the systematic gathering of parallels from Procopius to Philo's *Quaestiones* was accomplished by Wendland in 1891.[42] Like the catenae, Procopius cites *Quaes Gen* beginning with 1.55 and ending with 4.228, and cites *Quaes Ex* beginning with 2.2 and ending with 2.49.[43] The procedure utilized is, in principle, straightforward and similar to that used with the chains: one compares Procopius with the Armenian (or Latin) version of the *Quaestiones*, and where the correspondence is close one infers that Procopius has simply copied from Philo's Greek. Regrettably, however, Wendland prints, often with little or no textual discrimination, texts from Procopius which agree virtually exactly with the Armenian translation and which may thus be considered to be genuine Philo fragments, along with texts from Procopius which betray only the most remote connection with the

---

[39]The fragment appears not to come from any of the extant material of Philo. Didymus does show a knowledge of Philo's works (see *Sur la Genèse* 1:26–27), but the edition of Didymus adds the following note on this particular text (1:279, n. 3 on page 118 of the papyrus): "Nous n'avons pas trouvé cette affirmation dans les oeuvres conservées de Philon. Au contraire, dans *De sacr.* 11, il présente Caïn comme «l'aîné» d'Abel." However, Philo's words in *Sacr* 11 are hardly "contrary" to what Didymus reports Philo as saying; in fact, a little later, in *Sacr* 17, Philo says that Esau is older (πρεσβύτερος, as in *Sacr* 11) than Jacob, even though *they* are clearly twins.

[40]Devreesse, "Chaînes," 1087–88; *Les anciens commentateurs*, xi–xiv; Petit, *L'ancienne version* 1:23–25; *Quaestiones: Fragmenta Graeca*, 18–20; *Catena Sinaitica*, xx–xxi; Goodhart and Goodenough, *Bibliography*, 164–66.

[41]Harris, *Fragments*, 5: "The commentary of Procopius on the Pentateuch is full of passages and abridgments from Philo."

[42]*Fragmente*, 29–105.

[43]See my "Original Structure," 53, 56–57; Petit, *Quaestiones: Fragmenta Graeca*, 18–19, 231. Between *Quaes Gen* and *Quaes Ex* he utilizes *Jos* 175–76 and then turns to *Vita Mos* 1–2 (see Wendland, *Fragmente*, 91, 93–95; Cohn, *PCW* 4:xxvii–xxviii).

Armenian. Sometimes, indeed, the resemblance is only what might be expected from two comments on the same Biblical passage.[44] And in other cases, as Petit suggests, Procopius may be citing Philo via an intermediate source.[45]

The situation became worse when Marcus printed most of Wendland's parallels within his appendix of fragments, but ignored others,[46] again with very few textual remarks. Petit subsequently called attention to five of these "fragments" supposedly coming from the original book 6 of *Quaes Gen* (*Quaes Gen* 4.165, 188, 207, 208, 210), and remarked:

> On y trouve certes l'écho direct de l'exégèse philonienne, mais ce ne sont pas des fragments au sens strict, utiles à la reconstitution du texte original.[47]

Petit went on to note that the "fragment" assigned to *Quaes Gen* 4.210 is actually from Origen,[48] as is another text assigned by Wendland to *Quaes*

---

[44]Moreover, sometimes Wendland gratuitously supposes that some words in Procopius come from Philo. See, for example, the following: "Vielleicht philonisch sind im Folgenden die Worte S. 240B [*MPG* 87] μία δὲ τῆς ἁμαρτίας ἴασις ἡσυχία καὶ στάσις τοῦ πλημμελεῖν. Nachweisen kann ich sie freilich im armenischen Texte nicht, aber mancherlei weist ja darauf hin, dass derselbe an einzelnen Stellen lückenhaft ist" (*Fragmente*, 40). It is pointless to burden the study of Philo with such conjectures. See a similar claim in *Fragmente*, 47, n. 1. Occasionally, on the other hand, Wendland prints genuine fragments, but fails to locate them; see the text from *Quaes Gen* 2.74 noted at 61, n. 4 as simply "ein Philofr." Petit, *Quaestiones: Fragmenta Graeca*, 124–25, prints a fuller recension of the fragment, but does not refer to Wendland.

[45]Petit, *Quaestiones: Fragmenta Graeca*, 19. As one example among many, see her comments on *Quaes Gen* 4.86 (ibid., 172–73), in contrast to Wendland, *Fragmente*, 78–79, and Marcus, *Philo, Supplement* 2:221, who simply print Procopius's Greek.

[46]Examples are the fragment from *Quaes Gen* 1.3 (Wendland, *Fragmente*, 36; cf. Petit, *Quaestiones: Fragmenta Graeca*, 42, n. a) and the fragment from *Quaes Gen* 1.63 (Wendland, *Fragmente*, 39; cf. Petit, *Quaestiones: Fragmenta Graeca*, 61, n. a [at top]). Such omissions and other inadequacies in Marcus's collection of Greek fragments suggest that it was compiled in some haste.

[47]"Les fragments grecs," 119. These remarks come from a section which is entitled "Morceaux écartés" (119–21).

[48]Ibid., 120; idem, *L'ancienne version* 2:118. The text is found in Wend-

*Gen* 4.214.[49] And, further, she dismissed yet another citation from Procopius with the comment:

> Simple résonance philonienne également dans le texte de
> Procope parallèle au paragraphe 241.[50]

Of course, it is clear that these texts are to be located within Procopius's *Eclogae*, and thus the identification—at least on one level—has always been known. The unjustified attribution of certain lines within Procopius to Philo has arisen simply because editors, in their eagerness to discover ever more fragments of Philo, have failed to distinguish, as Petit notes, verbal resonance from genuine quotation.[51] And now the necessary discrimination throughout the *Quaestiones* is provided by Petit in her edition of the fragments. We will thus leave the problem of Procopius with the general observation that many of the "fragments" of Philo taken from Procopius by Wendland, and then printed by Marcus, are not really to be considered such, and that in every case a careful comparison with the Armenian (or Latin) must be made.

---

land, *Fragmente*, 88–89, and in Marcus, *Philo, Supplement* 2:231. Cf. also Petit, *Quaestiones: Fragmenta Graeca*, 209–10; by the way, the "citation . . . non identifiée" which Petit there cites from Harris, *Fragments*, 110.12 and says is parallel to a phrase of *Quaes Gen* 4.210, is in fact a quotation from *Post* 158 (as noted in the apparatus in *PCW*).

[49]Petit, "Les fragments grecs," 120; idem, *L'ancienne version* 2:124; Wendland, *Fragmente*, 114. Cf. also Petit, *Quaestiones: Fragmenta Graeca*, 210–11. In these last two cases Wendland thought that Origen had used Philo.

[50]"Les fragments grecs," 120; Wendland, *Fragmente*, 90. Cf. Petit, *Quaestiones: Fragmenta Graeca*, 213, n. a.

[51]Some of these incorrect identifications of Philo fragments within Procopius are also mentioned by Petit in her *Catena Sinaitica*: 64 (G 59; *Quaes Gen* 3.40), 80–81 (G 77; *Quaes Gen* 4.10), 88–90 (G 87; *Quaes Gen* 4.24), and 186–87 (G 192; *Quaes Gen* 4.73).

# THE FLORILEGIA

The majority of the fragments found to be spurious come from the florilegia, and thus a brief description of the major collections and the sources cited here is appropriate.[1] The largest and most important of these collections is the so-called *Sacra parallela*, which is generally attributed to John of Damascus. Originally this work was a collection known as Tὰ ἱερά, which was divided into three books: the first dealt with God, the second with man, and the third with vices and virtues in parallel chapters. Thus, the usual title derives from this third book. Throughout the work the compiler gathered texts from Scripture, from Christian writers, and from Philo and Josephus, and arranged them under various chapters, each treating a certain topic.[2]

This topic was designated by a title (τίτλος), and within the title one word is the key to an alphabetical arrangement of the material: all the chapters whose titles' key-words begin with the same letter were gathered into a

---

[1]See in general the masterly survey by Marcel Richard, "Florilèges spirituels, III. Florilèges grecs," *DSpir* 5 (1964): 475–512; reprinted in his *Opera minora*, vol. 1, no. 1 (with original column numbering), including additions and corrections in the "Appendice," i–iv. See further his "Les »Parallela« de saint Jean Damascène," *Actes du XIIe Congrès International d'Études byzantines (Ochride, 10–16 septembre 1961)*, vol. 2 (Belgrade: Comité Yougoslave des Études byzantines, 1963), 485–89. For Philo in particular see also Petit, *L'ancienne version* 1:25–28; *Quaestiones: Fragmenta Graeca*, 21–28; and "En marge de l'édition des fragments de Philon (Questions sur la Genèse et l'Exode): Les florilèges damascéniens," *Studia Patristica*, vol. 15, pt. 1, ed. Elizabeth A. Livingstone (TU, vol. 128; Berlin: Akademie-Verlag, 1984), 20–25. I may note also the references by Cohn in *PCW* 1:lxiii–lxix; Schürer, *Geschichte* 3:641, and n. 30 (–642); and idem, *History* 3.2:824, and n. 40 (–825). And Goodhart and Goodenough, *Bibliography*, 142–45, 156–57, again supply valuable information, which must be used with caution.

[2]The reconstruction of the original form of the Tὰ ἱερά was accomplished by Karl Holl, *Die Sacra Parallela des Johannes Damascenus* (TU, vol. 16, pt. 1; Leipzig: J. C. Hinrichs, 1897); see also Richard, "Florilèges," 475–86.

section (στοιχεῖον). And these sections were then written in alphabetical order (στοιχεῖον α, στοιχεῖον β, . . .).³ Fortunately for students of Philo, his works were extensively utilized in this collection.⁴ Moreover, the lemmata usually cite not only the author but also the name of the work from which the text (supposedly) comes.

The original florilegium has not survived, but a number of manuscripts preserve parts of it or later recensions of it. The only edition is that of Lequien,⁵ who prints—not always very accurately—the text of Vaticanus 1236, itself a copy of Ottobonianus 79.⁶ Lequien also added some selections from Codex Rupefucaldinus (now Berolinensis 46),⁷ a manuscript whose vast repertory of Philo texts has been explored by editors since Mangey.⁸ Further important manuscripts of the *Sacra parallela* are: Coislinianus 276 (also used

---

³The description in Petit, *Quaestiones: Fragmenta Graeca*, 21, is especially perspicuous.

⁴According to the information in Holl, *Die Sacra Parallela*, 183–84 and 201–2, Philo's name is cited 92 times in Coislinianus 276, third in frequency only to Gregory of Nazianzus (145 times) and Basil (106 times), and is cited 131 times in Vaticanus 1553, third again to Gregory of Nazianzus (237 times) and Basil (171 times).

⁵Michael Lequien, ed. and trans., *Sancti Patris nostri Joannis Damasceni . . . opera omnia quae exstant . . .* , vol. 2 (Paris: Delespine, 1712), 278–730. Lequien's edition is reprinted in *MPG* 95:1040–1588, and 96:9–442.

⁶That Vat. 1236 derives (most likely directly) from Ottob. 79 was demonstrated by Holl, *Die Sacra Parallela*, 11–15; cf. Richard, "Florilèges," 480. Ottob. 79 is a witness to what is called the Florilegium Vaticanum (ibid., 480–81), and in his examination of this recension, Richard says that Escurialensis Ω. III. 9 "est le meilleur exemplaire, peut-être l'ancêtre commun de toute la tradition de la Renaissance, au moins un proche parent de celui-ci" (ibid., 480). He also calls attention to Vindobonensis suppl. gr. 178. I have referred now and then to readings found in Escur. Ω. III. 9, Vindob. suppl. 178, and Ottob. 79.

⁷Lequien, *Joannis Damasceni opera* 2:731–90 (*MPG* 96:441–544).

⁸The source which Mangey calls "Johannes Monachus ineditus" (see *Philonis opera* 2:660–70, for Mangey's fragments from this source) has been identified as Codex Rupefucaldinus by Harris, *Fragments*, xix (cf. Schürer, Review of Harris, *Fragments of Philo Judaeus, TLZ* 11 [1886]: 481–82; idem, *Geschichte* 3:641, n. 30 [–642]; idem, *History* 3.2:824, n. 40). However, some of the texts which he gives from this source in fact come from Coisl. 276; see the following note.

by Mangey[9]), containing a recension of the first book;[10] Vaticanus 1553, containing a recension of the second book;[11] and Parisinus 923, drawing upon all three books.[12]

Probably modelled on this great collection, a number of other florilegia were constructed during the medieval period.[13] Their sources include manuscripts of the *Sacra parallela*, but they also gather texts from secular authors, in part through intermediaries such as Stobaeus. The texts are, again, arranged in chapters dealing with various topics, and in each chapter the texts often follow the order: Scripture, Christian writers, Philo and Josephus, and then secular authors. The most important of these florilegia for our purposes may be briefly identified:

1. A florilegium ascribed to Maximus Confessor,[14] first edited rather

---

[9]Although most of the texts which Mangey cites from his "Johannes Monachus ineditus" clearly do come from Codex Rupefucaldinus (see the preceding note), several others do not. Petit has conjectured that the other source somehow confused with that manuscript was in fact Coisl. 276, even though Mangey does not explicitly cite Coisl. 276; see her "Les fragments grecs," 115, n. 98 (−116). This confusion may be at least partially explained by the fact that the manuscripts have similar contents and were both, as it seems, in Paris at Mangey's time. By the way, already Harris, *Fragments*, xix, had noted the similarity of Mangey's description to Coisl. 276. And Friedrich Loofs, *Studien über die dem Johannes von Damaskus zugeschriebenen Parallelen* (Halle: Max Niemeyer, 1892), 61, no. 22, cites a text (actually *Quaes Ex* 2.55) from Coisl. 276, and notes: "Mangey II, 669 [i.e., 669.5], angeblich nach R [i.e., Ber. 46]; doch steht an der angegebnen Stelle das Citat nicht." For another example see chapter 1, note 16, above.

[10]See Richard, "Florilèges," 477–78. Selected fragments were printed by Pitra, *Analecta sacra* 2:304–10, nos. I–XXIII.

[11]See Richard, "Florilèges," 478–79. Selected fragments were printed by Angelo Mai, *Scriptorum veterum nova collectio e Vaticanis codicibus edita*, vol. 7 (Rome: Typis Vaticanis, 1833), 74–109, and this collection is reprinted in *MPG* 86.2:2017–2100.

[12]Extensive use of Par. 923 was made by Harris, *Fragments*. In fact, Par. 923 is a witness to what Holl called the Florilegium PML[b] (*Die Sacra Parallela*, 68–114) whose other witnesses are Marcianus 138 and Laurentianus pluteus VIII 22, ff. 46[r]–73[v] (see Richard, "Florilèges," 482–83). I have cited Marc. 138 for a few texts, although as it happens they are not contained in Laur. plut. VIII 22.

[13]See Richard, "Florilèges," 486–99.

[14]See ibid., 488–92.

badly by Conrad Gessner[15] in 1546,[16] subsequently edited much more adequately by Combefis in 1675,[17] and now most conveniently cited from *MPG* 91.[18] Several texts ascribed to Philo in an otherwise unknown Cairo manuscript of this florilegium were also published by Tischendorf.[19] Moreover,

---

[15]He is often cited as "Gesner," but I have here used "Gessner," following the "Vorbemerkungen zur Schreibweise von Gessners Namen," in Hans Fischer, et al., *Conrad Gessner 1516–1565: Universalgelehrter, Naturforscher, Arzt* (Zurich: Art. Institut Orell Füssli, 1967), 7. The spelling "Gesner" derives from his Latin name "Gesnerus."

[16]*Sententiarum sive capitum, theologicorum praecipue, ex sacris & profanis libris, Tomi tres, per Antonium & Maximum monachos olim collecti . . .* (Zurich: Christopher Froschauer, 1546), 163–213. See Richard, "Florilèges," 491–94. There are some brief remarks concerning this edition by Joachim Staedtke, "Conrad Gessner als Theologe," in Fischer, et al., *Conrad Gessner 1516–1565*, 26, and 29, n. 10, where a reference is made to a copy with Gessner's annotations in the Zurich Zentralbibliothek; see also 72 (and the plate of the title page on 73).

[17]Francis Combefis, ed. and trans., *S. Maximi Confessoris, Graecorum theologi eximiique philosophi, operum tomus secundus* (Paris: Cramoisy, 1675), 528–689.

[18]*MPG* 91:721–1018.

[19]These were published in Constantin Tischendorf, *Philonea, inedita altera, altera nunc demum recte ex vetere scriptura eruta* (Leipzig: Giesecke et Devrient, 1868), 152–55, as 16 "Philonis sententiae," which are described merely as being "Ex codice Cahirino saeculi decimi" (152, n. **). This is the edition universally cited for Philo. However, Tischendorf had earlier published 41 Philonic extracts from this same manuscript in his *Anecdota sacra et profana* (Leipzig: Emilius Graul, 1855), 171–74. Furthermore, in the 2d edition of that work (Leipzig: Hermann Fries, 1861), 171–74 are unaltered (and cited by Schürer, *Geschichte* 3:638, n. 13), but we find some added information on this manuscript on 217–22, including extracts from other authors. Tischendorf's description there (217: "Tituli sive capita scribuntur 71, quorum primum est: περὶ βίου ἀρετῆς καὶ κακίας, alterum περὶ φρονήσεως καὶ βουλῆς, ultimum περὶ ὅτι οὐκ ἀεὶ τὸ πλεῖον ἄριστον") makes clear that the manuscript was indeed one of Maximus, as noted by Curt Wachsmuth, *Studien zu den griechischen Florilegien* (Berlin: Weidmann, 1882), 81, 103–4. Also, Albert Ehrhard, "Zu den 'Sacra Parallela' des Johannes Damascenus und dem Florilegium des 'Maximos,' " *ByzZ* 10 (1901): 409, cites Tischendorf's manuscript as containing Maximus (although his note gives the date of

some extracts from Maximus (including a few attributed to Philo) are found in a manuscript partially edited by Cramer.[20]

2. A florilegium in two books ascribed to Antonius Melissa, also edited by Gessner in 1546, and now most conveniently found in *MPG* 136.[21]

3. A florilegium found in Baroccianus 143 and Monacensis 429.[22] This collection is unedited, but selections from Barocc. 143 have been printed by editors of Philo since Mangey, occasional use of Barocc. 143 and Mon. 429 was made in *PCW*, and Gessner made some additions and changes to his 1546 edition of Antonius and Maximus on the basis of Mon. 429.[23]

4. A florilegium ascribed to Johannes Georgides, edited from Parisinus 1166 by Boissonade,[24] and found also in Laurentianus pluteus VII 15, which was utilized by Lewy.[25]

Moreover, of some bibliographical interest are two editions[26] which appeared after Gessner's death in 1565, but were based on his 1546 edition of

---

Tischendorf's work as 1847). Petit, *Quaestiones: Fragmenta Graeca*, 26, n. 1, includes Tischendorf's citations in 1868 under her Pseudo-Maximus.

[20]John Anthony Cramer, ed., *Anecdota Graeca e codd. manuscriptis bibliothecarum Oxoniensium*, vol. 4 (Oxford: University Press, 1837), 247–55, prints some excerpts from Bodleianus Clarkianus 11. On the Philo citations (254) here, see the discussion of Fr. sp. 7 below.

[21]See Richard, "Florilèges," 492–94. The editio princeps is that of Gessner, *Sententiarum*, 1–162. *MPG* 136:765–1244, gives virtually the text of Gessner, but with some errors and some changes designed to bring the Greek into harmony with the Latin translation.

[22]See Richard, "Florilèges," 494–95, where three further manuscript witnesses to this florilegium are noted, and Cohn, "Die Philo-Handschriften in Oxford und Paris," *Phlgs* 51 [N.F. 5] (1892): 273.

[23]On this use of Mon. 429 see Richard, "Florilèges," 491; Wachsmuth, "De gnomologio Palatino inedito," in *Satura philologa Hermanno Sauppio obtulit amicorum conlegarum decas* (Berlin: Weidmann, 1879), 9–10; idem, *Studien*, 102–3, 106, n. 1.

[24]See Richard, "Florilèges," 498, as well as the earlier notice by Harris, *Fragments*, 5. The edition by Jean François Boissonade, *Anecdota Graeca e codicibus regiis*, 5 vols. (Paris: in Regio Typographeo, 1829–33), 1:1–108, is reprinted in *MPG* 117:1057–1164.

[25]"Neue Philontexte," 73.

[26]See Wachsmuth, *Studien*, 101; Anton Elter, *Gnomica homoeomata*, 5 vols. (Bonn: Carl Georgi, 1900–1904), 3:140, 154; Richard, "Florilèges," 491.

Antonius and Maximus as well as on his 1543 edition of Stobaeus.[27] In 1581 there was published a work which combined the florilegia of Stobaeus, Antonius, and Maximus into one volume by intercalating the chapters from Antonius and Maximus among the chapters from Stobaeus.[28] In most cases, indeed, the chapter from Antonius was conflated with the chapter on the same topic from Maximus, and then simply printed as "Ex Antonio & Maximo." Based upon this hybrid edition, a further edition was published in 1609 which separated out the chapters from Stobaeus and those from Antonius and Maximus.[29] Here occur first the chapters from Stobaeus's Florilegium, then his *Eclogae*, and then the chapters from Antonius and Maximus.[30] This last collection is now printed with the chapters numbered consecutively, but with many errors,[31] and of course most of the chapters are mixtures of

---

[27]*Ioannis Stobaei sententiae, ex thesauris Graecorum delectae . . .* (Zurich: Christopher Froschauer, 1543).

[28]*Loci communes sacri et profani sententiarum omnis generis ex authoribus Graecis plus quam trecentis congestarum per Ioannem Stobaeum, et veteres in Graecia monachos Antonium & Maximum: à Conrado Gesnero Tigurino Latinitate donati, & nunc primùm in unum volumen Graecis ac Latinis è regione positis coniuncti* (Frankfurt: Andreas Wechel, 1581).

[29]*Ioannis Stobaei sententiae, ex thesauris Graecorum delectae . . . , Huic editioni accesserunt eiusdem Ioannis Stobaei eclogarum physicarum et ethicarum libri duo, Item loci communes sententiarum, collecti per Antonium & Maximum Monachos, atque ad Stobaei locos relati* (Orleans: Franciscus Fabrus, 1609).

[30]These three parts have separate titles and separate pagination. The portion from Antonius and Maximus is at the end (1–305), with the title: *Loci communes sententiarum, ex S. Scriptura, veteribus theologis, et secularibus scriptoribus, collecti per Antonium et Maximum Monachos, atque ad Io. Stobaei locos relati.*

[31]The 1581 edition contains 308 chapters, but the 1609 edition has 125 chapters from Stobaeus and 182 from Antonius and Maximus. In the numeration of the chapters in 1609 some numbers are skipped and some are given twice, and there are discrepancies between the Greek and the Latin numerals as well as between the numerals in the chapters and those in the index. An indication of the carelessness with which the 1609 editor proceeded may be gained by observing what he did with the reference in 1581 to a lacuna in the text of Antonius (see *MPG* 136:995C6–8). The 1581 editor prints the first part of chapter 131, notes "Deest hic sermonis huius finis, & totus sequens CXXXII . . . ," and then prints chapter 133. Owing to the relocation of the

material from Antonius and Maximus. Such a creation would be merely a curiosity were it not for the fact that it is this edition of 1609 which was utilized by Mangey, who cites the chapters as "Ex Antonio," even when the texts come (as they often do) from the florilegium of Maximus.[32]

Now, the ways in which the material from Antonius and Maximus was transmitted in these editions are doubtless similar in general respects to the compilation techniques which were used during the period of manuscript transmission.[33] And such a history can hardly inspire complete confidence in the details of the final product. In particular, the lemmata in the florilegia are subject to the same sorts of errors as are the lemmata in the chains.[34] The lemmata can of course be misplaced.[35] And the loss of lemmata seems to be especially common; since several texts from one author will often be in sequence, either with only one lemma at the beginning or with τοῦ αὐτοῦ before the subsequent ones, the omission of a lemma will present the later reader or copier with what appears to be a normal sequence, where the text in question will simply be taken as belonging with the earlier ones, and thus as coming from the author whose name has occurred last in the manuscript. Fr. sp. 24 and 42 below are clear examples of such a process.

Moreover, there are two texts which stand immediately after spurious fragments, and which are therefore certainly doubtful. The first is: Μεγίστη συμφορὰ ἀνθρώπῳ δυσπραγοῦντι, καὶ ἡ ἐρημία τοῦ ἀνακτησομένου. This is found in both Antonius and Maximus,[36] and in each it immediately follows

----

chapters from Stobaeus, chapter 131 in 1581 becomes chapter 94 in 1609. But the 1609 editor prints the same note at the end of chapter 94 (with the reference to the following chapter 132!), and then proceeds to number the next chapter 95.

[32]The use by Mangey is noted in Elter, *Gnomica homoeomata* 3:174.

[33]Richard's examples throughout show how later florilegia drew upon several sources and combined them in a variety of ways.

[34]See Harris, *Fragments*, 85–86: "The ascription of passages in Florilegia is generally uncertain and the titles which are often written in after the body of the text have a tendency to slip from their proper positions." See also the comment by Chadwick cited in chapter 1, note 19, above.

[35]See Wachsmuth, *Studien*, 108: "Nichts ist ja überhaupt gewöhnlicher in den Florilegien, als ein solches Herunterrutschen oder Hinaufziehen von Lemmaten, namentlich das erstere, wobei oft selbst nicht ein eigentliches Verschreiben nöthig ist, sondern nur ein falsches Beziehen eines vorausgehenden Namens zu einer zufällig herrenlos gewordenen Sentenz."

[36]Gessner, 70 = *MPG* 136:981B5–6 (no lemma), from Antonius; Combefis, 589 = *MPG* 91:832A11–12 (no lemma), from Maximus.

Fr. sp. 37 and immediately precedes Fr. sp. 38, both of which are from Gregory (the Theologian) of Nazianzus. But I have been unable to find the above text in his writings. The second such text is: Σώματος παρακμὴ κατα-στολὴ παθῶν. This occurs in manuscripts of the *Sacra parallela*[37] immediately following Fr. sp. 47, which is from Chrysostom. But I have been unable to find this text in his writings. Now, it seems to me very likely that neither of these texts is from Philo, but it is possible that they are genuine, and that a spurious text has somehow found its way into the midst of genuine Philo fragments. Thus, the two texts cited here should, I believe, be retained as Philo fragments, albeit very doubtful ones.

Of course, in general the lemmata are transmitted correctly, although our concentration on spurious texts emphasizes the errors. And, as one might expect, errors of lemmata, like all types of scribal errors, appear in different manuscripts in varying degrees. Some manuscripts (or florilegia) have many errors, and some—as far as we can judge—have comparatively few. Indeed, with regard to the spurious texts listed below, we often see that the correct lemma is to be found in one manuscript or another, and frequently in a manuscript of the *Sacra parallela*. Moreover, it is significant that none of the fragments which are definitely assigned to Philo's *Quaestiones* appears in our list of spurious fragments.[38] Given the numbers of texts involved, this can hardly be coincidence.[39] Now, the ascriptions to specific works are characteristic of the *Sacra parallela*, while the chief source of the spurious fragments is clearly Maximus.[40] Thus, the lemmata in the manu-

---

[37]This is Harris 97.12, cited from Lequien, 404 = *MPG* 95:1308D4–5 (no lemma, follows Fr. sp. 47), and Par. 923, f. 105ʳB 1–3 (no lemma, follows Fr. sp. 47). Thus, this text occurs in both the Florilegium Vaticanum (see note 6 above) and the Florilegium PML^b (see note 12 above), and in fact is found at: Escur. Ω. III. 9, f. 58ʳ 24; Vindob. suppl. 178, f. 80ʳB 24–25; Ottob. 79, f. 79ᵛ 24; and Marc. 138, f. 105ʳB 16–17. In all of these it occurs with no lemma, and follows Fr. sp. 47, which follows an extract from *Abr* 271.

[38]Cf. Petit, *Quaestiones: Fragmenta Graeca*, 27: "Lorsqu'elles précisent le titre de l'ouvrage et la subdivision, les références des florilèges sont moins souvent fausses qu'on le croirait et on aurait tort de les négliger sous prétexte qu'elles ne sont pas toutes exactes."

[39]My attempts at identification have been, as far as possible, the same for all the unidentified texts.

[40]Holl, *Fragmente vornicänischer Kirchenväter aus den Sacra Parallela* (TU, vol. 20, pt. 2; Leipzig: J. C. Hinrichs, 1899), xxiii, comments: "In den Lemmata giebt (unser) Maximus (mit einer sehr interessanten Ausnahme) nur den Namen des Autors, Johannes Damascenus macht in den Lemmata,

scripts of the *Sacra parallela* would appear to be more trustworthy than those found in Maximus.[41] Of course, even the *Sacra parallela* witnesses are sometimes in error, but more often they retain the correct attribution when other manuscripts are incorrect. Consequently, I believe that one can be confident that at least most, and perhaps even all, of the fragments attributed to Philo's *Quaestiones* in the *Sacra parallela* but not yet localized in the Armenian or Latin in fact come from those portions of the *Quaestiones* which have otherwise completely disappeared.[42]

On the other hand, Petit is skeptical about the provenance of such fragments. She claims that:

> tous les efforts tentés pour retrouver dans les florilèges des fragments grecs qu'on pourrait avec quelque probabilité localiser dans les parties perdues de la version arménienne ont jusqu'à présent échoué.[43]

---

soweit wir sehen, überall genaue Angaben." (On this one exception, see xxviii–xxix.) Curiously enough, Holl believed that the *Sacra parallela* derived from Maximus, and that the longer lemmata were subsequently expanded from the shorter ones (*Die Sacra Parallela*, 382, 391–92; defended in *Fragmente*, xxi–xxxv). The primacy of Maximus is no longer defensible (Richard, "Florilèges," 487), and indeed was attacked early by both Cohn (Review of Holl, *Die Sacra Parallela*, *PhWoch* 17 [1897]: 488–93) and Wendland (Review of Holl, *Die Sacra Parallela*, *TLZ* 22 [1897]: 12–13), who mention particularly the implausibility that longer lemmata would come from shorter.

[41]See also Fabricius and Harles, *Bibliotheca Graeca* 9:635, n. q: "In locis communibus S. Maximi, auctorum nomina saepius permutata, confusa, deprauata deprehendi, notat *Tho. Gatakerus* . . . ."

[42]One such fragment (Harris 74.5) may quite likely be placed as coming from Philo's comment on Exod 13:2, which is lost in the Armenian; see my "Original Structure," 54, 61, and 74, n. 85, where I may now add the reference to Petit, *Quaestiones: Fragmenta Graeca*, 299–300, and to my "Further Greek Fragments," 145, n. 14. Two further fragments, incidentally, are not attributed to the *Quaestiones*, but may well come from identifiable sections not found in the Armenian: One (Harris 106.1) concerns the manna, and appears to relate to Exod 16:31; see "Original Structure," 58, 61, and 76, n. 105. The other (Harris 72.1) seems likely to be Philo's comment on Gen 14:20; see chapter 2, page 21, above.

[43]*Quaestiones: Fragmenta Graeca*, 28.

This ignores the fragment which may well be properly located at Philo's comment on Exod 13:2.[44] But in any case it is clear that independently of issues of genuineness one could hardly expect to make such identifications. For the florilegia present, in the vast majority of cases, brief sentences of a quite general ethical or spiritual import. It is the nature of such extracts that they thus do not betray their original context, and of course this independence makes it possible for the compiler to arrange them into chapters which make sense apart from their original context. Thus, while some of the extracts in the florilegia do make some references which could suggest their true locations,[45] many more do not.

In any case, Petit continues:

> Les florilèges n'ont donc pas connu les *QG* dans un état
> sensiblement plus complet que le témoin arménien, si ce
> n'est pour la dernière lacune à l'intérieur du livre VI (ad *Gn*
> 26, 19b–35) comblée par la version latine et trois fragments
> grecs.[46]

Of course, the exception of the Latin should give us some pause, since it is simply a fortunate accident which has supplied these missing sections. And of these three Greek fragments, the one from a florilegium (*Quaes Gen* 4.195.9\*) provides no clue of itself to its correct placement. Consequently, I see no reason to rule out the likelihood that we possess quite a few other fragments of the same sort, but lack the Armenian or Latin to locate them. This view is rejected, though, by Petit:

> En conclusion, il n'est guère probable que les fragments
> attribués par les florilèges à Philon avec référence aux
> *Questions*, mais qui n'ont pu y être repérés à l'aide de l'ar-

---

[44]This is the only one of the three fragments cited in note 42 above which comes from the florilegia. Similarly, Lewy ("Neue Philontexte," 29, n. 6) says: "Die Catenen und Florilegien enthalten (bis auf die Erklärung von Gen. 14$_{20}$, s. unten Nr. 39) zufällig kein Fragment aus dem verlorenen Teil der quaestiones." However, Lewy gives no support for his claim. (His reference is to the fragment from a chain on Hebrews, as mentioned above in chapter 2, page 21.)

[45]Indeed, the first Greek fragment of the *Quaestiones*, from *Quaes Gen* 1.1, includes the opening question which cites Gen 2:4, and goes on to cite again phrases from this verse; cf. Petit, *Quaestiones: Fragmenta Graeca*, 41–42.

[46]Ibid., 28.

> ménien ou du latin, soient tirés des parties perdues de cette
> oeuvre.[47]

By the way, the fact that three of Petit's unidentified fragments come from
the extant sections of the *Quaestiones* indicates that one should be cautious
about discarding such texts.[48]

Besides such possible fragments of the *Quaestiones*, there are also some
texts explicitly attributed to other works of Philo, but which cannot be located
in *PCW* or in the Armenian or Latin versions. It is interesting that among
our spurious fragments only four such explicit lemmata are found. One is
found on Fr. sp. 30: Φίλωνος ἐκ τοῦ δ´ τῆς νόμων ἱερῶν ἀλληγορίας.[49]
This text is always ascribed to Philo, even though it comes from Origen's
*Commentary on St. John*, and here we may well have simply a primitive error
in the *Sacra parallela*. The other three cases of explicit lemmata are Fr. sp. 6,
25, and 31, which all have the lemma: Φίλωνος ἐκ τοῦ περὶ (τῶν) γιγάντων.
It is very curious that all three of the texts attributed to *Gig* but not found in
*PCW* are spurious,[50] and come from three different sources. One of these

---

[47]Ibid.

[48]These three (her QE no. 33, p. 306; QG no. 7, p. 220; QE no. 27, p.
303) had been located by Früchtel as coming from *Quaes Gen* 1.49, *Quaes
Gen* 3.3, and *Quaes Ex* 2.110, respectively; see my "Further Greek Fragments," 148, n. 27, and 150–52. And Petit, in her review of Charles Mercier,
ed. and trans., *Quaestiones in Genesim I et II e versione Armeniaca*, *Mus* 92
(1979): 404, later independently identified the first of these as coming from
*Quaes Gen* 1.49. Note, though, that its lemma does not in fact refer to the
*Quaestiones*.

[49]This longest version of the lemma, found three times in Vat. 1553, is
surely the original one, since "das Längere in der Regel das Ältere ist" (Holl,
*Die Sacra Parallela*, 241, discussing other lemmata). For the other texts
which are assigned to the lost fourth book of the *Legum allegoriae*, see
Harris, *Fragments*, 6–8; and cf. Massebieau, "Le classement," 18, and n. 1;
Cohn, "Einteilung," 394; Schürer, *Geschichte* 3:651, n. 47; and idem, *History*
3.2:833, n. 66.

[50]Harris printed five texts (9.1–9.5) as coming "from the lost portion of
the book περὶ γιγάντων." Two of these (9.4 and 9.5) are from *Quod Deus*
(as noted in *PCW*; see *PCW* 2:xxii, n. 1), while the other three are shown here
to be spurious. The texts attributed to *Gig* but not found in either *Gig* or
*Quod Deus* have often been cited as evidence that some words of Philo have
been lost from those works: see Massebieau, "Le classement," 22 (and n. 3,
where he locates Harris 9.4 in *Quod Deus*); Cohn, "Einteilung," 397 (who

sources is again Origen's *Commentary on St. John*, but the other two sources
are, to say the least, unexpected: Pseudo-Aristotle's *De virtutibus et vitiis*, and
Pseudo-Philo's *De Sampsone*. In the latter case, we may postulate that the
*De Sampsone* was found ascribed to Philo. But how the same lemma became
attached to three such disparate texts is a puzzle.

Apart from such fragments ascribed to the *Quaestiones* or other specific
works, there are many more texts ascribed simply to Philo in the later florilegia. And, as we shall see in detail, these lemmata are often incorrect. But it
would be a mistake to think that all the unidentified texts preserved in such
sources under Philo's name may simply be disregarded. Harris, indeed, dismissed many of them from consideration with the remark:

> The unidentified passages in Maximus and Anton Melissa I
> have not thought it worth while to print.[51]

Of course, "unidentified" here refers to those fragments not identified
by Harris among the works of Philo preserved in Greek, Armenian, or Latin.
And such a dismissal would be justified only if Harris's attempts at identification within these works had really been thorough. Unfortunately, however,
Harris's work can hardly claim such completeness. Hampered by the lack of
any index to Philo, he printed a number of "fragments" which can in fact be
found in *PCW* (or, in Harris's time, in Mangey).[52] He also printed a few
texts as unidentified which can be localized within the *Quaestiones*.[53] And on

---

refers to "zwei Stellen," apparently Harris 9.1 and 9.2); Wendland, *PCW* 2:
xxii; Schürer, *Geschichte* 3:654, and n. 56; and idem, *History* 3.2:835, and n.
83. Moreover, all five of these texts are discussed by Maximilian Adler, *Studien zu Philon von Alexandreia* (Breslau: M. & H. Marcus, 1929), 45–46, who
notes that two are from *Quod Deus* (as cited in *PCW*).

[51]*Fragments*, 106. Elter found Harris's procedure praiseworthy (*Gnomica* 3:174):

> Wenn endlich J. Rendel Harris Fragments of Philo 1886 S.
> 106 schreibt: The unidentified passages in Maximus and
> Anton Melissa I have not thought it worth while to print, so
> sind die homoeomata Philos hiermit hoffentlich für alle
> Zeiten abgethan.

[52]Our Index locorum shows, for instance, that of the 30 "unidentified
passages" from Codex Rupefucaldinus which Harris prints (*Fragments*, 108–
10 [108.3–110.12]), 18 are located in *PCW*.

[53]From these same 30 passages in Harris, Früchtel discovered that 108.4
comes from *Quaes Ex* 2.110, and that 109.12 comes from *Quaes Ex* 2.13,
while I found that 110.6 comes from *Quaes Ex* 2.115; see my "Further Greek

occasion Harris duplicated under an "unidentified" heading lines which he had already localized.[54] Such oversights can readily be understood when one observes the sheer quantity of texts involved as well as the variety of sources to be disentangled. And of course one can expect that, even with indexes and all possible care, it is risky to ignore such potential Philo fragments.

Now, as it turned out, Harris's somewhat mechanical method of dismissing the fragments from Maximus and Antonius which he had not identified, while saving him from printing a number of spurious fragments which had been included by Mangey, also did not provide readers the opportunity to make fresh identifications. For example, he omitted the fragment, εὔπαιδες οἱ τῶν καλῶν καὶ ἀγαθῶν ἐπιστήμονες, which was printed by Mangey from Antonius. This unidentified text considered by Harris not "worth while to print" is from *Quaes Ex* 2.19.[55]

Consequently, it would be unwarranted simply to remove all the texts found in later florilegia which have not yet been identified. Also unwarranted would be the acceptance or rejection of texts based on the uniformity of the ascription to Philo.[56] For spurious fragments may be universally assigned to Philo by the lemmata,[57] and genuine fragments of Philo may be universally assigned to someone other than Philo.[58] In other cases, the mixture of

---

Fragments," 151–52. Of the remaining 9 passages, 2 are spurious (Fr. sp. 21 and 22) and 7 are so far unidentified.

[54]Harris printed (101.7) two lines from Codex Rupefucaldinus which he had earlier (64) printed from another manuscript within a wider citation from *Quaes Ex* 2.64; see my "Further Greek Fragments," 148, and n. 26.

[55]A brief discussion of the text may be found in my "Philo and the Immortality of the Race," *JSJ* 11 (1980): 36–37. Wendland (*Fragmente*, 140 n. 1) similarly criticized Harris for not printing these texts, since thereby a fragment from *Quaes Gen* 1.41 was omitted. For the attestation of each of these fragments, see my "Further Greek Fragments," 151 and 149.

[56]Harris seems from time to time to rely on this as a criterion; see his comment on *Fragments*, 77.2. It may also be worth noting that some errors were doubtless present in the original massive compilation of the Τὰ ἱερά; cf. Holl, *Fragmente*, xi, who remarks that "das Urexemplar weder im Text noch in den Lemmata fehlerfrei war—was an und für sich selbstverständlich ist und in einzelnen Fällen sich bestimmt nachweisen lässt— . . . ."

[57]Fr. sp. 30 below seems to be such a case.

[58]See the examples in chapter 2, note 7, above. These texts are from the catenae on Genesis, and thus the identification is possible by comparing the corresponding sections of the Armenian version. The identification of a genuine fragment found only in the florilegia but *never* assigned to Philo

ascriptions may be such as to leave us simply in doubt whether the text comes from Philo or someone else.[59] Moreover, since so much material of Philo and of early Christian writers (such as Clement, Origen, Irenaeus, and Didymus) has been lost, it may be that many fragments which actually come from such lost works will never be located.[60] Thus, there may be texts which are fated to remain always "fragmenta incerta" of Philo and such other writers. And in a few such cases, the mixture of attributions will result in the same text appearing in the lists of uncertain fragments of more than one author.

Good examples of such mixture are provided by two unlocated fragments which have been printed as belonging to Philo and also as fragments of Clement. These texts are:

1.      Τὸ εἰδέναι τινὰ ὅτι ἀγνοεῖ, σοφίας ἐστίν, ὡς καὶ
        τὸ εἰδέναι ὅτι ἠδίκησε, δικαιοσύνης.[61]

---

would be very difficult. In fact, I believe that the only such case is the Greek fragment of *Quaes Gen* 4.33 (b), located by Lewy (78.9). However, this text (found only in Ber. 46) follows the citation of *Quaes Gen* 4.33 (a), which is attributed to Philo in other manuscripts, and precedes other Philo texts. But in Ber. 46 there is no reference to Philo on this series of texts. Cf. Harris's identification of *Somn* 1.11, as discussed on pages 45–46 below.

[59]Harris, *Fragments*, 80, comments on the diversity of titles for a fragment of *Gaium* 140 (Harris 79.8) thus: "This is a very good specimen of the way the Titles in Collections of Parallels get misplaced. Almost all the confusions are between Philo and Clement or Evagrius or Nilus."

[60]For the later florilegia the losses from secular Greek literature (e.g., the pre-Socratics and Plutarch) must be kept in mind. Note that the fortunate preservation of the Armenian version of Philo has diminished considerably the list of unlocated fragments of Philo.

[61]This text is ascribed to Philo in Vat. 1236 (Lequien, 613 = *MPG* 96: 184B7–8), and was thus printed by Mangey, 651.11. The text is included by Harris (80.5), but he says it is "wrongly ascribed to Philo," noting that it is often ascribed to Didymus (as also in Vat. 1236 at Lequien, 693 = *MPG* 96: 360D7–8; and twice in Maximus: Combefis, 583 = *MPG* 91:821C3–4, and Combefis, 662 = *MPG* 91:968C12–13). It has also been included among the fragments of Clement; see Otto Stählin and Früchtel, eds. (prepared for publication by Ursula Treu), *Clemens Alexandrinus*, vol. 3: *Stromata Buch VII und VIII, Excerpta ex Theodoto, Eclogae propheticae, Quis dives salvetur, Fragmente*, 2d ed. (GCS, vol. 52, pt. 3; Berlin: Akademie-Verlag, 1970), xxxvi, no. 80 (among "Unechte Fragmente"), where we find: "anscheinend

2.  Μηδαμῶς τὴν φύσιν αἰτιώμεθα· πάντα γὰρ βίον
    ἡδὺν ἢ ἀηδῆ ἡ συνήθεια ποιεῖ.[62]

A third text is ascribed to Philo in Codex Rupefucaldinus, but elsewhere to Clement:

3.  Οὐχ ἡ τῶν πράξεων ἀποχὴ δικαιοῖ τὸν πιστόν,
    ἀλλ᾽ ἡ τῶν ἐννοιῶν ἀγνεία καὶ εἰλικρίνεια.[63]

Nevertheless, despite such uncertainties, a good deal of pruning of the various editions of fragments is possible. For example, as indeed we might expect from these last texts, this is the case with quite a few fragments which are locatable in the works of Philo, but which have been printed as fragments of Clement.[64] Furthermore, there is a text from Philo assigned to Justin

---

aus Didymos, noch nicht identifiziert." In the indices to his manuscript of Philo fragments Früchtel dismissed this text as "Clem. Al. fr. spur. 80."

[62]This text is ascribed to Philo in Maximus (Combefis, 674 = *MPG* 91:989D4–5), and is thus printed by Harris (88.2 and 105.4). It has also been included among the fragments of Clement; see Stählin and Früchtel, *Clemens Alexandrinus* 3:xxxvii, no. 86 (of the "Unechte Fragmente"), and also Holl, *Fragmente*, 15–16, no. 31. Früchtel similarly dismissed this from his collection of Philo fragments, noting that it is "Clem. Al. fr. spur. 86."

[63]This text is printed (as from Clement) in Holl, *Fragmente*, 119, no. 305; it does not, though, appear in any of the editions of Philo fragments. It is ascribed to Clement in Vat. 1236 (Lequien, 570 = *MPG* 96:89B13–14), in Maximus (Combefis, 669 = *MPG* 91:980C9–11), in Antonius (Gessner, 67 = *MPG* 136:972C7–8; and Gessner, 149 = *MPG* 136:1209C2–4), and in Digb. 6, f. 47ᵛ 4–6. The text is also found in Stählin and Früchtel, *Clemens Alexandrinus* 3:xxxvii, no. 88b (of the "Unechte Fragmente"), where we are referred to p. 228, and there it (no. 65) is printed as one of the "Fragmente ungewisser Herkunft." (Cf. Stählin and Früchtel, *Clemens Alexandrinus* 3:xxxviii, no. 90d.)

[64]See the convenient listing of "Unechte Fragmente" of Clement found in Stählin and Früchtel, *Clemens Alexandrinus* 3:xxx–xxxviii, where the following are noted to be in fact Philonic: no. 23, no. 24, no. 25, no. 35, no. 46c ( = 35), no. 53b ( = 25), no. 55a, no. 55b ( = 23), no. 56a (second part), no. 62c ( = 23), no. 62d ( = 24), no. 65c ( = 35), no. 68a, no. 69b ( = 25), no. 73, no. 75b ( = 56a [second part]), no. 79a. No. 72 = no. 89b is our Fr. sp. 40, and nos. 80, 86, and 88b are the three texts just examined.

Martyr,[65] and another which is printed as belonging to Cyril.[66] And there are doubtless many other examples of texts which can be correctly identified.[67] But we return to the texts which can be justifiably removed from the collections of Philo fragments.

In the following chapter are presented the fragmenta spuria along with their correct identifications. In many cases it is quite straightforward to see that the ascription to Philo is incorrect and that the true source is as stated, since the text occurs within a larger context.[68] But there are several groups of fragments stemming from the florilegia which pose special difficulties.

First, let us examine the ten fragments (Fr. sp. 8–17) which are ascribed to Philo within Maximus, but also appear as "Plutarch fragments" in Bernardakis's edition on the basis of the ascription to Plutarch in some florilegia.[69] Früchtel found seven of these in Mangey's edition, and, seeing them cited by Bernardakis as Plutarch, removed six of them (the other one, Fr. sp. 12, he

---

[65]This is a citation of *Leg All* 1.73, printed as a fragment of Justin (*MPG* 6:1600C3–5). It occurs in Antonius at Gessner, 87 = *MPG* 136:1032D8–10, without a lemma, but with the lemma Ἰουστίνου φιλοσόφου (Justini Philosophi) on the preceding text. Then the lemma Φίλωνος (Philonis) occurs on the next text, and so it clearly has been misplaced downward one text. In fact, this misplacement may have occurred within Gessner's edition, since the Justin text takes only one line but its lemma takes two lines; thus the following lemma may have been pushed down to make room. Note that this text from *Leg All* 1.73 is, of course, correctly assigned to Philo elsewhere, e.g., Combefis, 584 = *MPG* 91:821C9–11.

[66]This is *Anim* 100 (cf. Harris, 11.4), found also as one of the "Fragmenta ex reliquis S. Cyrilli Contra Julianum libris qui desiderantur" at *MPG* 76:1060A12–13.

[67]See, for example, Sebastian Haidacher, "Chrysostomos-Fragmente im Maximos-Florilegium und in den Sacra Parallela," *ByzZ* 16 (1907): 168–201; and Paul J. Fedwick, "The Citations of Basil of Caesarea in the Florilegium of the Pseudo-Antony Melissa," *OCP* 45 (1979): 32–44.

[68]In general, at least, there is no reason to imagine that the author is in fact quoting Philo.

[69]Gregorius N. Bernardakis, ed., *Plutarchi Chaeronensis moralia*, vol. 7: *Plutarchi fragmenta vera et spuria multis accessionibus locupletata* (Leipzig: B. G. Teubner, 1896), 150–82; the contents of this section are described as "Λείψανα συγγραμμάτων ἀδήλων Reliquiae incertorum librorum," while the page heading reads "Fragmenta incerta."

assigned to Democritus) in his indexes as really belonging to Plutarch.[70] But some additional explanation is surely needed. For these texts always occur as isolated fragments, rather than as parts of a continuous text. Thus, one might well doubt whether these are actually Plutarch fragments falsely ascribed to Philo, rather than Philo fragments falsely ascribed to Plutarch, or perhaps even fragments of some other writer(s) falsely ascribed to both Philo and Plutarch. Fortunately, though, there are further considerations which make it certain that the fragments are in any case not to be attributed to Philo.

The basic work on this issue is due to Elter,[71] whose studies Früchtel appears not to have known. Elter notes that Plutarch often follows Philo in the florilegia, and thus—as we have indicated above—the loss of the lemma ascribing (even incorrectly) certain texts to Plutarch would have resulted in those texts' becoming "Philo fragments" within the manuscript tradition. Elter summarizes his point in this way:

> In den Melissen pflegt Plutarch die profana zu eröffnen,
> P h i l o die sacra zu beschliessen. Eine Folge dieser Nach-
> barschaft ist es, dass durch Ausfall des Plutarchlemmas in
> den alten Drucken einzelne Plutarchhomoeomata unter die
> Philofragmente gerathen sind; was bei Plutarch zu wenig
> steht, steht hier also zu viel.[72]

What Elter says about the old printed editions can sometimes be seen very clearly,[73] but the omission of the lemma (or its being shifted downwards) could just as well occur in the manuscripts, and would have the same result.

The hypothesis that texts attributed earlier to Plutarch became attached to Philo later in the process of transmission receives convincing support from a discovery made by Elter concerning a collection of *sententiae* of various writers, both sacred and profane, which is found in Parisinus 1168,[74] and is

---

[70]Früchtel's procedure is puzzling since in "Nachweisungen zu Frag-mentsammlungen," *PhWoch* 56 (1936): 1439, he reports that five fragments which are found in Bernardakis's collection are "unecht," that is, not really from Plutarch. One would suppose that Früchtel would thus have considered the possibility that the "Philo fragments" are not really from Plutarch; but he provides no further explanation.

[71]*Gnomica homoeomata* 1–5.

[72]Ibid. 3:173–74.

[73]See Fr. sp. 14 below.

[74]Ibid. 1:67–74. See Richard, "Florilèges," 489; Cohn, *PCW* 1:lxviii; Wendland, "Zu Krumbachers Geschichte der Byzantinischen Litteratur[2] S. 600," *ByzZ* 7 (1898): 166–68; and Petit, *Quaestiones: Fragmenta Graeca*, 26

now known also to survive in Oxoniensis Digbeianus 6.[75]  This collection is arranged by author, instead of by Biblical order or spiritual topic.

Now, as Elter argues, Maximus is dependent for his texts from secular authors, at least,[76] on this collection of *sententiae*. Thus, the texts attributed to Plutarch in this collection were doubtless also attributed to him in the archetype of the florilegium of Maximus. And in fact the Pseudo-Plutarch fragments in which we are interested all occur in this collection assigned to Plutarch, whose lemma in Digb. 6 (<Π>λουτάρχου[77]) occurs at f. 55ʳ 18, followed by our "Plutarch" texts among others. (Then we have another lemma [<τ>οῦ αὐτοῦ ἀποφθέγματα] at f. 61ʳ 8 followed by yet more "Plutarch" texts.) Thus, even if the ascription to Plutarch is not correct—as may well be the case[78]—the ascription to Philo is secondary within the manuscript tradition, and thus is without foundation.

---

(and n. 3).  For convenience, my citations of Par. 1168 are taken from Leo Sternbach, ed., *Photii patriarchae opusculum paraeneticum, Appendix gnomica, Excerpta Parisina* (Cracow: Sumptibus Academiae Litterarum, 1893), 53–82.

[75]The discovery of the significance of this manuscript was made in 1958 by Gilberte Astruc-Morize, as noted by Richard, "Florilèges," 489.

[76]Holl, *Fragmente*, xxx–xxxv, argues vigorously against the claim that the sacra in Maximus also derive from this collection. Holl's arguments were approved by Ehrhard, "Zu den 'Sacra Parallela,'" 414, n. 2, and the restriction to the profana is clearly stated by Richard, "Florilèges," 489.

[77]The initial letter here is missing, as are the initial letters of most of the lemmata and indeed of the sayings themselves. Clearly, they were left to be rubricated.

[78]*Gnomica homoeomata* 3:171–73. As a consequence these fragments are omitted in F. H. Sandbach, ed., *Plutarchi moralia*, vol. 7 (Leipzig: B. G. Teubner, 1967), as discussed at v–vi; and in idem, ed. and trans., *Plutarch's Moralia*, vol. 15: *Fragments* (LCL; 1969), as discussed at xiii, 407–10. (In both places Sandbach refers to Früchtel's article cited above in note 70.) Some of the texts printed by Bernardakis had earlier been printed in Daniel Wyttenbach, ed., Πλουτάρχου τοῦ Χαιρωνέως τὰ ἠθικά, *Plutarchi Chaeronensis moralia*, vol. 5, pt. 2 (Oxford: Clarendon Press, 1800), 875–904. As Sandbach notes, though, Wyttenbach expresses his doubts about the fragments which he prints from the florilegia (878, n. on C.4 [–879]):

> Hi sex loci exstant sub Plutarchi nomine in Appendice Jo.
> Damasceni Parallel. Sacr. MS. Florent. Equidem neque de
> his, neque de sequentibus omnibus ex Maximo et Antonio
> depromtis, magnopere contendam eos Plutarchum habere

Consequently, those texts discussed by Elter (of which two had already been noted as spurious Philo fragments by Wachsmuth and Hense) are included below as fragmenta spuria even though they have not been definitely localized in another work.

By the way, the ascriptions in this collection seem to be, in general, highly trustworthy; at the very least they seem superior to those found in Maximus and Antonius. In fact, I have noted only four clear errors: Fr. sp. 18 is assigned to the wife of Philo, Fr. sp. 22 is ascribed to Solomon, Fr. sp. 28 is assigned to Philo (as well as correctly to Clement), and an extract from *Somn* 1.11, frequently found in florilegia under the name of Evagrius, is also assigned here to Evagrius.[79] On the other hand, the correct attributions are found for Fr. sp. 1, 2, 26, 28, 40, 41, and 42. I have accordingly cited Digb. 6 systematically for our fragmenta spuria, although it is only for the Pseudo-Plutarch fragments that its collection provides the crucial evidence.

Elter also discussed several fragments which are assigned to Philo in various editions of Antonius and Maximus, but which have not been included in collections of Philo fragments (probably through the oversight of the editors). These texts are Fr. sp. 13, 16, and 17.

Moreover, Elter mentions two texts which he claims are ascribed to Philo in Maximus, but which I have not been able to find so ascribed. These two are:

1.     Ὁ φρόνιμος ὥσπερ εἰς ὁδὸν τὸν βίον, οὐ τὰ πολ-
       λοῦ ἄξια συντίθησιν ἐφόδια, ἀλλὰ τὰ ἀναγκαιό-
       τερα.[80]

2.     Ἡ τρυφή, καθάπερ στρατοπέδου, τῆς τῶν ἀπαι-
       δεύτων ψυχῆς τὰ ἄριστα ἀφαιρεῖται.[81]

Whether I have overlooked these in some edition of Maximus, or Elter in some way slipped, I am fairly certain that, in any case, neither of these texts

---

auctorem: omittere eos non debui, quando adscripto Plutarchi nomine exstant.

[79]This is discussed on pages 45–46 below.

[80]See Elter, *Gnomica homoeomata* 5:26*, no. 132, where he says that this occurs "s. l. (post Philon.) Max. ed. pr.," i.e., "sine lemmate (post Philonea) Maximus editio princeps."

[81]Ibid. 5:5*, no. 20, where he says that this occurs "s. l. (post Philon.) Ma" (*sic*), i.e., "sine lemmate (post Philonea) Maximus." This is ascribed to Plutarch in Digb. 6, f. 58ʳ 14–15 = Par. 1168, f. 85ᵛ (Sternbach, 72, no. 47), and is in Combefis, p. 612 = *MPG* 91: 876A3–5 (Πλουτάρχ.).

has been printed within the Philo literature, and they are of course not from Philo.

Another group of spurious fragments are the four which are attributed to Evagrius Ponticus (Fr. sp. 40–43). These come from two small series of *sententiae*.[82] Now, it is certainly true that references to Philo and Evagrius are often confused in the florilegia,[83] and there is one particularly striking case which should be examined in detail. This is an excerpt which comes from Philo's *Somn* 1.11: ἀνθεῖ πρὸς ἐπιστήμην ψυχή, ὁπότε αἱ τοῦ σώματος ἀκμαὶ χρόνου μήκει μαραίνονται. Now, this text is correctly assigned to *Somn* 1.11 by Harris,[84] who found it in Par. 923 (f. 105ʳA [14] 14–19) and also in Lequien, 404 (= *MPG* 95:1308 [C9] C9–10), both times ascribed explicitly to Evagrius. A mystery here is how Harris noticed that this was really from Philo; presumably he was alerted to this text by the fact that in both his sources the immediately following text is *Abr* 271, which is explicitly assigned to Philo (Par. 923, f. 105ʳA [19] 20–34; Lequien, 404 [= *MPG* 95:1308 (C11) C11–D4]). In any case, though, this text is also ascribed to Evagrius in the collection found in Digb. 6 / Par. 1168, and from this latter manuscript it was printed by Elter along with the other texts assigned to Evagrius there.[85] Moreover, Elter argued that Maximus (which assigns this text to Evagrius) derived the sentence from the collection of Par. 1168, which in turn derived it from the *Sacra parallela*, which began the incorrect attribution to Evagrius.[86] Wendland cites this argument with approval,[87] and in *PCW* (3:207, apparatus) provides the evidence for the excerpt, where the assignment is always to Evagrius except for Vat. 1236: "praecedit in Dⱽ Euagrii sententia, sed Φίλωνος in margine adnotatum est." This reference occasioned a caustic reply from Holl, who notes that the text is correctly assigned to Philo in two manuscripts of the *Sacra parallela*,[88] and then adds on Wendland's remark on Dⱽ:

---

[82] These are found as *Spirituales sententiae* in *MPG* 40:1268C–69B, and *Aliae sententiae* in *MPG* 40:1269C–D. They are also edited by Elter, *Gnomica I: Sexti Pythagorici, Clitarchi, Evagrii Pontici sententiae* (Leipzig: B. G. Teubner, 1892), liii (series II), and liii–liv (series III).

[83] See Harris's comment in note 59 above.

[84] *Fragments*, 92.

[85] Elter, *Gnomica I*, liv (series IV).

[86] Ibid., il.

[87] "Zu Krumbachers Geschichte," 167–68 (including some other texts considered by Elter); see 168 for this particular case (where, though, the reference to Elter should be 'IL' instead of 'II').

[88] "Fragmente," xxxiii. These are Ottob. 79 and Ambrosianus H 26 inf.

"aber nicht etwa von einem Späteren, sondern von der ersten Hand, so wie im Vat. 1236 die Lemmata ebensohäufig am Rand, als im Texte stehen."[89] Holl then concludes that there has been a common error, but only between Maximus and some manuscripts (Par. 923 and Marc. 138) of the *Sacra parallela*, an error which may well have occurred independently.[90]

In the light of such a case, I suppose that one might wonder whether the *sententiae* in the two series really all come from Evagrius. However, as far as I can tell, no doubt has been raised concerning their origin with Evagrius.[91] And, in particular, Harris, Elter, and Holl identify one or more of our spurious texts as coming from these series, and without hesitation assign them to Evagrius. So, it seems that these two series have not been subject to the same vagaries as have the florilegia, and accordingly I believe that our four texts from these two series should be judged as spurious.

The final group of spurious fragments to which special attention should be directed consists of Fr. sp. 50–56. I have identified them as deriving from the very popular *Fürstenspiegel* of Agapetus, and have arranged them in the order in which they occur in his work. But here too there are complex issues to consider.

First, I may mention that my own discovery of Agapetus occurred as a result of following Harris's note on Fr. sp. 55.[92] Harris comments that the first part (ὁ μὲν θεὸς οὐδενὸς δεῖται, ὁ βασιλεὺς δὲ μόνου θεοῦ) "is based on an earlier gnomic saying," and refers the reader to Boissonade, *Anecdota Graeca* 1:45, which is in the edition of the gnomologium of Johannes Georgides.[93] There Boissonade prints the gnomic saying, Θεὸς δέεται [*sic*] μὲν οὐδενὸς [*sic*], σοφὸς δὲ δεῖται μόνου Θεοῦ,[94] and then in a note refers *inter alia* to "Agapetus cap. 63" as a parallel.[95] Now, though Boissonade does not refer to Philo here, just as Harris does not refer to Agapetus, when I turned to Agapetus all seven of our texts were quickly located there.

---

[89]Ibid., n. 1. Holl (xxxiii) also claims that Lequien took the incorrect lemma from Par. 923.

[90]Ibid., xxxiii–xxxiv.

[91]See Antoine and Claire Guillaumont, "Evagrius Ponticus," in *RAC* 6 (1966): 1092, concerning the three "Sentenzensammlungen" found in *MPG* 40:1264D–69D.

[92]*Fragments*, 104–5.

[93]On this florilegium see above, page 30.

[94]= *MPG* 117:1102D1–2. The same saying (but with δεῖται for δέεται μὲν) is edited by Wachsmuth, "De gnomologio Palatino inedito," 16, no. 11, and *Studien*, 167–68, no. 11.

[95]N. 3 = *MPG* 117:1102, n. 57 (–1103).

This work, entitled Ἔκθεσις κεφαλαίων παραινετικῶν, was dedicated by Agapetus, Diaconus in Constantinople, to the Emperor Justinian.[96] The 72 quite brief chapters, the initial letters of which form an acrostic,[97] present advice and exhortations to the ruler. The work was extensively copied during the succeeding centuries, and was often printed.[98] The most recent edition, however, remains that found in *MPG* 86.1:1163–86.

It is known that Agapetus was influenced by earlier writers in both the style and content of his work,[99] and perhaps even utilized sources now lost to us.[100] What is of interest to us here, of course, is the correspondence between Agapetus and our seven spurious fragments, and there have been, as I eventually discovered, scattered remarks noting this correspondence, some aspects of which have indeed been repeatedly discovered independently.

The first of these references[101] is by Boissonade in a later section of the volume to which Harris refers and concerns the same spurious text. Among

---

[96]On Agapetus generally, see Krumbacher, *Geschichte der byzantinischen Litteratur*, 456–57, and Pierre Hadot, "Fürstenspiegel," trans. Josef Engemann, *RAC* 8 (1972): 615–17. The attempts at further identification of Agapetus have failed; see Karl Praechter, Review of Antonio Bellomo, *Agapeto diacono e la sua scheda regia*, *ByzZ* 17 (1908): 163–64, and Patrick Henry III, "A Mirror for Justinian: The *Ekthesis* of Agapetus Diaconus," *GRBS* 8 (1967): 282–83. The dating of the work is similarly uncertain. Krumbacher, *Geschichte*, 456, assigns the work to "um die Zeit seines [Justinian's] Regierungsantrittes," i.e., 527. A date early in Justinian's reign seems plausible: see Praechter, Review, 162–63; Hadot, "Fürstenspiegel," 615; and Henry, "Mirror," 283–84.

[97]Hadot, "Fürstenspiegel," 615; Henry, "Mirror," 283. At least this is the case in most manuscripts; there are some different arrangements: see Praechter, Review, 154.

[98]See the list of manuscripts in *MPG* 86.1:1155–56, n. 2, and the list of editions at 1155–62.

[99]Bandur (cited at *MPG* 86.1:1153) mentions Isocrates and Gregory of Nazianzus. See also Henry, "Mirror," 297–98 (and especially 297, n. 47, for an intriguing suggestion).

[100]Praechter, "Der Roman Barlaam und Joasaph in seinem Verhältnis zu Agapets Königsspiegel," *ByzZ* 2 (1893): 459, argues that Agapetus and the author of *Barlaam and Ioasaph* used "eine gemeinsame Quelle." We will soon discuss *Barlaam* further.

[101]This is cited without discussion by Ihor Ševčenko, "A Neglected Byzantine Source of Muscovite Political Ideology," in *Harvard Slavic Studies*, vol. 2 (Cambridge: Harvard University Press, 1954), 147, n. 27.

the extracts edited there by Boissonade is a brief selection of ΓΝΩΜΑΙ
ΣΟΦΩΝ,[102] which includes (yet again): Ὁ μὲν Θεὸς οὐδενὸς δεῖται, ὁ δὲ
σοφὸς δεῖται μόνου τοῦ Θεοῦ.[103] And here Boissonade says in his note:

> Vide supra in Θεὸς p. 45, ubi quem adposui Agapeti locum
> exhibet, eumque pleniorem, Antonius Serm. 103, p. 172 [i.e.,
> Maximus[104]], praefixo male Philonis nomine. Excidit forsan
> ex Antonii codice locus Philonis De vita Mosis pag. 626 E
> [i.e., *Vita Mos* 1.157], ὁ μὲν γὰρ Θεὸς πάντα κεκτημένος
> οὐδενὸς δεῖται: et superstes tantum Philonis nomen Aga-
> peti verbis nunc legitur adpictum.[105]

Next, in his review of Bellomo's book, Praechter notes, almost in pas-
sing, that "einige Kapitel des Agapet auch in die Melissa des Antonios über-
gegangen sind."[106] In a note Praechter then adds:

> Da mir die Melissa zurzeit nicht zugänglich ist, so muß ich
> auf die Richtersche Philonausgabe verweisen, in welcher
> (VI, S. 233 ff.) "ex Antonio" eine Reihe von Philonfrag-
> menten abgedruckt ist, unter denen mehrere in Wirklichkeit
> Agapetsätze sind. Über das Lemma (Φίλωνος?) bei Anto-
> nios macht Richter keine Andeutung. Man vergleiche mit
> Ser. II Ag. 28, VIII Ag. 64, LII Ag. 12, LVII Ag. 23, CIV
> Ag. 21.[107]

---

[102]*Anecdota Graeca* 1:127–34 (from Par. 1630).

[103]Ibid. 1:127. At the similar text in Georgides Boissonade also refers
the reader to this text (although I did not turn to this until after reading Agapetus). See also ibid. 3:470, l. 13: Κύριος δεῖται οὐδενὸς [*sic*], σοφὸς δὲ
μόνου δεῖται Θεοῦ (one of the ΓΝΩΜΙΚΑ ΤΙΝΑ from Par. 2991 A).

[104]Boissonade, like Mangey, is citing Gessner's 1609 edition. This text
occurs only in Maximus.

[105]*Anecdota Graeca* 1:127, n. 3. Boissonade goes on to suggest reading
ἱκέτας (from Maximus) for οἰκέτας (in chap. 63 of the text of Agapetus), a
change which Henry ("Mirror," 290) independently approves: "The reading
of the fragment sounds more like Agapetus, since we would not expect the
deacon to repeat a phrase (περὶ τοὺς σοὺς οἰκέτας) which we have encoun-
tered already in § 23."

[106]Review, 153.

[107]Ibid., 153, n. 2. Praechter thus located Fr. sp. 50, 51, 52, 53, and 56.
He did not find Fr. sp. 54 and 55, since they are not in Mangey (or Richter).

The treatise of Agapetus was, as noted above, quite influential on later notions of kingship, and Philo's own writings, of course, discuss such issues. Consequently, one finds references to the Pseudo-Philo fragments alongside citations of genuine remarks of Philo. Goodenough, for example, cites Fr. sp. 51, 54, and 55 in his discussion of Philo's view of kingship. Furthermore, the work of Agapetus was influential, as it happens, on Muscovite ideology, and some of the literature on that subject has referred to the "Philo" fragments.

For instance, Kantorowicz cites Fr. sp. 51 as "a Philo fragment transmitted by Antonius Melissa," and comments:

> This passage is verbatim repeated by the composer of the Russian Laurentian Chronicle . . . who actually quotes Philo, though he purports to quote Chrysostom, when he writes: "By his earthly nature the Tsar is like all men; by the power of his rank, however, he is like God."[108]

Naturally, the influence is in fact from Agapetus, chap. 21.

This side of Agapetus's influence is explored more thoroughly by Ševčenko, who begins with the text (Fr. sp. 51) cited by Kantorowicz. Ševčenko finds that the Laurentian Chronicle is here dependent on a translation into Church Slavonic of an anthology similar to, but not identical with, the work of Pseudo-Antonius. (Although Ševčenko does not say so, this anthology must be that of Pseudo-Maximus, of course.) The Church Slavonic work was known, like that of Antonius, as the "Bee" (or "Pčela"), and was made in Kievan Rus'.[109] Ševčenko then informs us that, interestingly enough, this "Pčela" attributes our Fr. sp. 51 not to Philo but to "Agipitos,"[110] and goes

---

[108]Ernst H. Kantorowicz, "Deus per naturam, Deus per gratiam," *HTR* 45 (1952): 269, n. 55 (who cites, by the way, the "Philo" fragment from Goodenough, *Politics*, 99, and from *MPG* 136). Kantorowicz had earlier (265, n. 41) cited Philo's *Op* 148.

[109]Ševčenko, "Source," 142–43.

[110]One can most conveniently see the Slavonic and Greek texts in V. Semenov, ed., *Melissa* (reprinted with an introduction by Dmitrij Tschizhewskij; Slavische Propyläen, vol. 7; Munich: Wilhelm Fink, 1968), 111–12. There the Slavonic text has the lemma Агипитосъ ("Agipitos"), and the corresponding Greek text is given the lemma: < Ἀγαπητός>. (For Semenov's Greek sources, which evidently did not provide the lemma Ἀγαπητός, see the introduction by Tschizhewskij, xviii–xx; and on Fr. sp. 51 see p. xxiii and n. 35. Also, this introduction in general [ix–xxix] provides valuable information on the "Pčela"; note the brief reference in Richard, "Florilèges," 490.) It may be added that the other six spurious texts from Agapetus also

on to identify this text as coming from Agapetus's treatise, chap. 21.[111] He then says:

> Of course, this is not the only chapter of his *speculum principis* which entered into gnomic collections under the guise of Philo. Thus, to quote some examples, all the three "unidentified" passages of Harris' edition of Philonic fragments coincide in full with the three respective chapters of Agapetus, two of which are also given as Philonic by the Μελίσσα.[112]

In a note Ševčenko cites the identifications of Fr. sp. 52, 55, and 54, as coming from Agapetus, chaps. 23, 63, and 50. And he also remarks there:

> I see, after the completion of the present article, that K. Praechter, *Byzantinische Zeitschrift*, XVII (1908), 153, n.2 has already identified a number of "Philonic" fragments of Antonius as borrowed from Agapetus.[113]

Ševčenko continues by arguing that these texts should not be considered Philo fragments quoted by Agapetus, and his points will be considered below. He then turns to further treatment of Agapetus's influence, but there is one observation on Antonius which should be modified. After noting that the "Pčela" attributes Fr. sp. 51 to Agapetus, Ševčenko says:

---

appear in this Slavonic florilegium: Fr. sp. 50 on p. 125, Fr. sp. 52 on p. 83, Fr. sp. 53 on pp. 389–90, Fr. sp. 54 on pp. 87–88, Fr. sp. 55 on p. 100, and Fr. sp. 56 on p. 383. And each of these is explicitly ascribed to Philo, except for Fr. sp. 54, which, as in Maximus, follows an excerpt from *Quaes Ex* 2.6 which is explicitly assigned to Philo. Incidentally, in the related Serbian florilegium the text of Fr. sp. 51 is given the lemma Агапїдъ ("Agapidos"); see Mikhail Speranskij, ed., *Serbische und bulgarische Florilegien (Pchele) aus dem 13.–15. Jahrhundert* (reprinted with an introduction by Dmitrij Tschizhewskij; Slavische Propyläen, vol. 28; Munich: Wilhelm Fink, 1970), 80. (On this source, see the introduction by Tschizhewskij, v–viii.)

[111]Ševčenko, "Source," 145–46.

[112]Ibid., 146. The reference to "all the three" is to the texts published by Tischendorf but remaining unidentified by Harris (*Fragments*, 104–5). (Actually, although Harris says "three," there are four: 104.2 is genuine, and the three others are in the Slavonic florilegium.)

[113]Ševčenko, "Source," 146, n. 24; his reference is the same as our note 107 above.

I do not know on what authority, except that of editions of
Antonius, it found its way into Mangey's and Richter's collections of Philo's fragments and even into a recent treatise
on Philo's political theory. It must be said in Antonius'
defense, that he transmits the maxim anonymously. A cur-
sory survey of his edition by Gesner shows that the *lemma*
"Philonis" there stands in the margin of the Latin translation of the saying: rather flimsy grounds for determining
the authorship of the Greek text.[114]

Now, as Ševčenko mentions, he has seen only the 1609 edition of Gessner's work, along with the *MPG* reprint.[115] It is true that in these editions
the lemmata are placed alongside the Latin translation, although the fact that
*all* the lemmata are so placed should suggest that this was the decision of the
later editors, rather than the practice of the Greek manuscripts. In Gessner's
original edition the lemmata are in Greek, and Fr. sp. 51 is cited Φίλωνος.
And, of course, even in Harris's edition, cited by Ševčenko, sources other
than Antonius are given for these texts.[116]

Next, Henry considers in some detail these spurious texts.[117] He had
also found the correspondence independently, and only later learned of the
work of Praechter and Ševčenko.[118] Henry prints all seven texts with the
corresponding chapters in Agapetus, and also considers the two parallels in
*Barlaam and Ioasaph*.[119] He then summarizes Ševčenko's arguments that
these texts are from Agapetus,[120] but then brings forward some qualifications

---

[114]Ibid., 145. The "recent treatise" is, of course, that of Goodenough,
and (in n. 21) Ševčenko comments: "with conclusions on Philo's ideas drawn
from the passage in question and a reproach directed against J. Rendel
Harris for having omitted it from his collection of Philo's fragments."

[115]Ibid., n. 22.

[116]Henry, "Mirror," 292, cites Ševčenko's point, but also notes that the
Greek lemma is found in Maximus. However, Henry also (285, n. 14) relies
on the *MPG* reprint of Antonius, and so does not report on Greek lemmata
in Antonius.

[117]I learned of this article from Chadwick, "Florilegium," 1154, although
the reference there hardly indicates the importance of Henry's article for
Philo studies.

[118]"Mirror," 285.

[119]Ibid., 286–91.

[120]Ibid., 292.

to these arguments.[121] We shall consider Henry's arguments later, but will note here that he concludes: "The balance remains in favor of the view that the seven passages discussed above are not authentic Philo."[122]

Finally, Hadot briefly refers to texts found in Agapetus which are also ascribed to Philo.[123] Although his citations are not quite clear, he seems to refer to Fr. sp. 51, 52, 53 and 55,[124] and cites Praechter's review of Bellomo on this topic.[125] Hadot concludes: "Es ist fraglich, ob diese Fragmente tat-sächlich von Philon stammen u. einer verlorenen Abhandlung 'Über das Königtum' entnommen sind."[126]

Let us now turn briefly to these seven texts. First, the consistency of attribution of these seven texts to Philo is very curious. All are assigned to him in Maximus, five of the seven are assigned to him in Gessner's edition of Antonius, and the other two find their way under Philo's name by the edition in *MPG* 136. This latter movement indicates the direction of textual change. However, it is interesting that five texts from Agapetus should be uniformly ascribed to Philo in all the sources cited, and are scattered throughout the various florilegia. This situation is quite different from what we find with, say, our "Plutarch" fragments, which are often assigned to Plutarch rather than Philo, or the three texts from John Climacus, where the loss of just one lemma has caused the mistaken attribution. Furthermore, six of the seven Agapetus fragments (excepting Fr. sp. 54) are explicitly assigned to Philo in Maximus.

Accordingly, the sort of isolated loss or shifting of a lemma which we see elsewhere hardly accounts for what we see with the Agapetus texts. A possible explanation, although I can provide no evidence for it, is that these texts came into Maximus (at least) from a collection arranged as in Digb. 6 / Par. 1168, that is, with these seven texts all preceded by one lemma Ἀγαπη-τοῦ. If we suppose that this lemma was lost and that the preceding texts were from Philo, then we would have a global shift of these texts to Philo.

Another possibility, which I offer very hesitantly, is that at some point in the history of the florilegia someone failed to recognize the name Ἀγαπη-

---

[121]Ibid., 292–94.

[122]Ibid., 295.

[123]"Fürstenspiegel," 594, 616.

[124]At 594 Hadot refers to *MPG* 136:995–1011, while at 616 he refers to *MPG* 136:871D and 995–1011. Apparently he is citing the Latin columns.

[125]Ibid., 594.

[126]Ibid. Here Hadot also says that the Philo fragments appear "ano-nym" in Agapetus's *Fürstenspiegel*. This is at least misleading; they appear simply as part of Agapetus's text.

τοῦ, and seeing a connection between ἀγαπάω and φιλέω thought that this was meant to be Φίλωνος.[127] Naturally, such confusion could hardly have happened often, and perhaps the success of Agapetus's work speaks against its ever happening. But clearly some kind of confusion occurred, and it does seem as if a reader of florilegia would be surprised to find 'Αγαπητοῦ, which I don't recall ever seeing except on Fr. sp. 51, as noted below. And in fact, this lemma has occasioned some confusion in the literature. Gessner printed this text following two texts on the first of which was the lemma Κότυς. However, in his addenda, obviously on the basis of Mon. 429, he noted that the (spurious) text should receive the lemma 'Αγαπητοῦ.[128] Now, Wachsmuth somehow combined this correct lemma with the spurious ascription to Philo, and thus cited this text as occurring in Maximus with the lemma: 'Αγαπήτου Φίλωνος.[129] And this lemma was accordingly noted by Henry, who reasonably found it puzzling.[130]

In any case, though, there are several considerations which, taken together, may give us complete confidence that these seven texts are not from Philo, and indeed are, with the possible exception of Fr. sp. 56, from Agapetus.

---

[127]There is a partial parallel in the supposed misunderstanding of "ὑπὸ Φίλωνος" as "ab amicis" in the Muratorian Canon's listing of the Wisdom of Solomon; see Schürer, *Geschichte* 3:509; idem, *History* 3.1:574; Speyer, *Die literarische Fälschung*, 154, n. 6; and Bruns, "Philo Christianus," 143. Cf. also Henry's comment in note 130 below.

[128]See the references on this text in chapter 4 below. This lemma also occurs in Barocc. 143.

[129]*Studien*, 116 (with the accent as given). Wachsmuth cites this in his table as being the lemma on the text at Combefis, 561, ll. 21–28, although there the lemma is actually: Φίλων. Apparently Wachsmuth transferred Gessner's correction to the lemma in Antonius to the text as it stands in Maximus.

[130]Henry, "A Mirror," 292, n. 30 (–293), comments on the lemma on this spurious text, notes Wachsmuth's reference, thinks that perhaps Wachsmuth is drawing on manuscripts of Maximus, and then says:

> I do not know what to make of 'Αγαπήτου Φίλωνος. Perhaps some scribe thought it meant 'of the beloved Philo.' In this confusion there is probably some valuable clue to the way in which these sections came to be attributed to Philo, but I do not know how to follow up the hint.

I believe that this particular lemma is just an error by Wachsmuth, although it conflates the two lemmata which do stand in the florilegia.

1.   Five of the seven texts coincide precisely with chapters from Agapetus's work. And of the other two, Fr. sp. 50 omits some words and then the
final clause of chap. 12, while Fr. sp. 53 is merely the final third of chap. 28.
Hence, it is clear that the excerptor contented himself in most of the cases
with simply taking a chapter from Agapetus with no editing or rearranging.
That genuine Philo fragments would thus coincide could be explained only if
we imagine that the texts were already so divided in Agapetus's source. But
it seems an unbelievable sequence that the texts so existed, that Agapetus
used them (instead of Philo's then extant works[131]), and that they were eventually collected into florilegia and provided (again?) with Philo's name.[132]

2.   The texts occur only in late florilegia, not in the *Sacra parallela*.[133]
This fact very strongly suggests that the texts are not from Philo, since the
extensive excerpting of Philo clearly took place in the *Sacra parallela*,[134] and

---

[131]Ševčenko ("Source," 147) says that "no correspondence between him
and some authentic saying of Philo can be established." Henry ("Mirror,"
293) confirms this, and adds:

> It would be remarkable to find a deacon in sixth-century
> Constantinople acquainted with an entire work of Philo.
> The most we could expect is to find Agapetus using some
> fragment of Philo known to us to be authentic and available
> to Agapetus in a *florilegium*. I have gone carefully through
> the lists of Philo fragments, particularly all the ones identi-
> fied by Harris, and have not found any clearly authentic
> fragment which is also a maxim of Agapetus. Nonetheless,
> it is known that a good number of Philo's works are alto-
> gether lost, and there are also many unidentified Philo frag-
> ments which are not in Agapetus.

At this point it would be mere conjecture to suppose that these texts in Agapetus are from Philo.

[132]That the texts mostly coincide with Agapetus's chapters is emphasized by Ševčenko, "Source," 146–47, and by Henry, "Mirror," 292–93.

[133]We may suppose that Agapetus was too late to be included in the
*Sacra parallela*. On some (only) supposed occurrences of Agapetus in Stobaeus, see Fabricius and Harles, *Bibliotheca Graeca* 8:36, 9:570.

[134]Henry, "Mirror," 292, comments:

> I have been unable in a thorough search to locate any of
> these "Philo fragments" in the *Sacra Parallela*, which is
> thought to be earlier still and which does contain scores of
> authentic extracts from Philo. However, the whole third
> book of the *Sacra Parallela* is lost, and it may have included

it is at any rate unusual to find in later florilegia a genuine Philo fragment which does not occur in any manuscript of the *Sacra parallela*.

3. In several cases there are certain words or phrases which can plausibly be labelled Christian. With Fr. sp. 51 cf. Rom 9:5 (ὁ ὢν ἐπὶ πάντων θεός [noted already by Combefis]), which is also cited in chap. 37. In the same spurious text one finds the phrase κόνει χοϊκῇ,[135] which goes back to 1 Cor 15:47–49, and χοϊκός does not occur earlier than 1 Cor.[136] With Fr. sp. 52 cf. Matt 6:14–15, 7:2. And the reference to the divine wrath in Fr. sp. 56 is, while perhaps not impossible in Philo,[137] certainly more likely to be of Christian origin.[138]

4. There are many parallels between the seven texts and other sections of Agapetus's work. With κόλαξ in Fr. sp. 50, cf. chaps. 22, 31, and 56.[139] For ἀξίωμα in Fr. sp. 51, see chaps. 1 and 14. With the theme of Fr. sp. 52, cf. chap. 8. For βασιλεῦ in Fr. sp. 54, see chaps. 1, 11, etc. On the opening line of Fr. sp. 55, see chap. 68. And on πλημμελέω in Fr. sp. 56, see chaps. 28, 36, and 65.[140]

All of this evidence makes it implausible to think that these seven texts might come from Philo. There is, however, a complication. Two of the seven texts have parallels in *Barlaam*, which itself contains a brief *Fürstenspiegel* in

---

these passages which are preserved in the other two *florilegia*.

Of course, it seems very unlikely that all seven of these Agapetus texts would have chanced to be in portions of the *Sacra parallela* which have not survived (or are as yet unknown).

[135]Henry, "Mirror," 287, observes on this: "This latter reading seems much more characteristic of Agapetus, since the play on εἰκόνι θεϊκῇ . . . κόνει χοϊκῇ is thoroughly consonant with his style, while the repetition of a word is something he strives to avoid." But he fails to observe that χοϊκός itself is Christian.

[136]The reference in Liddell-Scott-Jones to Philo is to this text as printed in Mangey. The TLG confirms that all reported occurrences are Christian.

[137]See Erik Sjöberg and Gustav Stählin, "ὀργή D III," *TWNT* 5 (1954): 418.

[138]See Lampe, *A Patristic Greek Lexicon*, s.v. ὀργή C.

[139]Lewy, "Neue Philontexte," 81, refers to Philo, *Migr* 110–11.

[140]On this topic generally see also Ševčenko, "Source," 146: "All the 'Philonic' sentences which reappear as Agapetus' chapters display the very mannerisms peculiar to the whole of his [i.e., Agapetus's] work."

the speech to Barachias.[141]  This work seems to come from a time somewhat later than Agapetus,[142] and certainly bears some relation to Agapetus's work.[143]  Boissonade thought that the author of *Barlaam* had used Agapetus's work,[144] but later scholars were more cautious.  Praechter thought that a common source of both, rather than direct use of one by the other, was most likely.[145]

Now, while one of these texts, Fr. sp. 52, clearly derives from Agapetus, the other text presents some special difficulties.[146]  Our Fr. sp. 56 is identified as Agapetus, chap. 64.  However, the text of the fragment as found in the florilegia is in fact closer to what we find in *Barlaam* than to Agapetus.[147] (The Greek texts may be found under Fr. sp. 56 below.)  One observes that the ending of Agapetus, chap. 64 departs from the reading common to *Bar-*

---

[141]This section is found in Boissonade, *Anecdota Graeca* 4:331–35 ( = *MPG* 96:1204B1–1208B2).

[142]In general see Krumbacher, *Geschichte der byzantinischen Litteratur*, 886–91.  The traditional identification of the author with John of Damascus was defended by Franz Dölger, *Der griechische Barlaam-Roman: Ein Werk des H. Johannes von Damaskos* (Studia Patristica et Byzantina, vol. 1; Ettal: Buch-Kunstverlag, 1953).  See also his reply to reviews, *ByzZ* 48 (1955): 215; the introduction by D. M. Lang to G. R. Woodward and H. Mattingly, eds. and trans., *St. John Damascene, Barlaam and Ioasaph* (LCL; 1967), ix–xxxv; and the review of this work by Gérard Garitte, *Mus* 81 (1968): 277.

[143]At least some of the parallels are cited by Boissonade in his notes (*Anecdota Graeca* 4:331–34 [ = *MPG* 96:1203–6]).  Praechter, "Der Roman Barlaam und Joasaph," compares the works throughout, and Dölger, *Der Barlaam-Roman*, 100–104, presents numerous parallels between the two works.  Dölger seems indeed to write as though Agapetus were a source of *Barlaam*, since he says (65): "Wir wissen, daß der Barlaamroman . . . große Teile des Fürstenspiegels des Agapet . . . enthält . . . ."  On this claim Dölger refers (65, n. 2) to Praechter's article, who certainly did not assert a dependence (see note 100 above); perhaps "enthält" is meant to leave open the question of dependence.

[144]*Anecdota Graeca* 4:331, n. 2 (*MPG* 96:1203–4, n. 15): ". . . Agapetum c. 10, quem noster descripsit."

[145]Cf. note 100 above.  See also the comments on Agapetus and *Barlaam* by Ševčenko, "Source," 148, n. 30, and by Henry, "Mirror," 294.

[146]Henry, "Mirror," 291, discusses this text, and also follows Praechter's analysis of the textual relationships.

[147]Dölger, *Der Barlaam-Roman*, 104, in his listing of parallels between *Barlaam* and Agapetus silently "corrects" Agapetus to agree with *Barlaam*.

*laam* and the florilegia. And Praechter cites Bellomo as reporting that some manuscripts of Agapetus omit the final phrase (ἡ πρὸς θεὸν φιλία καὶ οἰκείωσις), and this omission from the usual text of Agapetus cannot be explained. However, the omission of the final phrase of *Barlaam* (τῆς δεσποτικῆς ὀργῆς γίνεται ἀπαλλαγή) would be readily explained as a result of homoeoteleuton (καταλλαγῇ . . . ἀπαλλαγή).[148] We may suppose, therefore, that chap. 64 of Agapetus originally ended as *Barlaam* does now, that the final phrase in Agapetus was accidentally omitted, and that the present final phrase was subsequently added in order to repair the sentence.[149] If we then postulate that both *Barlaam* and the ultimate source of the florilegia used Agapetus before the omission occurred, we have a coherent history of the existing texts.

The remaining differences are that *Barlaam* has τῆς δεσποτικῆς ὀργῆς where the florilegia have τῆς θείας ὀργῆς, and that *Barlaam* has τῇ καταλλαγῇ where the florilegia have ἡ καταλλαγή. Henry defends the readings of the florilegia as preserving the original text of Agapetus.[150] However, at the first variation, at least, I believe that *Barlaam* must be correct. Agapetus is speaking of an earthly δεσπότης, not of God or Christ, whereas the florilegia draw a spiritual lesson; note that they make the similar change from δεσπότην to θεόν in Fr. sp. 52.[151]

However we decide such details, though, there is no reason to suppose that this fragment or any of the other six derives from Philo.[152] What we

---

[148]See Praechter, Review, 159. (I have not seen Bellomo's book.)

[149]Praechter (ibid.) puts the point this way: "So [as in *Barlaam*] schloß also wohl das Kapitel auch bei Agapet, und das ἡ . . . οἰκείωσις ist nur Lückenbüßer und dazu noch ein herzlich schlechter; denn der Zusammenhang verlangt, daß von einer Leistung seitens der Gottheit gesprochen werde und nicht allgemein von Freundschaft mit Gott."

[150]"Mirror," 291: "One can go farther and say that the fragment is more nearly what Agapetus wrote than *Barlaam* is, since τῆς θείας ὀργῆς seems metrically better than τῆς δεσποτικῆς ὀργῆς (also, 'divine anger' is a more common notion than the anger of Christ), and ἡ καταλλαγή as the subject of γίνεται is smoother grammatically than the dative construction in Agapetus and *Barlaam*."

[151]Henry, "Mirror," 288, notes this change.

[152]Henry ("Mirror," 294) claims that "if the two authors [Agapetus and *Barlaam*] are dependent on a common source that source must have contained at least these two Philo fragments and the case for Philonic origin is considerably strengthened." I do not see why this is so. There is no reason to believe that a common source of Agapetus and *Barlaam* would be Philo or

doubtless have are seven excerpts from Agapetus, with, as one could expect, some confusions in the details of the textual transmission. In particular, it remains puzzling that they are ascribed to Philo. But many questions concerning texts and lemmata in the florilegia remain unanswered.[153] Nevertheless, we can dismiss these seven as spurious Philo fragments.

---

contain Philo; it might, of course, but this mere possibility cannot strengthen the case for Philonic origin.

[153]Cf. Henry, "Mirror," 295: "How are we to explain the transmission of seven gnomic sayings belonging to a work by a sixth-century deacon under the guise of the great first-century Alexandrian Jew? This question rather neatly characterizes the sort of cultural puzzles in which Byzantine history abounds."

4

# FRAGMENTA SPURIA

The fragments which have been assigned to Philo but which should definitely be removed from the list of "Philo fragments" are presented here. In order to provide some order to what often seems to be a mass of references to very diverse materials, I have arranged these fragments according to their correct identifications within the following categories: secular texts, Old Testament texts, texts from Jewish writers, and texts from Christian writers. Within each of these categories the texts are arranged in (at least roughly) chronological order. Indexes to the printed sources from which the fragments are taken may be found in the Appendix.

The following manuscripts are regularly cited: Barocc. 143, Ber. 46, Coisl. 276 (in which only Fr. sp. 27 and 31 occur), Digb. 6, Par. 923, and Vat. 1553 (in which only Fr. sp. 30 occurs). Earlier references to these manuscripts have been updated by precise citations of folios, columns (in the case of Par. 923), and lines. Occasional citations are made from related manuscripts of the florilegia: Escur. Ω. III. 9, Vindob. suppl. 178, Ottob. 79, Marc. 138, and Mon. 429. Since it is not intended to produce a critical edition of these fragments, textual variations are, in general, not reported, although a few of the less trivial variants are cited.

For the citations from printed editions, see the Appendix below (to which should be added that 'Holl' refers to Holl, *Fragmente*). The identifications assigned to Früchtel are all found in his collection of Philo fragments, and thus were made by 1963.

My attempts at locating fragments ascribed to Philo have utilized the usual lexica as well as (when possible) indexes to particular authors. I regret that I am not now able to reconstruct what clues first led me to some of these identifications, and hope that I have not failed to give appropriate credit to anyone. As a more systematic source of information, I was fortunate enough to be able to utilize the files which formed the basis of Lampe's *A Patristic Greek Lexicon*, although they did not lead directly to any fresh identifications.[1] However, toward the end of the preparation of this volume, I learned

---

[1] I must here express my appreciation to Professor Lampe, who told me

of the resources available through the Thesaurus Linguae Graecae, based at
the University of California, Irvine. Through the data there available, I was
able to identify several texts (a few from sources which I would hardly have
searched directly). These identifications are:  Fr. sp. 6, 19, 31, 33, 35, 36, 37,
46, and 47.[2]

---

of the existence of these files in the Bodleian Library, and to Mr. Barker-
Benfield, who made them available to me.

[2]The TLG continues to add texts to its data bank, and I hope that perhaps through its use I may be able to identify yet other spurious texts. At the
very least, of course, the information gathered there will permit more confident judgment concerning the authenticity of various texts than would otherwise be possible.

Fr. sp. 1

Οἱ ἡμερήσιοι ὕπνοι σώματος ὄχλησιν ἢ ψυχῆς ἀδημοσύνην ἢ ἀργίην ἢ ἀπαιδευσίην σημαίνουσιν.

Gessner, 51 = *MPG* 136:921A9–11 (no lemma; follows Fr. sp. 59), from Antonius.[3]

Combefis, 616 = *MPG* 91:881B12–13 (no lemma; on previous text [B10]: Δημοκρίτ.), from Maximus.

Barocc. 143, f. 152ᵛ (2) 3–5: Δημοκρίτου.

Ascribed to Democritus (Δημοκρίτου γνῶμαι, f. 67ʳ 18) in Digb. 6, f. 69ʳ 2–4 = Par. 1168, f. 95ᵛ (Sternbach, 77, no. 36).

Removed as = Democritus, fragment 212, from Stobaeus 3.6.27: Δημοκρίτου.[4]

---

[3]In his addenda, 296–97, Gessner writes: "al. ἡμερούσια, tribuit autem Democrito."

[4]Found in Hermann Diels and Walther Kranz, eds., *Die Fragmente der Vorsokratiker* (2 vols.; 6th ed.; Dublin and Zurich: Weidmann, 1951–52), 2:188.

Fr. sp. 2

'Υπὸ γυναικὸς ἄρχεσθαι ὕβρις ἂν εἴη ἐσχάτη.

Gessner, 107 = *MPG* 136:1089D12 (Philonis), from Antonius.
Combefis, 631 = *MPG* 91:912B6–7 (Δημοκρίτ.), from Maximus.
Ascribed to Democritus (Δημοκρίτου γνῶμαι, f. 67ʳ 18) in Digb. 6, f. 69ʳ 14 = Par. 1168, f. 96ʳ (Sternbach, 77, no. 41).

Removed by Wachsmuth[5] as = Democritus, fragment 111, from Stobaeus 4.23.39: Δημοκρίτου.[6]

---

[5]*Studien*, 207 (no. 268), where the text is ascribed to Democritus and the lemma Φίλωνος is noted with "!" Boissonade, *Anecdota Graeca* 3:465, n. 3, cites this text (with ἀνδρὶ for ἂν εἴη) and adds: "Quae sententia exstat apud Democratem p. 631, et apud Antonium S. 124, p. 97, sub Philonis nomine; nec utrobique sine varietate."
[6]Diels and Kranz, *Fragmente der Vorsokratiker* 2:164.

Fr. sp. 3

'Ασκητέον ὀλίγων δεηθῆναι· τοῦτο γὰρ ἐγγυτάτω θεῷ, τὸ δὲ ἐναν-
τίον μακροτάτω.

Gessner, 38 = *MPG* 136:881A10–11 (no lemma; follows two Philo texts
[A4]: Philonis), from Antonius.
Mangey, 666.3, from Ber. 46, f. 220ʳ (34) 35–36: τοῦ αὐτοῦ (Φίλωνος, l.
14).
Harris, 101.11, from Mangey, Ber. 46, and Antonius.

Removed by Früchtel as = Crates, *Epistle* 11.[7] By the way, it is strange
to find this secular text in Ber. 46; see the comments on Fr. sp. 6 below.

---

[7]Found in Rudolf Hercher, *Epistolographi Graeci* (Paris: A. F. Didot,
1873), 210, but with ἀσκεῖτε for ἀσκητέον.

Fr. sp. 4

Οὐ ποιεῖ ἀγρὸς φαύλους, οὐδὲ ἄστυ σπουδαίους, ἀλλ᾽ ἡ μετὰ τοιῶνδε συνδιατριβή.

Gessner, 109 = *MPG* 136:1096D9–10 (no lemma; follows a Philo text [D6]: Philonis), from Antonius.
Mangey, 671.3b, "ex Antonio."

Removed by Früchtel as = Crates, *Epistle* 12.[8]

---

[8]Ibid., where we find: Οὐ ποιεῖ ἀγρὸς σπουδαίους, οὐδὲ ἄστυ φαύλους, ἀλλ᾽ αἱ σὺν τοῖς ἀγαθοῖς καὶ κακοῖς διατριβαί.

Fr. sp. 5

Πλοῦτος κακίας μᾶλλον ἢ καλοκαγαθίας ἐστὶν ὑπηρέτης.

Gessner, 39 = *MPG* 136:885A6–7 (no lemma; on previous text [A4]: Chilonis), from Antonius.

Gessner, 40 (Χείλονος [*sic*]) = *MPG* 136:889A1–2 (Philonis), from Antonius.

Lequien, 418 = *MPG* 95:1340A4–5 (no lemma; on previous text [A3]: Cyril.), from Vat. 1236.

Ber. 46, f. 252$^r$ (10) 10–11: Φίλωνος ὡς ἀπὸ Σωκράτους.

Removed as = Isocrates 1.6 (πρὸς Δημόνικον). The genuineness of this letter is disputed, but it is hardly by Philo in any case.[9] Incidentally, in the British Library copy of Gessner's 1546 edition (which was owned by Charles Burney), the second occurrence of this text has received the marginal comment: Ἰσοκράτους πρὸς Δημ. The text may also be found in Stobaeus 4.31.77. By the way, the confusion between Φίλωνος and Χείλονος here is paralleled by an error cited by Sternbach[10] from Vat. 1144, f. 232$^v$, where Sternbach prints the lemma Χίλων, but notes: "Χίλων] Φίλων (contra ordinem alphabeticum)." Perhaps more likely than a simple *lapsus calami* would be that the initial letter at some point in the textual transmission was left to be written later by a rubricator, and was then supplied incorrectly. But such a sequence could hardly have occurred between Gessner's 1546 edition and the later reprint. It is again curious to find a secular text in Ber. 46 and Vat. 1236; see the comments on Fr. sp. 6 below.

---

[9]Chadwick, "Florilegium," 1136: "Obwohl die Rede ad Demonicum nicht als authentisches Werk des Isokrates angesehen werden kann, gehört sie in das 4. Jh. vC. u. ist die erste förmliche Sammlung von Lebensregeln in Prosaform."

[10]*Gnomologium Parisinum ineditum* (Cracow: Sumptibus Academiae Litterarum, 1893), 84, no. 146. Similar errors are noted by Sternbach in his *Gnomologium Vaticanum e codice Vaticano Graeco 743* (foreword by Otto Luschnat; Texte und Kommentare, vol. 2; Berlin: Walter de Gruyter, 1963), 197, no. 549, and 198, no. 553.

Fr. sp. 6

Ἀνδρείας ἐστὶ τὸ δύσπληκτον εἶναι ὑπὸ φόβων τῶν περὶ θάνατον καὶ τὸ εὔθαρσῆ ἐν τοῖς δεινοῖς καὶ τὸ εὔτολμον ἐν τοῖς κινδύνοις καὶ τὸ μᾶλλον αἱρεῖσθαι τεθνάναι καλῶς ἢ αἰσχρῶς σωθῆναι καὶ τὸ νίκης αἴτιον εἶναι. παρέπεται δὲ τῇ ἀνδρείᾳ ἡ εὐτολμία καὶ εὐψυχία καὶ τὸ θάρσος.

Mangey, 665.1, from Ber. 46, f. 185ʳ (7) 8–11: Φίλωνος ἐκ τοῦ περὶ γιγάντων.
Harris, 9.2, from Mangey and Ber. 46.

Removed as = Pseudo-Aristotle, *De virtutibus et vitiis* 4.1250ᵃ44–ᵇ5. This treatise has been dated to the late fourth century or early third century B.C.[11] There we find δυσέκπληκτον for δύσπληκτον, and, along with a few minor differences, the addition after the second εἶναι of ἔστι δὲ ἀνδρείας καὶ τὸ πονεῖν καὶ καρτερεῖν καὶ [αἱρεῖσθαι] ἀνδραγαθίζεσθαι.[12]

It is remarkable that this text (like Fr. sp. 3 and 5) is found, under any name at all, in a manuscript of the *Sacra parallela*. For that work is always reported to contain no secular citations at all.[13] Thus, we must assume that this selection was placed into the *Sacra parallela* in the belief that it came from a work of a Church writer or Philo or Josephus. Now, the work attributed to Aristotle seems to have circulated with the title περὶ ἀρετῶν καὶ κακιῶν or περὶ ἀρετῆς or περὶ ἀρετῶν.[14] And there are two works of Philo with

---

[11]See the comments by Ernst A. Schmidt, trans., *Aristoteles, Über die Tugend, Aristoteles Werke in deutscher Übersetzung*, ed. Ernst Grumach, vol. 18: *Opuscula*, pt. 1 (Berlin: Akademie-Verlag, 1965), 23–28.

[12]See the evidence in Franz Susemihl, ed., *[Aristotelis Ethica Eudemia,] Eudemi Rhodii Ethica, adiecto de virtutibus et vitiis libello* (Leipzig: B. G. Teubner, 1884), 185–86 (the treatise occupies 181–94; for the manuscripts see the preface, xxxi–xxxvii). The omission, which is perhaps due to homoeoteleuton, is also found in Pseudo-Andronicus, Περὶ παθῶν; however, Pseudo-Andronicus reads before the omission αἴτιον διὰ παντὸς γίνεσθαι.

[13]Indeed, the absence of secular authors distinguishes the *Sacra parallela* from the sacro-profane collections such as Maximus and Antonius. In the lists of authors cited in various manuscripts of the *Sacra parallela*, I have found no secular writer: see, e.g., Holl, *Die Sacra Parallela*, 183–84, 201–2; Loofs, *Studien*, 100–102. Naturally, it is always possible that some of the other unidentified texts in fact come from secular authors.

[14]See the evidence in Schmidt, *Aristoteles*, 13–16. By the way, this treatise was among the third group of works translated into Armenian by the

titles sometimes similar to the third form: *Gaium*[15] and *Virt*.[16] Of course, the usual title of this latter work begins περὶ ἀρετῶν, and even has a section περὶ ἀνδρείας, all of which would fit nicely with our spurious text. One would be tempted, thus, to suppose that someone thought that the Pseudo-Aristotelian work was by Philo, and then made this brief extract for the *Sacra parallela*. But we then would have the difficulty that the text does not appear with the lemma Φίλωνος ἐκ τοῦ περὶ ἀρετῶν, and so would have to suppose yet another error with the lemma. And we have already noted that precisely the lemma Φίλωνος ἐκ τοῦ περὶ γιγάντων is problematic.[17]

---

Hellenizing School: see Terian, *Philonis Alexandrini de animalibus*, 7–8, who follows Arevšatyan, "Platoni erkeri Hayeren t'argmanowt'yan žamanakə," where (17) the title of this work is given as "yałags aīak'inowt'ean" (= περὶ ἀρετῆς).

[15]See the evidence in *PCW* 6:lviii–lx, and the apparatus at 6:155. One manuscript (M) in fact reads: Φίλωνος περὶ ἀρετῶν ὅ ἐστι τῆς αὐτοῦ πρεσβείας πρὸς γάϊον.

[16]See the evidence in *PCW* 5:xxvi–xxviii, and the apparatus at 5:266.

[17]See chapter 3, pages 36–37, above.

Fr. sp. 7

Τὸ μὴ αἰσχύνεσθαι κακὸν ὄντα κακίας ὑπερβολή.

Gessner, 135 = *MPG* 136:1169D8 (no lemma; on previous text [D4]: Aristotelis), from Antonius.

Combefis, 633 = *MPG* 91:916B8–9 (᾽Αριστοτέλ.), from Maximus.

Cramer, *Anecdota Graeca* 4:254, fragment 7 (no lemma; follows two Philo texts with lemma: Φίλωνος), from Oxoniensis Clarkianus 11, f. 63ᵛ (15) 23: Φίλωνος.

Harris, 106.2, from Cramer.

Barocc. 143, f. 137ʳ (19) 23–24: Φιλιστίωνος.

Removed as = Aristotle (?), fragment. This is a very interesting case. The text is printed from Maximus as an Aristotle fragment by Valentin Rose in his collection.[18] It is, I suppose, not at all clear that this text is from Aristotle.[19] But, in any case, the attribution to Philo has arisen from a scribal error in the following manner. The manuscript, Clark. 11, contains various excerpts in no apparent order.[20] However, Wachsmuth observed that the texts on f. 63ᵛ are in fact simply selected from several chapters of Maximus, retaining the earlier order.[21] For our purposes the relevant data are:

| | *MPG* 91:916 | Clark. 11, f. 63ᵛ | Cramer, 254 |
|---|---|---|---|
| *Leg All* 2.65 | A9–12 | 16–18 | 10–12 |
| *Quaes Gen* 4.99 | A13–B3 | 18–22 | 13–17 |
| Fr. sp. 7 | B8–9 | 23 | 18 |

---

[18]*Aristoteles pseudepigraphus* (Leipzig: B. G. Teubner, 1863), 610, no. 17. This is among 22 extracts printed from florilegia (606–11).

[19]The TLG confirms that it is not, at any rate, found in the usual works of Aristotle.

[20]Richard, "Florilèges," 498, reports that he has found no sense to this manuscript. Similarly, Petit, *Quaestiones: Fragmenta Graeca*, 27, calls it "un florilège anonyme anarchique"; she cites it for *Quaes Gen* 4.99 only (ibid., 175–76).

[21]*Studien*, 138: "Der 'unbestimmte Autor' bei Cramer An. Oxon. IV p. 254, 4 ist aber wiederum kein anderer als Maximus. Die Excerpte nämlich, die im cod. Bodl. Clark. 11ᵇ fol. 63 [sic] stehen, sind der Reihe nach aus einem Maximus genommen—was freilich auch andern entgangen ist—; . . . ." Wachsmuth (138–39) then gives a list showing the locations in Maximus of the texts found in Cramer, 253, l. 18 – 254, l. 24.

Consequently, either the excerptor himself or some later scribe has simply skipped the lemma in Maximus ascribing our text to Aristotle. Since there is no further evidence that the text is from Philo, we may remove it.

There is, however, another curious point. In his index to the fragments in Harris's edition, Früchtel identified this text as being *Spec Leg* 3.54, where we find: τὸ γὰρ μέχρι τέλους ἀναισχυντεῖν ὑπερβολὴ κακίας. Although there is some similarity here, it is not sufficient to justify us in believing that the text really has this origin.

Fr. sp. 8

Ἐκ χρυσοῦ ποτηρίου πίνειν φάρμακον καὶ ἐκ φίλου ἀγνώμονος συμβουλίαν λαμβάνειν ταὐτόν ἐστιν.

Gessner, 29 = *MPG* 136:852C13–D1 (no lemma; on third previous text [C7]: Solonis), from Antonius.

Combefis, 548 = *MPG* 91:757D1–2 (no lemma; follows a Philo text [C11]: Φίλωνος), from Maximus.

Mangey, 673.6a, "ex Antonio."

Barocc. 143, f. 78ʳ (3) 7–9: Πλουτάρχου.

Ascribed to Plutarch (<Π>λουτάρχου, f. 55ʳ 18) in Digb. 6, f. 55ᵛ 8–10 = Par. 1168, f. 83ʳ (Sternbach, 69, no. 4).

Removed by Elter[22] as = Pseudo-Plutarch, fragment 87 (Bernardakis, 160).

---

[22]*Gnomica* 3:174, and *Gnomica* 5:24*–25*, no. 127.

Fr. sp. 9

Σκεύη μὲν τὰ καινὰ κρείττονα, φιλία δὲ ἡ παλαιοτέρα.

Gessner, 28 = *MPG* 136:849B1–2 (no lemma; on previous text [A10]: Plutarchi), from Antonius.

Combefis, 548 = *MPG* 91:757D3–4 (no lemma; follows Fr. sp. 8), from Maximus.

Boissonade, 82 = *MPG* 117:1140A9–10 (Σέκστου), from Johannes Georgides.

Mangey, 673.6b, "ex Antonio."

Barocc. 143, f. 78ʳ (3) 12–13: Πλουτάρχου.

Ascribed to Plutarch (<Π>λουτάρχου, f. 55ʳ 18) in Digb. 6, f. 56ʳ 13–14 = Par. 1168, f. 83ᵛ (Sternbach, 70, no. 13).

Removed by Elter[23] as = Pseudo-Plutarch, fragment 52 (Bernardakis, 157; Wyttenbach, 885, no. 51).

---

[23]*Gnomica* 3:174, and *Gnomica* 5:9*–10*, no. 43.

Fr. sp. 10

Οἱ μὲν ἐκ τῆς γῆς καρποὶ κατ᾽ ἐνιαυτόν, οἱ δὲ ἐκ τῆς φιλίας κατὰ πάντα καιρὸν φύονται.

Combefis, 548 = *MPG* 91:757D5–6 (no lemma; follows Fr. sp. 9), from Maximus.
Mangey, 673.6c, "ex Antonio."
Barocc. 143, f. 78ʳ (3) 14–16: Πλουτάρχου.
Ascribed to Plutarch (<Π>λουτάρχου, f. 55ʳ 18) in Digb. 6, f. 56ᵛ 16–18 = Par. 1168, f. 84ʳ (Sternbach, 70, no. 21).

Removed by Elter[24] as = Pseudo-Plutarch, fragment 102 (Bernardakis, 161).

---

[24]*Gnomica* 3:174, and *Gnomica* 5:21*, no. 110.

Fr. sp. 11

Πολλοὶ φίλους αἱροῦνται οὐ τοὺς ἀρίστους ἀλλὰ πλουτοῦντας.

Gessner, 28 = *MPG* 136:849B3–4 (no lemma; follows Fr. sp. 9), from Antonius.

Combefis, 548 = *MPG* 91:757D7–8 (no lemma; follows Fr. sp. 10), from Maximus.

Mangey, 673.6d, "ex Antonio."

Barocc. 143, f. 78ʳ (3) 17–18: Πλουτάρχου.

Ascribed to Plutarch (<Π>λουτάρχου, f. 55ʳ 18) in Digb. 6, f. 60ʳ 15–16 = Par. 1168, f. 87ʳ (Sternbach, 73, no. 75).

Removed by Elter[25] as = Pseudo-Plutarch, fragment 118 (Bernardakis, 163).

_____

[25]*Gnomica* 3:174, and 5:38*, no. 20 (incorrectly referred to in vol. 3 as no. 23).

Fr. sp. 12

Πολλοὶ δοκοῦντες εἶναι φίλοι οὐκ εἰσί, καὶ οὐ δοκοῦντες εἰσί· σοφοῦ οὖν ἐστι γινώσκειν ἕκαστον.

Combefis, 548 = *MPG* 91:760A1–2 (no lemma; follows Fr. sp. 11), from Maximus.

Mangey, 673.6e, "ex Antonio."

Barocc. 143, f. 78ʳ (3) 18–20: Πλουτάρχου.

Ascribed to Plutarch (<Π>λουτάρχου, f. 55ʳ 18) in Digb. 6, f. 60ʳ 17–19 = Par. 1168, f. 87ʳ (Sternbach, 73, no. 76).

Removed by Wachsmuth,[26] who notes that this text occurs in Maximus "ex coll. Democr.-Epictetea, sed post Philonea, inde falso adscriptum Philoni."[27] Elter also discusses the text,[28] noting that it is ascribed to Philo by Mangey. It is also printed as Pseudo-Plutarch, fragment 117 (Bernardakis, 163).

Früchtel, in his manuscript, had identified the text as Democritus, fragment 97 (Diels-Kranz, *Fragmente* 2:162), which is taken from Δημοκράτους γνῶμαι, but which omits σοφοῦ — ἕκαστον.

---

[26]"De gnomologio Palatino inedito," 31, no. 119.

[27]Wachsmuth makes a similar remark in his *Studien*, 192, no. 159.

[28]*Gnomica* 3:174, and 5:38*, no. 21 (incorrectly referred to in vol. 3 as no. 24).

Fr. sp. 13

Φεύγειν δεῖ τὴν φιλίαν, ὧντινων ἀμφίβολος ἡ διάθεσις.

Gessner, 30 = *MPG* 136:853A11 (Plutarchi), from Antonius.

Combefis, 548 = *MPG* 91:760A3–4 (no lemma; follows Fr. sp. 12), from Maximus.

Barocc. 143, f. 78ʳ (3) 21–22: Πλουτάρχου.

Ascribed to Plutarch (<Π>λουτάρχου, f. 55ʳ 18) in Digb. 6, f. 60ᵛ 1–2 = Par. 1168, f. 87ʳ (Sternbach, 74, no. 77).

Removed by Elter,[29] noting that this text comes after Fr. sp. 12 in Maximus, but that Mangey failed to include it.[30] The text is also found as Pseudo-Plutarch, fragment 53 (Bernardakis, 157; Wyttenbach, 885, no. 52).

---

[29]*Gnomica* 3:174 (referred to as "fr. 53," according to Bernardakis).

[30]Elter also edits the text in *Gnomica* 5:38*, no. 22, but no reference to Philo is there given.

Fr. sp. 14

Οὔτε ἀρρώστου πληγὴν οὔτε ἀνοήτου ἀπειλὴν δεῖ εὐλαβεῖσθαι.

Gessner, 134 = *MPG* 136:1165B13–14 (no lemma; on second previous text [B8]: Chabrias), from Antonius.

Combefis, 670 = *MPG* 91:984B4–5 (no lemma; follows three Philo texts [A10]: Φίλωνος), from Maximus.[31]

Mangey, 671.4a, "ex Antonio."

Ascribed to Plutarch (<Π>λουτάρχου, f. 55ʳ 18) in Digb. 6, f. 57ᵛ 12–13 = Par. 1168, f. 85ʳ (Sternbach, 71, no. 37).

Removed by Elter[32] as = Pseudo-Plutarch, fragment 107 (Bernardakis, 162).

---

[31]Incidentally, in Gessner's 1546 edition of Maximus, 208, this text follows the same three Philo texts, but correctly has the lemma Πλουτάρχου. This is the only case I have noted where Gessner's edition of Maximus is more accurate than Combefis's.

[32]*Gnomica* 3:174, and *Gnomica* 5:23*, no. 117.

Fr. sp. 15

Οἱ ἐλαφροὶ τῶν ἀνθρώπων, ὥσπερ τὰ κενὰ τῶν ἀγγείων, εὐβάστακτοι τοῖς ὠτίοις εἰσίν.

Gessner (1581), 109 (no lemma; follows Fr. sp. 14), from Maximus.

Combefis, 670 = *MPG* 91:984B10–11 (no lemma; on second previous text [B6]: Πλουτάρχ.), from Maximus.

Mangey, 671.4b, "ex Antonio."

Ascribed to Plutarch (<Π>λουτάρχου, f. 55ʳ 18) in Digb. 6, f. 58ᵛ 5–6 = Par. 1168, f. 85ᵛ (Sternbach, 72, no. 51).

Removed by Otto Hense[33] as = Pseudo-Plutarch, fragment 101 (Bernardakis, 161).[34]

---

[33]"Bion bei Philon," *RhMus*, N.F. 47 (1892): 229, and n. 1. Hense cites the text from Par. 1168 and remarks: "Mit Philon hat dieser Satz nichts zu thun, obwohl er bei Mangey II p. 671 'ex Antonio' unter die Fragmente Philons gestellt wurde."

[34]This identification, with the reference to Gessner (1581), is noted by Elter, *Gnomica* 5:9*, no. 41ᵃ.

Fr. sp. 16

Κακόσιτός ἐστι πρὸς τὸν συμφέροντα λόγον ἡ τῶν ἀνοήτων ψυχή, οὐ παραδεχομένη τὸν σῴζοντα νοῦν ὥσπερ φάρμακον.

Gessner (1581), 109 (no lemma; follows Fr. sp. 15), from Maximus.
Combefis, 670 = *MPG* 91:984B12–14 (no lemma; follows Fr. sp. 15), from Maximus.
Ascribed to Plutarch (<Π>λουτάρχου, f. 55ʳ 18) in Digb. 6, f. 58ᵛ 9–11 = Par. 1168, ff. 85ᵛ – 86ʳ (Sternbach, 72, no. 53).

Removed by Elter[35] as = Pseudo-Plutarch, fragment 92 (Bernardakis, 160).

---

[35]*Gnomica* 3:174, and *Gnomica* 5:11*, no. 51.

Fr. sp. 17

Ἡ χάρις, ὥσπερ ἡ σελήνη, ὅταν τελεία γένηται, τότε καλὴ φαίνεται.

Combefis, 556 = *MPG* 91:773B7–8 (follows Fr. sp. 54; τοῦ αὐτοῦ [scil. Φίλωνος, A12], ἄλλ. Πλουτ.), from Maximus.

Boissonade, 41 = *MPG* 117:1097C6–7 (Δημοκρίτου), from Johannes Georgides.

Ascribed to Plutarch (<Π>λουτάρχου, f. 55ʳ 18) in Digb. 6, ff. 59ᵛ 18 – 60ʳ 1 = Par. 1168, f. 86ᵛ (Sternbach, 73, no. 70).

Removed by Elter[36] as = Pseudo-Plutarch, fragment 37 (Bernardakis, 155; Wyttenbach, 883, no. 36).

---

[36]*Gnomica* 5:10*, no. 45ᵃ.

Fr. sp. 18

Ἡ Φίλωνος γυνὴ ἐρωτηθεῖσα ἐν συνόδῳ πλειόνων γυναικῶν, διὰ τί μόνη τῶν ἄλλων οὐ φορεῖ κόσμον χρυσοῦν, ἔφη ὅτι αὐτάρκης κόσμος ἐστὶ γυναικὶ ἡ τοῦ ἀνδρὸς ἀρετή.

Gessner, 105 = *MPG* 136:1088A12–B2 (no lemma; follows two Philo texts [A7]: Philonis), from Antonius.

Combefis, 632 = *MPG* 91:912C1–4 (Πουλχερία, reading Αὕτη for Ἡ Φίλωνος γυνὴ), from Maximus.

Mangey, 673.4, "ex Antonio."

Ascribed to Philo's wife (τῆς Φίλωνος γυναικός, f. 100ᵛ 14) in Digb. 6, f. 100ᵛ 15–19 = Par. 1168, cap. 82, no. 545 (Sternbach, 58, n. 4 [–59]).

Removed by Jacob Bernays[37] as = fragment concerning the wife of Phocion. In Stobaeus, 4.23.54, this fragment occurs ascribed to the wife of Philo, although one manuscript and a marginal note in another ascribe it to the wife of Phocion. Stobaeus, 3.5.37 (quoted below), also refers to the wife of Phocion and her κόσμον χρυσοῦν, and it was surely the reading Φωκίωνος which was the source of the reading Φίλωνος.[38] However, there is a legend about Philo's baptism which mentions his wife, and such an account may have facilitated the ascription.[39] In any case, the text is clearly not *by* Philo of Alexandria, although Mangey not only printed the fragment but referred to it at the beginning of his preface: "In re lauta fuisse Philonem indicio esse videtur egregium ejus uxoris responsum, quae interrogata *Cur ornamenta aurea non gestat*, respondit *Mariti virtus mulieris ornamentum sufficiens*."[40]

---

[37]*Phokion und seine neueren Beurtheiler: Ein Beitrag zur Geschichte der griechischen Philosophie und Politik* (Berlin: Wilhelm Hertz, 1881), 125–26.

[38]Wachsmuth, *Studien*, 152, n. 1, suggests that the reading Φίλωνος is a common error in Stobaeus, Antonius, and Maximus (although the latter does not have that reading). Wachsmuth also there states that the reading Φωκίωνος in one manuscript of Stobaeus arose "nur aus Conjektur." (There is a further reference to this text in *Studien*, 215, n. 5.)

[39]In the *Acts of John* of Pseudo-Prochorus, cited by Bruns, "Philo Christianus," 142, from Theodor Zahn, ed., *Acta Joannis* (Erlangen: Andreas Deichert, 1880), 111, l. 18 – 112, l. 4: εἰσελθόντων δὲ ἡμῶν ἐν τῷ οἴκῳ Φίλωνος ἡ γυνὴ αὐτοῦ ἀκούσασα τῆς διδαχῆς Ἰωάννου ᾐτήσατο αὐτόν, δοῦναι αὐτῇ τὴν ἐν Χριστῷ σφραγῖδα· ἦν γὰρ λεπρὰ ὡσεὶ χιὼν ὅλη. καὶ δεξαμένη τὴν ἐν Χριστῷ σφραγῖδα παρὰ Ἰωάννου εὐθέως ἐκαθαρίσθη τῆς λέπρας.

[40]*Philonis opera* 1:i.

Bernays presents an extensive analysis of the history of this text:

> Die wegen ihrer sittsamen Einfachheit vielbelobte zweite Frau des Phokion . . . haben in Folge eines Schreibfehlers einiger Handschriften des Stobäus neuere Verfasser von Geschichten der Juden zur Frau des Juden Philon gemacht. In Stobäus' Florilegium bieten nämlich die gangbaren Ausgaben 74, 54: ἡ Φίλωνος γυνὴ ἐρωτηθεῖσα, διὰ τί μόνη τῶν ἄλλων ἐν συνόδῳ οὐ φορεῖ χρυσοῦν κόσμον, ἔφη· ὅτι αὐτάρκης κόσμος μοί ἐστιν ἡ τοῦ ἀνδρὸς ἀρετή. Eine Gaisford'sche Handschrift hat jedoch statt Φίλωνος den offenbar richtigen Namen Φωκίωνος, und die Anekdote ist dieselbe, welche Plutarch an zwei Stellen mit etwas lebhafterer Färbung erzählt, im Leben des Phokion c. 19: ἡ γυνὴ [τοῦ Φωκίωνος] ξένης τινὸς Ἰωνικῆς ἐπιδειξαμένης χρυσοῦν καὶ λιθοκόλλητον κόσμον ἐν πλοκίοις καὶ περιδεραίοις, 'ἐμοὶ δέ', ἔφη, 'κόσμος ἐστὶ Φωκίων εἰκοστὸν ἔτος ἤδη στρατηγῶν Ἀθηναίων', und de musica c. 1 z. A.: ἡ μὲν Φωκίωνος τοῦ χρηστοῦ γυνὴ κόσμον αὐτῆς ἔλεγεν εἶναι τὰ Φωκίωνος στρατηγήματα. Der Mönch Antonius benutzte nun aber eine Handschrift des Stobäus mit der falschen Lesart Φίλωνος, und er hat daher in den zweiten Theil seiner Melissa (sermo 33 p. 105 Zeile 7 v. u. der Züricher Ausgabe von 1546) die Fassung des Stobäus mit ganz unerheblichen stilistischen Abweichungen folgendermaassen [sic] aufgenommen: ἡ Φίλωνος γυνὴ ἐρωτηθεῖσα ἐν συνόδῳ πλειόνων γυναικῶν διὰ τί μόνη τῶν ἄλλων οὐ φορεῖ χρυσοῦν κόσμον, ἔφη· αὐτάρκης κόσμος ἐστὶ γυναικὶ ἡ τοῦ ἀνδρὸς ἀρετή. Aus des Antonius Melissa hat dann Mangey, der sie nach der Genfer Ausgabe hinter dem Stobäus von 1609 (sermo 123 p. 196) citirt, das Geschichtchen unter die Fragmente des Juden Philon versetzt (vol. 2 p. 673 mit kleinen Ungenauigkeiten, κόσμον χρυσοῦν statt χρυσοῦν κόσμον und ἀνδρὸς statt τοῦ ἀνδρός); und im guten Glauben an Mangey hat endlich Ewald (Geschichte Israels 6, 262 der dritten Ausgabe) den Lebensabriss des Juden Philon mit dieser schönen Aeusserung seiner vermeintlichen Frau ausgeschmückt. Ewald sind dann Andere gefolgt.[41]

---

[41]*Phokion*, 125–26 (the first brackets are by Bernays); his references to Plutarch are to *Phocion* 750d and to *De musica* 1131b. An example of the

All that needs to be added is that while it seems clear that the first Plutarch passage cited by Bernays is the ultimate source of our spurious text, it is interesting that the other anecdote in Stobaeus (3.5.37) is more directly based on that same passage:

> ἡ Φωκίωνος γυνὴ πρὸς τὴν ἐπιδεικνυμένην αὐτῇ τὸν κό-
> σμον χρυσοῦν ὄντα καὶ διάλιθον "ἐμοὶ δ'" ἔφη "κόσμος
> ὑπέρλαμπρός ἐστι Φωκίων πένης ὢν καὶ εἰκοστὸν ἤδη
> τοῦτο ἔτος Ἀθηναίων στρατηγῶν."[42]

Also, Sternbach[43] prints a similar text which is ascribed to the mother of Alexander. In his *Photii opusculum*, 58, n. 4 (–59), Sternbach comments: "cap. LXXXII de Philonis Iudaei uxore cogitare noli; apophthegma ipsum . . . tractavi ad Gnom. Vat. 576, u[b]i Φωκίωνος pro Φίλωνος reponendum esse significavi."

In his manuscript Früchtel placed this fragment in brackets as the last of the unidentified fragments. In his apparatus he gave its source as Stobaeus, 4.23.54, but then added, "alii rectius Φωκίωνος," referring to Stobaeus, 3.5.37.

By the way, I can find no explanation of Maximus's attribution of this text to "Pulcheria." Presumably this should be taken as referring to Pulcheria Aelia Augusta (A.D. 399–453).

---

use of this story is H. Graetz, *Geschichte der Juden von den ältesten Zeiten bis auf die Gegenwart*, 4th ed., vol. 3: *Geschichte der Judäer von dem Tode Juda Makkabi's bis zum Untergange des judäischen Staates* (2 pts.; Leipzig: Oskar Leiner, 1888), pt. 1, 338:

> Seine Frau war stolz auf ihn und eiferte ihm in Lebens-
> einfachheit nach. Als sie putzsüchtige Frauen einst fragten,
> warum sie, obwohl so reich, es verschmähe, goldenen
> Schmuck zu tragen, antwortete sie: "Die Tugend des Ehe-
> gatten ist ein hinlänglicher Schmuck für die Frau".

Graetz gives as his reference (n. 3): "Fragment aus Antonius' Homilien bei Mangey II. 673."

[42]This pair of anecdotes (with trivial textual variations) can be found in the gnomologium in Par. suppl. 134, ff. 232ᵛ – 271ʳ, as edited by Sternbach, *Gnomologium Parisinum ineditum*, 1–37. Our spurious text is found at f. 256ᵛ (ibid., 23, no. 221), while the other anecdote is found at ff. 267ʳ⁻ᵛ (ibid., 32, no. 316).

[43]*Gnomologium Vaticanum e codice Vaticano Graeco 743*, 204, no. 576, with references to many parallels, to which I might add Xenophon, *Anabasis* 1.9.23.

Fr. sp. 19

Νεότης πονεῖν οὐκ ἐθέλουσα πρὸς τὸ γῆρας κακοπραγεῖ.

Gessner, 97 (Φίλωνος) = *MPG* 136:1061D5–6 (no lemma; follows a Philo text [D3]: Philonis), from Antonius.
Mangey, 673.7, "ex Antonio."

Removed as = Aphthonius, *Fable* 1.[44]

---

[44]The text can be found in August Hausrath, *Corpus fabularum Aesopi-carum*, vol. 1, fasc. 2 (2d ed., ed. Herbert Hunger; Leipzig: B. G. Teubner, 1959), 133, *Fabula* 1, ll. 9–10 (adding οὕτως at the beginning). On the author, who seems to have lived in the fourth to fifth centuries A.D., see Francesco Sbordone, "Recensioni retoriche delle favole esopiane," *Rivista indo-greco-italica* 16 (1932), fasc. iii–iv, pp. 45–46, with *Fabula* 1 edited on p. 47; Hausrath, "Phaedrus," *PW* 19.2 (1938): 1492–93; idem, *Corpus fabularum Aesopicarum*, vol. 1, fasc. 1 (Leipzig: B. G. Teubner, 1940), xxi–ii; and Hans Gärtner, "Aphthonius," in *KP* 1 (1964): 431.

Fr. sp. 20

'Εσχάρα ἄνθραξι, καὶ ξύλα πυρί, ἀνὴρ δὲ λοίδορος εἰς ταραχὴν μάχης.

Pitra, xxiii.III, from Vaticanus Reginensis 77, f. 660.
Harris, 83.6, from Pitra.

Removed by Harris[45] as = Prov 26:21.

_____

[45]*Fragments*, 83.

Fr. sp. 21

'Απὸ ἑνὸς συνετοῦ συνοικισθήσεται πόλις.

Gessner, 112 (Ἐκκλησιαστοῦ)[46] = *MPG* 136:1105B8 (no lemma; on third previous text [B5]: Prov. II), from Antonius.

Combefis, 689 = *MPG* 91:1017A5 (Σιρὰχ ιϛ´ on previous text; in margin: Eccl. 16.5), from Maximus.

Lequien, 693 = *MPG* 96:360C7 (Eccli. XVI, 5), from Vat. 1236.

Harris, 110.9, from Ber. 46, f. 261ᵛ (12) 12–13: τοῦ αὐτοῦ (Φίλωνος, l. 12).

Ber. 46, f. 33ʳ (34) 35: τῶν αὐτῶν (παροιμιῶν, l. 31).

Par. 923, f. 332ʳA 31–33 (no lemma; on earlier text [l. 24]: Φίλωνος).

Removed by Früchtel as = Sir 16:4. This is also independently identified by Junod, "Les fragments grecs," 11.

---

[46]In *MPG* 136 this lemma has moved to the following text (1105B9–C2), which has 'Eccle.,' but is without a lemma in Gessner.

Fr. sp. 22

Οὐκ ἔστιν ἀντάλλαγμα πεπαιδευμένης ψυχῆς.

Gessner, 55 = *MPG* 136:932C7–8 (Solomon.), from Antonius.

Combefis, 582 = *MPG* 91:820A10–11 (Σιφὰχ κϛ´; in margin: Eccl. 26.18), from Maximus.

Lequien, 693 = *MPG* 96:360D1 (Eccli. XXVI, 18), from Vat. 1236.

Harris, 110.10, from Ber. 46, f. 261ᵛ (13) 13 (follows Fr. sp. 21; τοῦ αὐτοῦ [Φίλωνος, l. 12]).

Par. 923, f. 332ʳA 33–35 (no lemma; follows Fr. sp. 21).

Ascribed to Solomon (<τ>οῦ Σολομόντος [*sic*], f. 35ʳ 4) in Digb. 6, f. 37ʳ 8–9.

Removed by Früchtel as = Sir 26:14. This is also independently identified by Junod, "Les fragments grecs," 11.

Fr. sp. 23

Μὴ δοξάζου ἐν ἀτιμίᾳ πατρός σου. ἡ γὰρ δόξα ἀνθρώπων ἐκ τιμῆς πατρὸς αὐτῶν.

Gessner, 93 (no lemma; on previous text: Σιρὰχ γ) = *MPG* 136: 1049D4–5 (Philonis), from Antonius.
Barocc. 143, f. 234ʳ (233ᵛ 15) 9–10: τοῦ Σιράχ.

Removed as = Sir 3:10a, 11.[47]

---

[47]Here we have a clear case of the movement of a lemma from Gessner's edition to *MPG* 136. This text is subsumed under the previous (correct) lemma in Gessner, and the following text (*Dec* 110) is correctly given the lemma Φίλωνος. In *MPG* the latter lemma moves upward to our spurious text, and the genuine Philo text follows without a lemma.

Fr. sp. 24

Περισσὸς ὑπὲρ τοῦ τὰ δέοντα ποιεῖν πᾶς ὁ λόγος ὅταν ἡ τῶν ἀκουόν-
των πρὸς τὸ χεῖρον ὁμόνοια ᾖ.

Gessner, 128 = *MPG* 136:1153B2–3 (no lemma; follows a Philo text
[A14]: Philonis), from Antonius.
Mangey, 671.5c, "ex Antonio."
Ber. 46, f. 26ᵛ (13) 13–15: Ἰωσήππου [*sic*].

Removed as = Josephus, *Bellum Iudaicum* 2.345.

Fr. sp. 25

Πέφυκε τοῖς μεγάλοις ἀκολουθεῖν φθόνος.

Mangey, 668.4, from Ber. 46, f. 270ᵛ (11) 12: Φίλωνος.
Harris, 9.3, from Mangey and Par. 923, f. 355ʳA (2) 3–4: τοῦ αὐτοῦ
(Φίλωνος, f. 354ᵛB 33) ἐκ τοῦ περὶ τῶν γιγάντων.⁴⁸
Barocc. 143, f. 223ʳ (f. 222ᵛ 23) 1–2: Φίλωνος.

Removed as = Pseudo-Philo, *De Sampsone* 20 (Aucher, *Paralipomena
Armena*, 560). Harris printed this text among the five fragments which he
assigned to the lost portion of Philo's *De gigantibus*,⁴⁹ and commented on it:

> It should be noticed that the sentiment is found also in the
> *De Sampsone*, edited by Aucher from the Armenian (II.
> 560), "Quoniam, ut dicitur, solet magnum virum sequi invi-
> dia."⁵⁰

While this remark clearly suggests the correct identification of this fragment,
the correspondence is much closer than Harris's reference to "sentiment"
indicates. His failure to compare the Greek directly with the Armenian pre-
vented him from seeing that in fact the Greek is certainly the original of the
Armenian.⁵¹ A brief justification of the close correspondence between the
Greek fragment and the Armenian may be useful.

---

⁴⁸In Marc. 138 this text occurs at f. 265ᵛB (18–20) 21–22: τοῦ αὐτοῦ
(Φίλωνος, ll. 13–14) ἐκ τοῦ περὶ τῶν γιγάντων. (On this manuscript see
chapter 3, note 12, above.)

⁴⁹See chapter 3, pages 36–37, above.

⁵⁰*Fragments*, 9.

⁵¹I believe that Harris never demonstrates any direct knowledge of the
Armenian, although he frequently does make textual observations and conjectures based on Aucher's Latin. In fact, Harris does not even cite the Latin
from Aucher's own editions, but uses the later stereotype edition. This can
be seen as follows. The editions of Mangey and Aucher formed the basis of
*Philonis Iudaei opera omnia*, edited by C. E. Richter (8 vols.; Leipzig: E. B.
Schwickert, 1828–30). This was then reprinted as *Philonis Iudaei opera
omnia* (8 vols.; Leipzig: Carl Tauchnitz, 1851–53), which itself was reprinted
as *Philonis Iudaei opera omnia* (8 vols.; Leipzig: Otto Holtze, 1880–93). Although I have not seen the 1851–53 edition, the following evidence from
Aucher's *Paralipomena Armena*, the 1828–30 (vol. 7, 1830) edition, the 1880–
93 edition (vol. 7, 1893), and Harris's edition is conclusive:

Aucher's Armenian text reads as follows, where the first three words are not included in the Greek excerpt:

(k'anzi orpês asi) bnaworeal imn ê mecanecac' zhet ert'al naxanj.[52]

Now, using standard Armenian-Greek equivalents we find that "bnaworeal ê" corresponds to πέφυκε,[53] that "mecanecac'" corresponds to τοῖς μεγάλοις,[54]

Quaes Ex 2.63:

| | |
|---|---|
| Aucher (512): | Aurum symbolum est pretiosae substantiae; tornatile vero artificiosae, ac intelligentia praeditae naturae. |
| 1830 (319): | Aurum symbolum est pretiosae substantiae; tornatile vero artificiosae atque intelligentia praeditae naturae. |
| 1893 (359): | *Aurum* symbolum est pretiosae substantiae, *tornatile* vero artificiosae ac intelligentia praeditae naturae. |
| Harris (64): | *Aurum* symbolum est pretiosae substantiae, *tornatile* vero artificiosae ac intelligentia praeditae naturae. |

Quaes Ex 2.68:

| | |
|---|---|
| Aucher (515): | Quod si itaque accurate haec perspicere, ac intelligere quis poterit horum naturas . . . . |
| 1830 (321): | Quod si [*sic*, omitting 'itaque'] accurate haec perspicere atque intelligere quis poterit horum naturas . . . . |
| 1893 (361): | Quod si itaque accurate haec perspicere atque intelligere quis poterit horum naturas . . . . |
| Harris (66–67): | Quod si itaque accurate haec perspicere atque intelligere quis poterit horum naturas . . . . |

It is thus clear that Harris has used the edition of 1851–53, which must be identical in these passages with that of 1893.

[52]The German translation of this phrase found in Siegert, trans., *Drei hellenistisch-jüdische Predigten, Ps.-Philon, "Über Jona", "Über Simson", und "Über die Gottesbezeichnung 'wohltätig verzehrendes Feuer' ", I: Übersetzung aus dem Armenischen und sprachliche Erläuterungen* (WUNT, vol. 20; 1980), 63, reads: "Man sagt ja, es sei nur natürlich, daß auf große (Taten) der Neid folgt."

[53]See Awetik'ean, Siwrmêlean, and Awgerean, "Nor baṙgirk'" 1:498C; Marcus, "Index," 259.

[54]"Nor baṙgirk'" 2:238A; Marcus, "Index," 272. Armenian does not have genders or anything quite corresponding to the Greek definite article; "mecanecac'" is the genitive-dative-ablative plural of "mecanec," which corresponds to μέγας. Aucher took the sentence as referring to great men,

that "zhet ert'al" corresponds to ἀκολουθεῖν,[55] and that "naxanj" corresponds to φθόνος.[56] The Armenian is therefore a literal version of the Greek text, with each word of the Greek having its equivalent word(s) in the same order.[57]

The only (very slight) difficulty is the presence of "imn" in the Armenian. This is the indefinite article (τις),[58] but "imn" is also an adverb which means "really, in effect."[59] And at least once in Philo (*Quaes Gen* 4.184) it translates πως. However, in at least three cases (*Quaes Gen* 3.58, 4.69; *Quaes Ex* 2.10) "imn" occurs in the Armenian with nothing in the Greek corresponding to it. Thus, its presence in *De Sampsone* 20 may well simply reflect a stylistic preference of the translators.[60]

Therefore, what we have is a Greek text and an Armenian text which corresponds perfectly (or virtually perfectly) with it. And the Greek text is ascribed to Philo, while the Armenian text occurs within a work circulating with the works of Philo. The only reasonable conclusion from these facts is

---

but Siegert more plausibly takes the reference to be to great deeds. Note that in the next sentence of the Armenian "irac'" occurs, and "ir" corresponds to πράγμα ("Nor baïgirk'" 1:870A; Marcus, "Index," 265). Thus, in the Greek πράγμασιν could be understood after τοῖς μεγάλοις.

[55]"Nor baïgirk'" 1:738B; not in Marcus, "Index." (On the use of the participle in Armenian for the infinitive in Greek, see, e.g., *Quaes Gen* 1.21.)

[56]"Nor baïgirk'" 2:393A; Marcus, "Index," 274 (ζῆλος is the more common equivalent).

[57]Note that Aucher's Latin is similarly literal (although Harris didn't recognize that). The Armenian translation of the works of Philo usually is quite literal, of course, and the translation of the *De Sampsone* is from the same school that translated the genuine works of Philo; see Siegert, *Predigten*, 3.

[58]As, e.g., in *Quaes Ex* 2.118. In *Provid* "imn" occurs three times where the Greek is extant: for τινί (2.51), τινα (2.100), and τι (2.107).

[59]As cited in Matat'ia Petrosean [Matthias Bedrossian], *New Dictionary Armenian-English* (Venice: S. Lazarus Armenian Academy, 1875–79), 243A. The "Nor baïgirk'" (1:852C) gives no Greek equivalent for this use, and the word is not cited by Marcus, "Index."

[60]Alternatively, of course, there may have been something (such as πως) in the Greek *Vorlage* of the Armenian, which was then omitted when this text was excerpted in the *Sacra parallela*. Dr. Siegert has also suggested to me that the presence of "imn" may indicate the impersonal use of πέφυκε, rather than the personal.

that the Greek text is indeed a fragment of the lost original *De Sampsone*. And it would then follow that the compiler of the *Sacra parallela* had available to him the Greek *De Sampsone* under Philo's name.[61] Thus, the ascription to Philo, while incorrect, has ancient authority.

---

[61]At least, this seems rather more likely than that the lemma "Philo" became accidentally attached within the Greek tradition of the *Sacra parallela* to a text which, within the Armenian tradition, was associated with works of Philo. See also the remarks and references on the *De Sampsone* in chapter 5 below.

Fr. sp. 26

Οὐ τὸ κολάζεσθαι ἐνταῦθα κακόν, ἀλλὰ τὸ ἄξιον τῆς ἐκεῖσε γενέσθαι κολάσεως.

Combefis, 642 = *MPG* 91:932B5–6 (no lemma; follows an unidentified text [A11]: Φίλωνος), from Maximus.

Lequien, 349 = *MPG* 95:1188A3–4 (Dion. Areop. De div. nominib. cap. 4), from Vat. 1236.

Mangey, 673.8, "ex Antonio."[62]

Ber. 46, f. 80ʳ (8) 8–9: τοῦ αὐτοῦ (τοῦ Χρυσοστόμου, f. 79ᵛ 30).

Par. 923, f. 68ᵛB (21) 22–25: Διονυσίου τοῦ ᾿Αρεοπαγίτου.

Ascribed to Dionysius the Areopagite (<Δ>ιονύσου [*sic*] τοῦ ᾿Αρειοπαγήτου [*sic*], f. 47ᵛ 16) in Digb. 6, f. 47ᵛ 17–18.

Removed by Früchtel as = Pseudo-Dionysius the Areopagite, *De divinis nominibus* 4.22 (*MPG* 3:724B15–C1).

---

[62]Mangey notes: "Poenas ergo damnatorum in saeculo futuro astruit Philo."

Fr. sp. 27

Αὐτὸς πάντα οἶδεν, ὁ ποιήσας τάδε ἀπ' ἀρχῆς μόνος.

Pitra, 310.XXIII, from Coisl. 276, f. 34ᵛ (17) 17–18: ἐκ τῶν δι' ἐπῶν κεφαλαίων (following several Philo texts).[63]

Harris, 85.7, from Pitra and Ber. 46, f. 51ʳ 37 (no lemma, following several Philo texts; l. 23: Φίλωνος).

Removed by Harris[64] as = *Oracula Sibyllina*, fragment 3, l. 16.[65] Harris notes that in Ber. 46 the text immediately follows a text from Philo[66] and precedes ones from the Clementine homilies.[67] Harris then suggests that the text might indeed be Philonic, concluding: "We shall simply say that we do not see any reason why this Proemium [of the *Oracula Sibyllina*] may not be referred very nearly to Philo in time, place, language, and range of ideas."

---

[63]Pitra remarks: "Ex fol. 34, sub ambiguo titulo brevis locus caeteris miscetur Philoni jure ascriptis. Nec puto ibi senarios latere."

[64]*Fragments*, 85–86 (who refers to it as the second fragment according to an earlier edition).

[65]The text is found in Johannes Geffcken, *Die Oracula Sibyllina* (GCS, vol. 8; Leipzig: J. C. Hinrichs, 1902), 231; ll. 15–16 there read:
τίς γὰρ σάρξ δύναται θνητῶν γνῶναι τάδ' ἅπαντα;
ἀλλ' αὐτὸς μόνος οἶδεν ὁ ποιήσας τάδ' ἀπ' ἀρχῆς.

[66]In fact, the sequence in both Coisl. 276 and Ber. 46 is: *Leg All* 3.4, *Quod Det* 61, *Quod Deus* 29, an unidentified text also ascribed to Philo elsewhere (= Harris 73.5; see chapter 1, page 6, above), and then this spurious text. Clearly, Ber. 46 has omitted the final lemma here which Coisl. 276 has retained.

[67]Loofs, *Studien*, 59, n. *, refers to this text in Coisl. 276 and Harris's edition, and says: "das für philonisch zu halten (vgl. Harris), die Hs. kein Recht giebt." Of course, at least Ber. 46 does give some justification.

Fr. sp. 28

Φοβηθῶμεν, οὐχὶ νόσον τὴν ἔξωθεν, ἀλλ᾽ ἁμαρτήματα, δι᾽ ἃ ἡ νόσος· καὶ νόσον ψυχῆς οὐ σώματος.

Gessner, 19 = *MPG* 136:824A12–14 (Clementis), from Antonius (Gessner has Φοβηθῶμεν — νόσος only).

Combefis, 610 = *MPG* 91:869C10–72A2 (Κλήμεντος), from Maximus.

Lequien, 341 = *MPG* 95:1169C12–D1 (Clem. Alex. Ecclog. 20; note k: "In Rup. fragmentum istud dicitur ἐκ τοῦ η΄ Στρωμ., ex VIII *Strom*. Exstat vero in Eclogis Clementis §20."), from Vat. 1236.

Lequien, 751 = *MPG* 96:476B (9) 11–13, from Ber. 46, f. 39ʳ (27) 28: Κλήμεντος ἐκ τοῦ η΄ στρωμάτου (Φοβηθῶμεν — νόσος only).

Mangey, 674.5, from Barocc. 143, ff. 102ʳ 25 – 102ᵛ 2 (no lemma; follows a Philo text [f. 102ʳ 21]: Φίλωνος).

Harris, 77.3, from Par. 923, f. 62ᵛB (28) 29–34: Φίλωνος; from Lequien, 341 and 751; from Mangey, and from Maximus.

Holl, 110, no. 279.

Ascribed to Philo (<Φ>ίλωνος, f. 39ʳ 12) in Digb. 6, f. 41ᵛ 12–14.

Ascribed to Clement (<τ>οῦ Κλήμεντος, f. 47ʳ 5) in Digb. 6, ff. 47ʳ 18 – 47ᵛ 2.

Removed by Harris[68] as = Clement of Alexandria, *Eclogae* 11 (*MPG* 9: 704A7–9). Harris refers the identification to Zahn,[69] who however, like Lequien, does not note the attribution to Philo.

---

[68]*Fragments*, 77.

[69]Theodor Zahn, *Forschungen zur Geschichte des neutestamentlichen Kanons und der altkirchlichen Literatur*, pt. 3: *Supplementum Clementinum* (Erlangen: Andreas Deichert, 1884), 29.

Fr. sp. 29

Ὁ γὰρ ὕπνος ὥσπερ τελώνης τὸν ἥμισυν ἡμῖν τοῦ βίου συνδιαιρεῖται χρόνον.

Gessner, 51 = *MPG* 136:920D12–13 (no lemma; follows an unidentified text [D7]: Philonis), from Antonius.

Combefis, 616 = *MPG* 91:881B5–6 (no lemma; on second previous text [A14]: Κλήμεντ.), from Maximus.

Removed as = Clement of Alexandria, *Paedagogus* 2.9 (*MPG* 8: 496B14–15).

Fr. sp. 30

Ἀμήχανον συνυπάρχειν τὴν πρὸς κόσμον ἀγάπην τῇ πρὸς τὸν θεὸν ἀγάπῃ, ὡς ἀμήχανον συνυπάρχειν ἀλλήλοις φῶς καὶ σκότος.

Lequien, 370 = *MPG* 95:1233C4–6 (Philonis; note t: "In Rup haec inscriptio est; sed Christiani hominis sententia est, non Judaei."), from Vat. 1236.

Lequien, 382 = *MPG* 95:1260C2–4 (Philonis; note x: "Ejusmodi sententiae quibus amor mundi dilectioni Dei et charitati opponi dicuntur, Christianum auctorem potius quam Judaeum produnt."), from Vat. 1236.

Mangey, 649.9, from Lequien, 370 (note h refers to 1 John 2:15).

Mai, 98b = *MPG* 86.2:2069 (C13) D1–3, from Vat. 1553, f. 93$^r$ (8) 9–11: Φίλωνος ἐκ τοῦ δ´ τῆς νόμων ἱερῶν ἀλληγορίας, and f. 111$^r$ (3) 4–6: same lemma, and f. 115$^v$ (19) 20–22: same lemma.

Harris, 7.1, from Lequien, 370 and 382; from Par. 923, f. 22$^r$B (10) 11–17: Φίλωνος, and f. 24$^r$A (10) 11–16: Φίλωνος ἐκ τῆς νόμων ἀλληγορίας; and from Mai (incorrectly cited as 95), ascribing the text to the lost fourth book of *Leg All.*[70]

Ber. 46, f. 42$^r$ (4) 4–6: Φίλωνος.

Ber. 46, f. 45$^v$ (20) 20–21: Φίλωνος.

Removed by Wendland[71] as = Origen, *Commentary on St. John* 19.21 (*MPG* 14:565C6–9). From the comments cited above, one can see that the Christian element in this text was often noted.[72] Also, note that, apart from the three texts ascribed to Philo's *Gig*, this is the only one of the fragmenta spuria which is assigned to a specific work of Philo.[73]

---

[70]Harris, 7, says: "Lequien prints this passage with a note of suspicion on account of the apparently Christian sentiment which it contains." But Harris goes on to mention that this text occurs frequently in several manuscripts always ascribed to Philo, and even to this lost book. This text is cited by C. G. Montefiore, "Florilegium Philonis," *JQR* 7 (1894): 543, and n. 7, where doubts are expressed concerning its genuineness.

[71]In Erwin Preuschen, ed., *Origenes Werke*, vol. 4: *Der Johanneskommentar* (GCS, vol. 10; Leipzig: J. C. Hinrichs, 1903), 323, ll. 2–4 (the note is by Wendland; see cviii and 2). I owe this reference to Früchtel.

[72]Incidentally, this is the text cited in translation by Goodenough, *Politics*, 72, although the source is given (n. 42) as "Mang. II, 651."

[73]See chapter 3, page 36, above.

Fr. sp. 31

'Αδύνατον οἶμαι μηδὲν ῥυπωθῆναι τῆς ψυχῆς, μηδὲ τὰ τελευταῖα καὶ κατωτάτω αὐτῆς, καὶ ἂν ὡς ἐν ἀνθρώποις τέλειος εἶναι δοκῇ.

Mangey, 662.5, from Ber. 46, f. 67ᵛ (37) 37–39: (Φίλωνος, l. 33) ἐκ τοῦ περὶ τῶν γιγάντων.

Pitra, 309.XVII, from Coisl. 276, f. 47ʳ (2) 3–5: (Φίλωνος, f. 46ᵛ 22) ἐκ τοῦ περὶ τῶν γιγάντων.

Harris, 9.1, from Mangey and Ber. 46, and from Pitra.

Removed as = Origen, *Commentary on St. John* 32.2 (*MPG* 14:744A2–4).[74] This is the final one of the three fragmenta spuria assigned to *Gig.*[75]

---

[74]The text is in Preuschen, ed., *Origenes Werke* 4:427, ll. 11–14.
[75]See chapter 3, pages 36–37, above.

Fr. sp. 32

Τὴν εὐκατάπρηστον ὕλην ἐπιμελὲς ἡμῖν ὅτι πορρωτάτω τοῦ πυρὸς ἀποτίθεσθαι.

Pitra, xxiii.V, from Vaticanus Reginensis 77, f. 660 [sic].
Harris, 103.2, from Pitra.
Wendland, *PCW* 2:xviii, from Vat. Reg. 77.[76]
Goodhart and Goodenough, *Bibliography*, 168, no. 229 (Vat. Reg. 77).[77]

Removed by Früchtel as = Basil the Great, *Homilia de invidia* 11.4 (*MPG* 31:377D9–10).[78]

---

[76]Wendland notes: "quod fragmentum in traditis Philonis scriptis non legitur; quin Philonis sit, non est quod dubitemus. nam ἐπιμελὲς cum dativo coniunctum omissa copula saepius adhibet, saepius etiam verbo ἀποτίθεσθαι utitur." At *PCW* 2:224, apparatus, Wendland gives f. 669ᵛ [sic] as the place of the preceding text, which is from *Sobr* 43.

[77]They cite the text and call it "another extract not preserved in extant treatises of Philo."

[78]The text is also cited by Petit, *Quaestiones: Fragmenta Graeca*, 190, n. d, in connection with *Quaes Gen* 4.172.

Fr. sp. 33

Ζητοῦσιν βρῶσιν ψυχαὶ αἱ ἄξιον θεοῦ λόγον ἔχουσαι ἐκ τοῦ διανεστη-
κέναι τῷ φρονήματι καὶ τὸ πολίτευμα ἔχειν ἐν οὐρανοῖς.

Pitra, 310.Ia, from Vat. Reg. 40, f. 224: Φίλωνος (first part of text).
Harris, 103.3a, from Pitra (first part of text).
Cohn, *PCW* 1:lix, from Pitra (first part of text).

Removed as = Basil the Great, *Commentarius in Isaiam prophetam*
9.228 (*MPG* 30:517A7–10), which reads:

Καὶ αἱ κέδροι λαμβάνονται μέν ποτε καὶ εἰς εἰκόνα ψυχῶν
μεγάλων, καὶ ἀξιόλογον ἐχουσῶν δίαρμα, ἐκ τοῦ διανε-
στηκέναι τῷ φρονήματι, καὶ τὸ πολίτευμα ἔχειν ἐν οὐρα-
νοῖς· κτλ.

The manner in which this passage in Basil became transformed into part of a
"Philo fragment" is somewhat involved. Pitra is citing a catena on Ps 103:21–
22 (LXX), and the editors print the spurious text as simply the first portion of
a larger text, where the spurious text above is followed immediately by these
words:

ὥσπερ γὰρ ἀνατείλας ὁ ἥλιος τὸν ζόφον τοῦ ἀέρος φωτὸς
ἐνέπλησεν, οὕτως καὶ ἀρετὴ ἀνατείλασα ἐν ψυχῇ τὴν ἀχ-
λὺν αὐτῆς αὐγάζεται καὶ τὸ σκότος σκεδάννυσιν, καὶ τὰ
τῶν παθῶν θηρία κοιμίζει.

Now Harris places in the margin to the earlier part a reference to Phil
3:20,[79] and comments on the entire text:

The passage is certainly Philo, however much the first words
suggest the New Testament; and the last part is very like I.
*Alleg. Sac. Leg.* § 14.

This is in fact a reference to *Leg All* 1.46, and Cohn more straightforwardly
says:

verba ὥσπερ γὰρ ἀνατείλας ὁ ἥλιος — καὶ τὸ σκότος σκεδάννυσιν e Philonis *legum allegoriarum* lib. I § 46 (p. 72,17–
20) desumpta sunt.

---

[79]This reads: ἡμῶν γὰρ τὸ πολίτευμα ἐν οὐρανοῖς ὑπάρχει. Pitra had
also noted "fere ut epistola ad Phil. III, 20."

It is thus clear that what was printed by Pitra, Harris, and Cohn as one fragment is in fact two comments which have been combined in this catena under
the lemma which should go with the second. Indeed, we can see that the
above spurious text is more precisely a comment on Ps 103:21b, where the
opening words are taken from the Biblical text (καὶ ζητῆσαι παρὰ τοῦ θεοῦ
βρῶσιν αὐτοῖς), and grafted, with some further alteration, onto some words
from the above work by Basil.[80] Originally the resulting comment (our spurious text) was doubtless accompanied by the lemma Βασιλείου. Then, on Ps
103:22 (ἀνέτειλεν ὁ ἥλιος κτλ.) the catena presented the text taken from *Leg
All* 1.46, with the lemma Φίλωνος. To this quotation also were added some
words (καὶ τὰ τῶν παθῶν θηρία κοιμίζει), which derive from Ps 103:20:

> ἔθου σκότος, καὶ ἐγένετο νύξ,
> ἐν αὐτῇ διελεύσονται πάντα τὰ θηρία τοῦ δρυμοῦ.

The development continued with the loss of the first lemma, and the shifting
of the second lemma to the two combined texts. All that remained, then, was
that a later collector of Philo fragments should find this combined text and
print it.

---

[80]Basil goes on in the next few lines to cite Ps 103:16.

Fr. sp. 34

Τέκνων ἀρετὴ δόξα πατέρων.

Gessner, 93 = *MPG* 136:1052B1 (no lemma; on previous text [A11]: Theologi; on following Philo text [B2]: Philonis), from Antonius.

Lequien, 701 = *MPG* 96:377D6 (no lemma; follows Sir 4:13 with lemma [D3]: Eccli. IV, 13), from Vat. 1236.

Mangey, 673.5a, "ex Antonio" (with ἀρεταὶ for ἀρετὴ).

Par. 923, f. 346ʳB (13) 14–15: τοῦ θεολόγου ἐκ τῆς ρϛ´ ἐπιστολῆς.

Removed by Früchtel as = Gregory (the Theologian) of Nazianzus, *Epistle* 3 (*MPG* 37:24B2–3), reading ἀρετή.

Fr. sp. 35

Οὐ μὴ τὸ ἀλγεῖν ἀπαραμύθητον, εἰ μήτε τὸ εὖ πράττειν ἀπαιδαγώγητον.

Gessner, 70 (no lemma; incipit ἀλγεῖν) = *MPG* 136:981A12 (no lemma, no Greek), from Antonius.[81]

Combefis, 580 = *MPG* 91:817A4–5 (Θεολ.), from Maximus (reading μήτε for οὐ μή, and omitting εἰ), from Maximus.

Combefis, 588 = *MPG* 91:832A5–6 (no lemma; follows a Philo text [A3]: Φίλων.), from Maximus.

Barocc. 143, f. 120ᵛ (5) 6–7: τοῦ θεολόγου (reading μήτε for οὐ μή, and omitting εἰ).

Removed as = Gregory (the Theologian) of Nazianzus, *Oratio* 17.4 (*MPG* 35:972A10–11), where the text has μήτε τὸ ἀλγεῖν ἀπαραμύθητον ᾖ, μήτε τὸ εὖ πράττειν ἀπαιδαγώγητον.

---

[81]This is the first text in Gessner's chapter A.οʹ, which is mutilated at the beginning. Gessner notes "Λείπει ἡ ἀρχή," and *MPG* reports (981A11) "Λείπει τι ἐνταῦθα." Indeed, *MPG* omits the Greek of this first text completely, but does include its Latin translation. And in his addenda (297) Gessner gives the following note: "Initium sermonis 70. sic legito: μήτε τὸ ἀλγεῖν ἀπαραμύθητον ᾖ, μήτε, &c." This is in fact the reading in Gregory.

Fr. sp. 36

Μεγίστη γὰρ ἐπικουρία τοῖς ἀτυχοῦσι, μεταβολῆς ἐλπίς, καὶ τὸ κρεῖττον ἐν ὀφθαλμοῖς κείμενον.

Gessner, 8 = *MPG* 136:788C10–11 (no lemma; on previous text [C8]: Theologi), from Antonius.

Gessner, 70 = *MPG* 136:981B1–2 (no lemma; follows Fr. sp. 35), from Antonius.

Combefis, 588 = *MPG* 91:832A7–8 (no lemma; follows Fr. sp. 35), from Maximus.

Boissonade, 57 = *MPG* 117:1113C10–11 (no lemma; on previous text [C3]: Τοῦ Θεολόγου), from Johannes Georgides, identifying the text as "Gregor. Naz. Orat. XII, p. 203 A."

Removed as = Gregory (the Theologian) of Nazianzus, *Oratio* 6.19 (*MPG* 35:748A7–9).

Fr. sp. 37

Πληγὴ τοῖς εὖ φρονοῦσι παίδευμα γίνεται, καὶ κρείττων εὐημερίας πολλάκις κακοπάθεια.

Gessner, 70 = *MPG* 136:981B3–4 (no lemma; follows Fr. sp. 36), from Antonius.

Combefis, 588–89 = *MPG* 91:832A9–10 (no lemma; follows Fr. sp. 36), from Maximus.

Lequien, 674 = *MPG* 96:317C8–10 (Theologi), from Vat. 1236 (reads ὄντως πληγὴ τοῖς κτλ.).

Removed as = Gregory (the Theologian) of Nazianzus, *Oratio* 43.55 (*MPG* 36:565B8–10), which reads as in Lequien.

Fr. sp. 38

Μέγα τῷ ἀτυχοῦντι φάρμακον ἔλεος ἀπὸ ψυχῆς εἰσφερόμενος· καὶ τὸ συναλγεῖν γνησίως, πολύ τι κουφίζει τῆς συμφορᾶς.

Gessner, 70 = *MPG* 136:981B7–9 (no lemma; follows an unidentified text which follows Fr. sp. 37), from Antonius.

Combefis, 589 = *MPG* 91:832B1–3 (no lemma; follows an unidentified text which follows Fr. sp. 37), from Maximus.

Lequien, 679 = *MPG* 96:329A8–10 (no lemma; on previous text [A6]: S. Greg. Naz. orat. XVI), from Vat. 1236.

Removed as = Gregory (the Theologian) of Nazianzus, *Oratio* 14.28 (*MPG* 35:896B9–11).[82]

---

[82]For the text which comes between Fr. sp. 37 and Fr. sp. 38 in both Maximus and Antonius, see chapter 3, pages 32–33, above.

Fr. sp. 39

Ἄγγελος ἦν ὁ παλαίσας μετὰ Ἰακὼβ καὶ οὐ θεὸς ὡς ἐνόμισεν ὁ Ἰακώβ· λέγει γὰρ τελευτῶν, "ὁ ἄγγελος ὁ ῥυσάμενός με ἐκ νεότητός μου"· καὶ αὐτὸς ᾔδει ὅτι ἄγγελος μὲν ἦν, θεὸς δὲ δι' ἀγγέλου εἰργάζετο· καὶ εἶπεν, "ἀπόστειλόν με"· ὁ δὲ εἶπεν, "οὐ μή σε ἀποστείλω" καὶ τὰ ἑξῆς· ἆρα γὰρ ἀναχωρεῖν οὐκ ἠδύνατο; ἀλλὰ διδοὺς χώραν αὐτῷ εἰπεῖν· πάντως γὰρ ἤθελεν εἰπεῖν, ὤκνει δέ· λαβὼν δὲ παρρησίαν, φησίν, "οὐ μή σε ἀποστείλω."

*Catena Lipsiensis* 1:397E1–Z2: ΦΙΛΩΝΟΣ ΕΒΡΑΙΟΥ.
Harris, 107.4, from *Catena Lipsiensis*.

Removed by Devreesse[83] as = Eusebius of Emesa, fragment. The text is quoted by Devreesse from Barberinus 569, f. 200ʳ (Εὐσεβίου); Basiliensis 1, f. 156ᵛ (Εὐσ. ἐπισκ. Ἐμίσης); Par. 128, f. 142ʳ margin (Εὐσεβίου); Vat. 746, f. 111ʳ (Εὐσεβίου); *Catena Lipsiensis*; and Procopius (according to Monacensis 358, f. 138ʳ). Moreover, Barb. 569, Basil. 1, and Monac. 358 preserve a fuller recension of this text,[84] which cites John 1:18 at the end. Thus, the text is in fact Christian, and it doubtless comes from Eusebius of Emesa's lost commentary on Genesis.

---

[83]"Anciens commentateurs grecs," 208 (citing Barb. 569, Vat. 746, *Catena Lipsiensis*, and Procopius); *Les anciens commentateurs*, 78 (citing all the sources listed here).

[84]This fuller text is:

Ἄγγελος ἦν ὁ παλαίσας μετὰ Ἰακώβ, καὶ οὐ Θεός, ὡς ἐνόμισεν ὁ Ἰακώβ· λέγει γὰρ τελευτῶν "ὁ ἄγγελος ὁ ῥυσάμενός με ἐκ νεότητός" μου. καὶ αὐτὸς ᾔδει ὅτι ἄγγελος μὲν ἦν, Θεὸς δὲ δι' ἀγγέλου εἰργάζετο. διὰ τί οὖν ἐνταῦθα τὸ "'Ισραὴλ ἔσται τὸ ὄνομά σου"; Ἰσραὴλ Θεὸν ὁρῶν κατὰ τὴν πίστιν. ποίαν; λέγει ὁ ἄγγελος "ἀπόστειλόν με." ἆρα γὰρ ἀναχωρεῖν οὐκ ἠδύνατο, εἰ μὴ "ἀπόστειλόν με" εἶπεν; ἀλλὰ διδοὺς χώραν εἰπεῖν ἃ εἶπεν· πάντως γὰρ ἤθελε μὲν εἰπεῖν, ὤκνει δέ. λαβὼν δὲ παρρησίαν φησίν "οὐ μή σε ἀποστείλω, ἐὰν μή με εὐλογήσῃς." διὰ ταύτην τὴν πίστιν Ἰσραὴλ ἐκλήθη· "Θεὸν" γὰρ "οὐδεὶς ἑώρακεν πώποτε."

This is the text as Devreesse edits it; see his apparatus for the variants.

Fr. sp. 40

Ἄτοπόν ἐστι τὸν διώκοντα τὰς τιμὰς φεύγειν τοὺς πόνους δι᾽ ὧν αἱ τιμαὶ πεφύκασι γίνεσθαι.

Gessner, 86 = MPG 136:1029A1–2 (Evagrii), from Antonius.
Combefis, 621 = MPG 91:889D1–2 (Εὐαγρίου), from Maximus.
Lequien, 518 (Εὐαγρίου) = MPG 95:1556C3–4 (Ejusd. [scil. (A9): S. Nili]), from Vat. 1236.
Lequien, 713 = MPG 96:401D13–14 (Evagrii), from Vat. 1236.
Mangey, 668.6, from Ber. 46, f. 274$^v$ (1) 1–2: τοῦ αὐτοῦ (Φίλωνος, f. 274$^r$ 22).
Harris, 81.4, from Mangey; Ber. 46, f. 274$^v$ (cited above); Lequien, 713 ("referred to Evagrius"), and Par. 923 ("to Clem. Alex. Quis Dives, which belongs to a previous sentence"), i.e., Par. 923, f. 363$^r$B (20) 21–24: (Κλήμεντος, l. 4) ἐκ τοῦ τίς ὁ σῳζόμενος πλούσιος; and Maximus ("it is given to Evagrius").
Holl, 126–27, no. 338.
Par. 923, f. 195$^r$A (27) 28–32: Εὐαγρίου.
Ber. 46, f. 177$^v$ (19) 19: Εὐαγρίου.
Ascribed to Evagrius (Εὐαγρίου, f. 44$^v$ 7) in Digb. 6, f. 44$^v$ 8–9.

Removed by Elter[85] as = Evagrius Ponticus, Spirituales sententiae 1 (MPG 40:1268C1–2). Holl[86] notes that the text stands in Ber. 46 after a series of Philo texts, and adds: "hier ist wohl ein vorausgehendes Euagrius-citat übersprungen worden."
It will have been observed that the attribution of the first occurrence of this text in Lequien (518) differs from that found in MPG 95:1556C3–4. Of course, errors in lemmata may occur, as we have already seen, within the tradition of printed books as well as of the manuscripts. As one detailed

---

[85]Gnomica I, liii (series II, no. 25), where he notes that the text appears in Harris. The text is also ascribed to Evagrius in Par. 1168 (ibid., liv [series IV, no. 1]). And, as mentioned above in chapter 3, note 64, this text is one of the "Unechte Fragmente" in Stählin and Früchtel, Clemens Alexandrinus 3:xxxv, no. 72, and 3:xxxvii, no. 89b. At the first occurrence we find this note by Früchtel: "von St[ählin] als Euagrios Sent. 25 Elter bezeichnet, inhaltlich aber Thuc. II 63, 1 μὴ φεύγειν τοὺς πόνους ἢ μηδὲ τὰς τιμὰς διώκειν."
[86]Fragmente, 126–27.

example of such errors, let us note the fate of the lemmata on this text within just one recension of the *Sacra parallela*, the Florilegium Vaticanum.[87]

The most relevant manuscripts here are Escur. Ω. III. 9, Ottob. 79, and Vindob. suppl. 178 (hereafter referred to as E, O, and V, respectively). And, while examining their lemmata on this spurious text, we can also note the evidence for a genuine Philo fragment.[88] A portion of *Quaes Gen* 4.40 (νόμος — ἀορασίας) appears twice in the Florilegium Vaticanum (see *MPG* 95: 1169D2–4, and 1556C5–7), the second time immediately after the first occurrence of Fr. sp. 40. The evidence is as follows:

|  | E | O | V |
|---|---|---|---|
|  | f. 122ᵛ | f. 171ʳ | f. 150ᵛB |
| Fr. sp. 40 (a)<br>(*MPG* 95:1556C3–4) | Εὐαγρίου<br>33–34 | Εὐαγρίου<br>5–6 | no lemma<br>upper mg |
| *Quaes Gen* 4.40<br>(*MPG* 95:1556C5–7) | no lemma<br>34–35 | no lemma<br>6–8 | Εὐαγρίου<br>14–18 |
|  | · · | · | · |
|  | · | · | · |
|  | · | · | · |
|  | f. 234ᵛ<br>Εὐαγρίου | f. 322ᵛ<br>Εὐαγρίου | f. 282ᵛB<br>τοῦ αὐτοῦ<br>(Κλήμεντος) |
| Fr. sp. 40 (b)<br>(*MPG* 96:401D13–14) | 6–7 | 7–8 | 13–15 |

Evidently, then, the scribe of V initially skipped the text but not the lemma of the first occurrence of this spurious fragment, with the result that the lemma shifted to the genuine Philo fragment. And clearly the genuine fragment had previously lost its lemma Φίλωνος in some ancestor of the Florilegium Vaticanum. For the fragment is correctly assigned to Philo (and indeed precisely to the fourth book of *Quaes Gen*) in several witnesses of the *Sacra parallela*.[89]

---

[87]See chapter 3, note 6, above for the manuscripts cited here.

[88]Petit, *Quaestiones: Fragmenta Graeca*, 154, and n. a, prints the text from Vat. 1236.

[89]See the evidence in Petit, ibid.

Fr. sp. 41

Λάλει ἃ δεῖ, καὶ ὅτε δεῖ, καὶ ὑπὲρ ὧν δεῖ, καὶ οὐκ ἀκούσεις ἃ μὴ δεῖ.

Gessner, 135 = *MPG* 136:1168D3–4 (Evagrii), from Antonius.

Combefis, 647 = *MPG* 91:940B10–11 (Εὐαγρίου), from Maximus.

Lequien, 357 = *MPG* 95:1205C6–7 (no lemma; on preceding text [C5]: Εὐαγρίου), from Vat. 1236 (omits καὶ ὑπὲρ ὧν δεῖ).

Lequien, 563 = *MPG* 96:76A6–7 (Philonis), from Vat. 1236 (omits καὶ ὑπὲρ ὧν δεῖ).

Mangey, 651.6, from Lequien.

Harris, 79.5, from Lequien, Maximus, and Par. 923 (unspecified text).

Par. 923, f. 73ʳB (17) 19–21: Εὐαγρίου ἐκ τῶν γνωμῶν (omits καὶ ὅτε δεῖ, καὶ ὑπὲρ ὧν δεῖ).

Par. 923, f. 215ʳA (29) 30–32: τοῦ αὐτοῦ (Εὐαγρίου, l. 27; omits καὶ ὑπὲρ ὧν δεῖ).

Ber. 46, f. 72ᵛ (9) 9–10: Εὐαγρίου ἐκ τῶν γνωμῶν (omits καὶ ὑπὲρ ὧν δεῖ).

Barocc. 143, f. 166ᵛ (23) 24–25: Εὐαγρίου.

Ascribed to Evagrius (Εὐαγρίου, f. 44ᵛ 7) in Digb. 6, f. 45ʳ 17–18 (omits καὶ ὑπὲρ ὧν δεῖ).

Removed by Harris[90] as = Evagrius Ponticus, *Spirituales sententiae* 11 (*MPG* 40:1268D4–5).[91]

---

[90]*Fragments*, 79.

[91]The text (without καὶ ὑπὲρ ὧν δεῖ) is edited by Elter, *Gnomica I*, liii (series II, no. 35), is found ascribed to Evagrius in Par. 1168 (ibid., liv [series IV, no. 10]), and is also found in Photius, *Opusculum paraeneticum*, no. 102 (Sternbach, *Photii opusculum*, 13).

Fr. sp. 42

Τὸ ἔντιμον ἐν γήρᾳ εἶναι ἀπόδειξις τοῦ φιλόπονον πρὸ γήρως γεγο-
νέναι· τὸ δὲ σπουδαῖον ἐν νέῳ ἐχέγγυον τοῦ ἔντιμον ἐν γήρᾳ ἔσεσθαι.

Combefis, 635 = *MPG* 91:917C1–3 (Εὐαγρίου; follows a Philo text
[B11]: Φίλωνος), from Maximus.
Lewy, 83.29, from Laur. plut. VII 15, f. 206ʳ ("hinter Philonzitat ohne
Lemma").
Ascribed to Evagrius (Εὐαγρίου, f. 44ᵛ 7) in Digb. 6, f. 44ᵛ 12–15.

Removed as = Evagrius Ponticus, *Spirituales sententiae* 19–20 (*MPG* 40:
1269A10–B2).[92]

---

[92]The text is also edited by Elter, *Gnomica I*, liii (series II, no. 43), is
ascribed to Evagrius in Par. 1168 (ibid., liv [series IV, no. 3]), and also found
in Photius, *Opusculum paraeneticum*, no. 110 (Sternbach, *Photii opusculum*,
14). Of course, Elter did not find this ascribed to Philo anywhere.

Fr. sp. 43

Λεία ὁδὸς ὑπὸ ἐλεημοσύνης γίνεται.

Lequien, 481 = *MPG* 95:1473D6–7 (no lemma; on previous text [D5]: Evagrii), from Vat. 1236.

Harris, 105.2, from Lequien; Par. 923, f. 179ᵛB (28) 29–31: Φίλωνος; and Barocc. 143, f. 17ʳ 17–18 (no lemma; follows Fr. sp. 52).[93]

Removed by Elter[94] as = Evagrius Ponticus, *Aliae sententiae* 4 (*MPG* 40:1269C2–3).

---

[93]Harris adds: "I do not think it is Philo."

[94]*Gnomica I*, liii (series III, no. 52), where a reference is made to the text in Harris.

Fr. sp. 44

In their classification of the catenae, Karo and Lietzmann note that extracts from "Philon" are contained in three manuscripts of their class V of the catenae on the Song of Songs.[95] Accordingly, Goodhart and Goodenough cite these three manuscripts, as well as two others which they found catalogued elsewhere, under their "Greek Manuscripts, I," and comment: "Codices containing a *Catena on the Song of Songs* in which Philo is cited."[96] Furthermore, they note that this catena was published in 1617 by Ioannes Meursius.[97] Now, in fact, the chain as printed by Meursius has 39 texts which are ascribed to Philo.[98] These texts (never printed within the literature on Philo of Alexandria) are treated here collectively.

Removed as = texts from Philo of Carpasia, *Enarratio in Canticum Canticorum* (*MPG* 40:27–154).

An examination of Meursius makes clear that the texts come from a Christian writer, and indeed from Philo of Carpasia.[99] The first fragment,

---

[95]"Catenarum catalogus," 318–19.

[96]*Bibliography*, 169; their nos. 235–37 are Karo and Lietzmann's manuscripts, while nos. 238–39 are added.

[97]*Eusebii, Polychronii, Pselli, in Canticum Canticorum Expositiones Graecè [sic]* (Leiden: Ex Officinâ Elzeviriana, 1617). The catena is on 1–74.

[98]All have the lemma Φίλωνος, except for one occurrence on 29 of τοῦ αὐτοῦ. Theodor Zahn, *Forschungen zur Geschichte des neutestamentlichen Kanons und der altkirchlichen Literatur*, pt. 2: *Der Evangeliencommentar des Theophilus von Antiochien* (Erlangen: Andreas Deichert, 1883), 240, says that Philo is cited 37 times in Meursius's catena, a number supported by Faulhaber, *Hohelied-Catenen*, 56 (his count, however, is from Ottob. 305, a manuscript of type E as is the Meursius catena; see 53). Similarly, Aldo Ceresa-Gastaldo, "Philon de Carpasia (saint)," *DSpir* 12.1 (1984): 1376, says that there are 37 extracts in Meursius. Despite their agreement, I am confident that the Meursius catena (if not the manuscripts) has 38 occurrences of Φίλωνος and the 1 occurrence of τοῦ αὐτοῦ. By the way, Fabricius and Harles, *Bibliotheca Graeca* 10:479, writing of Philo of Carpasia, report on Meursius's edition: "Nusquam autem Philo Carpathius, sed tantum Philo ibi adpellatur."

[99]In their index ("Catenarum catalogus," 614) Karo and Lietzmann say simply that "Philo" is cited (in their catalogue) on 314 and 318, while "Philo (episcopus Carpathius)" is cited on 306 and 314. The explicit reference to Philo of Carpasia comes in the prologue to class II of the catena (by Proco-

for instance, reads (Meursius, 13): Οἱ μαζοί, αἱ δύο διαθῆκαι [sic], αἱ ὑπὲρ τὸν ἐπίγειον λόγον. With this text may be compared MPG 40:36B2: Δύο μαστοὺς τὰς δύο Διαθήκας ῥητέον.[100] And the third fragment begins (Meursius, 16): Υἱοὶ μητρὸς οἱ ἀπόστολοι. κατὰ τὸ [sic], οὐκ ἦλθον βαλεῖν εἰρήνην ἐπὶ τῆς γῆς, ἀλλὰ μάχαιραν. With this text one may compare MPG 40:48B1–2: Υἱοὺς μητρὸς αὐτῆς οἶμαι τοὺς σοφοὺς τῆς ἐπουρανίου βασιλείας υἱοὺς [sic], τοὺς ἀποστόλους λέγειν.

There are, to be sure, divergences between the texts in Meursius and those in MPG 40, but these differences have simply arisen within the textual traditions of these editions.[101] However, that the ultimate source of these 39 texts is really Philo of Carpasia and not Philo of Alexandria, can scarcely be doubted. Perhaps Goodhart and Goodenough did not examine the Meursius edition; presumably even the most ardent collector of fragments of Philo of Alexandria would hesitate to assign to him the third text, which refers to the Apostles and quotes Matt 10:34.

---

pius), where we find Φίλωνος τοῦ Καρπαθίου (314); the citation of "Philo" apparently just reflects the lemma Φίλωνος (318) as found in the class V manuscripts and Meursius. Karo and Lietzmann doubtless knew that this "Philo" was not Philo of Alexandria, but Goodhart and Goodenough made the unjustified identification. On the other hand, Karo and Lietzmann also cite under "Philo (episcopus Carpathius)" the references to Φίλωνος ἐπισκόπου in the catenae on the Octateuch, although these are all (as it seems) references to Philo of Alexandria; see the comments in chapter 1, notes 3 and 50, and chapter 2, note 23, above.

[100]This is noted as an example of influence by Hippolytus's commentary on Philo of Carpasia by G. Nath. Bonwetsch and Hans Achelis, eds., Hippolytus Werke, vol. 1 (GCS, vol. 1, pt. 1; Leipzig: J. C. Hinrichs, 1897), xxiii.

[101]See Zahn, Der Evangeliencommentar des Theophilus von Antiochien, 238–56; Philo of Carpasia is explicitly noted as the Philo here (240). Faulhaber (Hohelied-Catenen, 47–49, 53–54) has valuable information on the catenae on the Song of Songs generally, and on the Meursius edition in particular. Faulhaber (35) is also clear that Philo of Carpasia is involved, not Philo of Alexandria.

Fr. sp. 45

Πρὸς τὰς τῶν ἠθῶν καταστάσεις τυποῦται τοῖς πολλοῖς τὰ ἐνύπνια· ἄλλα τοῦ ἀνδρείου καὶ ἄλλα τοῦ δειλοῦ τὰ φαντάσματα, ἄλλοι τοῦ ἀκολάστου ὄνειροι καὶ ἄλλοι τοῦ σώφρονος· ἐν ἑτέροις φαντασιοῦται ὁ ἄπληστος οὐδαμοῦ τῆς διανοίας, ἀλλὰ τῆς ἀλογωτέρας ἐν τῇ ψυχῇ διαθέσεως τὰς τοιαύτας φαντασίας ἀνατυπούσης.

Lewy, 81.19, from Laur. plut. VII 15, f. 82ʳ ("nach einem Philonzitat, ohne Lemma").[102]

Removed by Früchtel as = Gregory of Nyssa, *De hominis opificio* 13 (*MPG* 44:173B15–C6), where there is an addition after ἑτέροις of ὁ μεταδοτικὸς καὶ ἐν ἑτέροις, which Lewy's manuscript has omitted by homoeoteleuton.

---

[102]Lewy notes: "Das Zitat stammt vielleicht aus dem verlorenen Teil der Schrift de somniis, . . ."

Fr. sp. 46

Ψεῦδός ἐστι φαντασία τις περὶ τὸ μὴ ὂν ἐγγενομένη τῇ διανοίᾳ, ὡς ὑφεστῶτος τοῦ μὴ ὑπάρχοντος.

Gessner, 27 = *MPG* 136:845A13–B2 (no lemma; follows a Philo text [A11]: Philonis), from Antonius.

Removed as = Gregory of Nyssa, *Mystica interpretatio vitae Moysis* (*MPG* 44:333A10–12).

Fr. sp. 47

Ἀκύμαντος λιμὴν πολιά.

Lequien, 404 = *MPG* 95:1308D4 (no lemma; follows *Abr* 271: Philon.), from Vat. 1236.
Mangey, 650.5, from Lequien.
Harris, 97.11, from Lequien and Par. 923, f. 105ʳA 35 – B 1 (no lemma; follows *Abr* 271 [19]: Φίλωνος).

Removed as = John Chrysostom, *Sermo cum presbyter fuit ordinatus* (*MPG* 48:698, ll. 22–23). There we read: ἡ δὲ πολιὰ ὥσπερ εἰς λιμένα ἀκύμαντον τὰς τῶν γεγηρακότων ὁρμίζει ψυχάς, . . .[103]

---

[103]Chrysostom frequently uses ἀκύμαντος and λιμήν together.

Fr. sp. 48

Ἡ τῆς ἀρχῆς ἐξουσία, εἰ μὴ κέκραται ἡμερότητι καὶ ἐπανθεῖ αὐτῇ ἡ θεῷ διακονοῦσα πρόνοια, ἀπονοίας μᾶλλόν ἐστιν ἀγριότης. εἰ δὲ τῷ πράῳ μιγείη καὶ τούτῳ ἰθύνοι τὸ δίκαιον, καὶ εὐθύτης ἐστὶ καὶ χρηστότης καὶ ὁδὸς εὐνομίας καὶ πραγμάτων γαλήνη.

Cohn, *PCW* 1:lix, from Urbinas 125, f. 308ᵛ (follows *Quod Omn* 38).[104]

Removed as = Isidore of Pelusium, *Epistle* 1.47 (*MPG* 78:212B2–7). The text there reads:

Ἡ τῆς ἀρχῆς ἐξουσία, εἰ μὴ κέκραται ἡμερότητι, καὶ ἐπανθεῖ αὐτῇ ἡ θεῷ διακονοῦσα προσήνεια, ἀπόνοιά ἐστι μᾶλλον καὶ ἀγριότης. εἰ δὲ τῷ πράῳ μιγείη, καὶ τούτῳ ἰθύνει τὸ δίκαιον, καὶ εὐθύτης ἐστὶ καὶ χρηστότης καὶ ὁδὸς εὐνομίας καὶ πραγμάτων γαλήνη.

By the way, note 46 there (before μᾶλλον) reads: "Locus hic in codd. Alt. et Vat. 649 hoc modo exstat ἀπονοίας μᾶλλόν ἐστιν ἀγριότης." Apparently, therefore, Cohn's manuscript took its excerpt from a related manuscript of Isidore.

---

[104]Cohn notes: "sequitur fragmentum alibi, ut videtur, non traditum, quod an Philonis sit dubito."

Fr. sp. 49

Ὅταν ἄνθρωπος κατορθώσῃ βίον ἐνάρετον δι᾿ ἀσκήσεως καὶ ἀγαθῆς πολιτείας, καὶ ἔστιν ὑπὸ πάντων ἐγνωσμένος, ὅτι ἐστὶν εὐσεβὴς καὶ φοβούμενος τὸν θεόν, καὶ ἐκπέσῃ εἰς ἁμαρτίαν· τοῦτό ἐστι παράπτωμα. ἀνῆλθεν γὰρ εἰς τὸ ὕψος τοῦ οὐρανοῦ, καὶ πέπτωκεν εἰς τὸν πυθμένα τοῦ ᾅδου.

Lequien, 343 = *MPG* 95:1176A6–11 (no lemma; follows a Philo text [A1]: Philonis), from Vat. 1236.
Lequien, 597 = *MPG* 96:148C9–D1 (Eusebii), from Vat. 1236.
Mangey, 648.4, from Lequien, 343.
Harris, 77.4, from Lequien, 343.[105]
Holl, 222–23, no. 482, who does not note Lequien, 343, or the ascription to Philo.

Removed by Früchtel as = Eusebius of Alexandria, *Sermo* 6 (*MPG* 86.1: 352D6–353A1).[106] The text printed at Lequien, 343, and then reprinted by Mangey and Harris, is only the opening portion of the text at Lequien, 597, which is reprinted by Holl.

---

[105]Harris comments: "In Dam. Par. [i.e., Lequien] 597 it is however expressly given to *Eusebius*, and so in Reg. 923 [i.e., Par. 923, f. 388ᵛA (32) 33 – B 12: Εὐσεβίου], and should therefore probably be removed."
[106]This is a text cited (from Mangey) by C. G. L. Grossmann, *De Iudaeorum disciplina arcani* (2 pts.; Leipzig: University of Leipzig, 1833–34), 1:27 (n. 120), in order to illustrate that Philo agreed with the doctrine of the Pharisees "de futuris bonorum malorumque praemiis iustissimis" (1:16).

Fr. sp. 50

'Αποστρέφου τῶν κολάκων τοὺς ἀπατηλοὺς λόγους· ἐξαμβλύνοντες γὰρ τοὺς τῆς ψυχῆς λογισμοὺς οὐ συγχωροῦσι τῶν πραγμάτων τὴν ἀλήθειαν· ἢ γὰρ ἐπαινοῦσι τὰ ψόγου ἄξια ἢ ψέγουσι πολλάκις τὰ ἐπαίνων κρείττονα.

Gessner, 59 = *MPG* 136:941D11–44A3 (Philonis), from Antonius.
Combefis, 567 = *MPG* 91:792C5–9 (Φίλωνος), from Maximus.[107]
Mangey, 671.9, "ex Antonio."
Lewy, 81.20, from Maximus, Barberinus I 158, f. 39ʳ (Φίλωνος), Antonius, and Laur. plut. VII 15, f. 144ʳ (Φίλωνος).
Barocc. 143, f. 173ʳ (4) 5–10: Φίλωνος.

Removed as = Agapetus, *Capita admonitoria* 12 (*MPG* 86.1:1168C8–D1).[108]

---

[107]Combefis conjectures < ἰδεῖν > after συγχωροῦσι, and Agapetus in fact has ὁρᾶν.

[108]Agapetus in fact reads, among other slight variations: . . . ἀπατηλοὺς λόγους, ὥσπερ τῶν κοράκων τοὺς ἁρπακτικοὺς τρόπους· οἱ μὲν γὰρ τοὺς τοῦ σώματος ἐξορύττουσιν ὀφθαλμούς· οἱ δὲ τοὺς τῆς ψυχῆς ἐξαμβλύνουσι λογισμούς, . . . We perhaps have another example of homoeoteleuton here (from λόγους to ὀφθαλμούς). However, the excerpt also omits some words at the end.

Fr. sp. 51

Τῇ μὲν οὐσίᾳ τοῦ σώματος, ἴσος παντὸς ἀνθρώπου ὁ βασιλεύς, τῇ ἐξουσίᾳ δὲ τοῦ ἀξιώματος ὅμοιός ἐστι τῷ ἐπὶ πάντων θεῷ· οὐκ ἔχει γὰρ ἐπὶ γῆς αὐτοῦ ὑψηλότερον. χρὴ τοίνυν καὶ ὡς θνητὸν μὴ ἐπαίρεσθαι καὶ ὡς θεὸν μὴ ὀργίζεσθαι. εἰ γὰρ καὶ εἰκόνι θεϊκῇ τετίμηται, ἀλλὰ καὶ κόνει χοϊκῇ συμπέπλεκται, δι᾽ ἧς ἐκδιδάσκεται τὴν πρὸς πάντας ἁπλότητα.

Gessner, 80 (Ἀγαπητοῦ)[109] = *MPG* 136:1012B8–C1 (no lemma; follows a Philo text [B6]: Philonis), from Antonius.[110]
Combefis, 561 = *MPG* 91:781C5–12 (Φίλων.), from Maximus.[111]
Mangey, 673.1, "ex Antonio."
Barocc. 143, f. 191ʳ (19) 20–28: Ἀγαπητοῦ.

Removed as = Agapetus, *Capita admonitoria* 21 (*MPG* 86.1:1172A2–

---

[109]This lemma is found in Gessner's addenda, 298, where he notes: "pag. 80. uer. 1. scribe in margine ἀγαπητοῦ." Clearly this correct lemma was taken from Mon. 429. At p. 80 the text occurs (starting on line 1) with no lemma, but on the second previous text: Κότυς.

[110]The relation here between Gessner's edition and *MPG* 136 is confused. In the 1546 edition the sequence is as follows: Chapter B.α´ ends with two texts with the lemma Κότυς (Cotyis; = *MPG* 136:1009C3–6, C7–8), our spurious text (without a lemma), and finally six more texts (= *MPG* 136:1012C2–D1). Then occurs chapter B.β´, which concludes with the citation of *Gaium* 190 (= *MPG* 136:1012B6–7). Now in *MPG* 136, the sequence is: Chapter B.α´ concludes with the two texts with the lemma Κότυς (Cotyis; = *MPG* 136:1009C3–6, C7–8). Then chapter B.β´ begins as in Gessner, then has *Gaium* 190 (= *MPG* 136:1012B6–7), our spurious text (without a lemma), and finally the six other texts (= *MPG* 136:1012C2–D1). This relocation of the spurious text has resulted in its being subsumed under the lemma on *Gaium* 190, i.e., in its becoming ascribed to Philo. Perhaps this dislocation of text was in some way occasioned by the fact that the two texts with the lemma Κότυς (Cotyis) end p. 79 in Gessner's edition. It appears that the seven texts at the top of p. 80 were first skipped, and then retrieved but inserted at the wrong place. And in any case Gessner's note in his addenda, which in this case provided the true source of our spurious text, was ignored.

[111]Combefis has a marginal note to Rom 9:5. Also he suggests ὁμοιότητα for ἁπλότητα, while Agapetus has ἰσότητα (cf. Henry, "Mirror," 287).

9).[112] Of our seven texts from Agapetus, this is the only one which I have found ascribed to him in the manuscripts. In fact, this ascription is not peculiar to Barocc. 143; in Mon. 429, f. 89$^r$ (1) 1–5, the text occurs with the same lemma.[113]

---

[112]Goodenough, *Politics*, 99–100, cites this passage in English, and says that "Philo's attitude [toward kingship] is best summarized" in it. At 99, n. 72, Goodenough cites the Greek from Mangey, and adds: "This is one of the many fragments which Harris (*Fragments*, 106) for some reason 'thought it not worth while to print.' "

[113]On these two manuscripts see chapter 3, page 30, above.

Fr. sp. 52

Τοιοῦτος γίνου περὶ τοὺς σοὺς οἰκέτας οἷον εὔχῃ σοὶ τὸν θεὸν γενέσθαι· ὡς γὰρ ἀκούομεν ἀκουσθησόμεθα ὑπὸ τοῦ θεοῦ, καὶ ὡς ὁρῶμεν ὁραθησόμεθα ὑπ᾽ αὐτοῦ· προσενέγκωμεν οὖν τοῦ ἐλέου τὸν ἔλεον, ἵνα τῷ ὁμοίῳ τὸ ὅμοιον ἀντιλάβωμεν.

Gessner, 35 = *MPG* 136:872D1–5 (Philonis), from Antonius.

Combefis, 554–55 = *MPG* 91:769C1–6 (Φίλωνος), from Maximus.

Mangey, 672.1, "ex Antonio."[114]

Tischendorf, 153.5, "Ex codice Cahirino."

Harris, 104.1, from Barocc. 143, Tischendorf, and Maximus.

Barocc. 143, f. 17ʳ (10) 11–17: Φίλωνος.

Removed as = Agapetus, *Capita admonitoria* 23 (*MPG* 86.1:1172B3–8). This has a parallel in *Barlaam*.[115] But the spurious text agrees with Agapetus against *Barlaam*.[116]

---

[114]Mangey refers to Matt 7:1, and notes that the text is also in Barocc. 143. This text is also cited by Montefiore, "Florilegium Philonis," 543.

[115]See Boissonade, *Anecdota Graeca* 4:333 (= *MPG* 96:1205B13–C2):

Καὶ ὡς ἀκούομεν ἀκουσθησόμεθα, ὡς ὁρῶμεν ὁραθησό-μεθα ὑπὸ τοῦ θείου καὶ παντεφόρου βλέμματος. προεισ-ενέγκωμεν οὖν τοῦ ἐλέου τὸν ἔλεον, ἵνα τῷ ὁμοίῳ τὸ ὅμοιον ἀντιλάβωμεν.

This parallel is not cited by Boissonade, but is noted by Dölger, *Der Barlaam-Roman*, 103, and by Henry, "Mirror," 288.

[116]Agapetus and the florilegia have ὡς γάρ instead of *Barlaam*'s καὶ ὡς, and have καὶ ὡς ὁρῶμεν instead of *Barlaam*'s ὡς ὁρῶμεν.

Fr. sp. 53

Εἰ βούλει διττῶς εὐδοκιμεῖν, καὶ τοὺς κάλλιστα ποιοῦντας προτίμα, καὶ τοὺς τὰ χείρονα πράττοντας ἐπιτίμα.

Combefis, 685 = *MPG* 91:1012A1–3 (Φίλωνος), from Maximus.
Mangey, 670.4, "ex Antonio."[117]
Lewy, 82.23, from Maximus, Barberinus I 158, f. 153ᵛ (Φίλωνος), and Laur. plut. VII 15, f. 246ʳ (Φίλωνος).

Removed as = Agapetus, *Capita admonitoria* 28 (*MPG* 86.1:1173A7–9).[118]

---

[117]This text does not occur in Antonius, and Mangey's source is, of course, the 1609 edition of Gessner. Henry comments ("Mirror," 288, n. 19): "I have searched thoroughly the *PG* Ant. Mel. and have been unable to find this fragment."

[118]Here the excerpt contains only about the last third of the Agapetus chapter.

Fr. sp. 54

Πλέον ἀγάπα, βασιλεῦ, τοὺς λαμβάνειν παρὰ σοῦ χάριτας ἱκετεύον-
τας ἤπερ τοὺς σπουδάζοντας δωρεάς σοι προσφέρειν· τοῖς μὲν γὰρ ὀφει-
λέτης ἀμοιβῆς καθίστασαι, οἱ δέ σοι τὸν ὀφειλέτην ποιήσουσι τὸν οἰκειού-
μενον τὰ εἰς αὐτοὺς γινόμενα καὶ ἀμειβόμενον ἀγαθαῖς ἀντιδόσεσιν τὸν
φιλάνθρωπόν σου σκοπόν.

Combefis, 556 = *MPG* 91:773A14–B6 (no lemma; follows a Philo text
[A12]: Φίλωνος), from Maximus.
Tischendorf, 155.16, "Ex codice Cahirino."
Harris, 105.1, from Maximus and Tischendorf.

Removed as = Agapetus, *Capita admonitoria* 50 (*MPG* 86.1:1180A8–
14).[119]

---

[119]Agapetus reads at the end: τὸν φιλόθεον καὶ φιλάνθρωπόν σου σκοπόν, so we seem to have here an omission by homoeoarcton. The spurious
text is cited by Goodenough, *Politics*, 95 (and n. 47), for Philo's theory of
kingship.

Fr. sp. 55

'Ο μὲν θεὸς οὐδενὸς δεῖται, ὁ βασιλεὺς δὲ μόνου θεοῦ· μιμοῦ τοί
νυν τὸν οὐδενὸς δεόμενον καὶ δαψιλεύου τοῖς αἰτοῦσι τὸ ἔλεος, μὴ ἀκρι
βολογούμενος περὶ τοὺς σοὺς ἱκέτας ἀλλὰ πᾶσι παρέχων τὰς πρὸς τὸ ζῆν
αἰτήσεις· πολὺ γὰρ κρεῖττόν ἐστι διὰ τοὺς ἀξίους ἐλεεῖν καὶ τοὺς ἀναξί
ους, καὶ μὴ τοὺς ἀξίους ἀποστερῆσαι διὰ τοὺς ἀναξίους.

Gessner, 77 = *MPG* 136:1004B7–11 (Philonis), from Antonius ('Ο μὲν
— αἰτήσεις only).
Combefis, 559 = *MPG* 91:777D4–80A1 (Φίλων.), from Maximus.
Tischendorf, 155.14, "Ex codice Cahirino."
Harris, 104.3, from Maximus and Tischendorf.[120]
Barocc. 143, f. 17ᵛ (10) 11–19: Πλουτάρχου .

Removed as = Agapetus, *Capita admonitoria* 63 (*MPG* 86.1:1184A2–8).
As noted in chapter 3, I found Agapetus as a source of spurious Philo texts by
following Harris's note on this text.[121]

---

[120]Harris (*Fragments*, 104–5) notes that the first part ('Ο μὲν — θεοῦ)
"is based on an earlier gnomic saying," and refers to Boissonade, *Anecdota
Graeca* 1:45. He also says: "I believe it is found in this form also in Philo."
Perhaps he was thinking of *Vita Mos* 1.157 or *Plant* 51.

[121]There is a brief reference to it by Goodenough, *Politics*, 97, and n. 58.

Fr. sp. 56

Συγγνώμην αἰτούμενος ἁμαρτημάτων συγγίνωσκε καὶ αὐτὸς τοῖς εἰς σὲ πλημμελοῦσιν· ὅτι ἀφέσει ἀντιδίδοται ἄφεσις, καὶ ἡ πρὸς τοὺς ὁμοδούλους ἡμῶν καταλλαγὴ τῆς θείας ὀργῆς γίνεται ἀπαλλαγή.

Gessner, 123 (Φίλωνος)[122] = MPG 136:1137C4–8 (on ninth previous text [1136C12]: S. Basilii), from Antonius.

Combefis, 681 = MPG 91:1004B6–10 (Φίλωνος), from Maximus.

Mangey, 670.5, "ex Antonio."[123]

Barocc. 143, ff. 210ʳ (25) 26 – 210ᵛ 2: Φίλωνος.

Removed as = Agapetus, *Capita admonitoria* 64 (*MPG* 86.1:1184A10–14).[124] A parallel is also found in *Barlaam*.[125] On the textual relations

---

[122]The lemma is corrected by Gessner in his addenda, 298; the text on 123 occurs without a lemma (as in *MPG*). Consequently, this text is included by Fedwick, "The Citations of Basil," 42, marked with brackets as being "not identified or belonging to other writers" (35).

[123]Mangey notes: "Sententia haec Philoni quoque tribuitur in Cod. Barocc. Nᵒ 143."

[124]In fact, Agapetus reads:
Συγγνώμην αἰτούμενος ἁμαρτημάτων, συγγίνωσκε καὶ αὐτὸς τοῖς εἰς σὲ πλημμελοῦσιν· ὅτι ἀφέσει ἀντιδίδοται ἄφεσις, καὶ τῇ πρὸς τοὺς ὁμοδούλους ἡμῶν καταλλαγῇ, ἡ πρὸς θεὸν φιλία καὶ οἰκείωσις.
By the way, I have examined one manuscript of Agapetus, Baroccianus 51, which is of the fifteenth century and contains chaps. 27 (end) – 72. However, chap. 40 in the manuscript is chap. 23 of *MPG*, and two chapters are numbered 56, causing *MPG* chaps. 57–72 to appear as 56–71. Therefore, it does not contain Fr. sp. 50 or 51, but does contain the other five. However, the variants are rather minor, and I have not bothered to cite them generally. I will note, though, that for chap. 64, Barocc. 51 reads exactly as does *MPG*. Also, a manuscript cited by Bandur (*MPG* 86.1:1183–84, n. 17) has καὶ ὁμοίωσις γίνεται in place of καὶ οἰκείωσις. This agrees with *Barlaam* in having γίνεται, which could, of course, be an independent addition.

[125]See Boissonade, *Anecdota Graeca* 4:334 (= *MPG* 96:1205C8–12):
συγγνώμην αἰτούμενος ἁμαρτημάτων, συγγίνωσκε καὶ αὐτὸς τοῖς εἰς σὲ πλημμελοῦσιν, ὅτι ἀφέσει ἀντιδίδοται

among Agapetus, *Barlaam*, and this excerpt, see chapter 3, pages 56–57, above.

---

ἄφεσις, καὶ τῇ πρὸς τοὺς ὁμοδούλους ἡμῶν καταλλαγῇ
τῆς δεσποτικῆς ὀργῆς γίνεται ἀπαλλαγή.
The parallel is already noted by Boissonade, and then later by Dölger, *Der Barlaam-Roman*, 104, and Henry, "Mirror," 291.

Fr. sp. 57

Ὕπνος ἐστὶ φύσεως ποσῆς σύστασις, εἰκὼν θανάτου, αἰσθήσεων ἀργία.

Gessner, 51 = *MPG* 136:920D14–15 (no lemma; follows Fr. sp. 29), from Antonius.
Mangey, 672.2a, "ex Antonio."
Barocc. 143, f. 152ᵛ (24) 26 – 153ʳ 2: Μενάνδρου.

Removed as = John Climacus, *Scala Paradisi*, Gradus 19 (*MPG* 88: 937A6–7).

Fr. sp. 58

Εἷς μὲν ὁ ὕπνος, πολλὰς δὲ ὑποθέσεις καὶ ἡ ἐπιθυμία ἔχει, λέγω δὴ ἐκ φύσεως, ἐκ βρωμάτων, ἐκ δαιμόνων, ἢ τάχα καὶ ἄκρας καὶ ἐπιτεταμένης νηστείας, ἐξ ἧς ἐξατονοῦσα ἡ σὰρξ διὰ ὕπνου λοιπὸν αὐτὴν παραμυθήσασθαι βούλεται.

Gessner, 51 = *MPG* 136:921A1–5 (no lemma; follows Fr. sp. 57), from Antonius.
Mangey, 672.2b, "ex Antonio."

Removed as = John Climacus, *Scala Paradisi*, Gradus 19 (*MPG* 88: 937A7–12).

Fr. sp. 59

Ὥσπερ ἡ πολυποσία συνήθεια εἴρηται, οὕτως καὶ πολυυπνία· χαλε-
πὸν οὖν συνήθειαν μακρὰν ἰάσασθαι.

Gessner, 51 = *MPG* 136:921A6–8 (no lemma; follows Fr. sp. 58), from
Antonius.[126]
Mangey, 672.2c, "ex Antonio."

**Removed as** = John Climacus, *Scala Paradisi*, Gradus 19 (*MPG* 88:
937A12–13, B1).

---

[126]Gessner prints πολυπλασία, and notes: "forte πολυποσία."

Fr. sp. 60

Τῶν ἀπορρήτων ἃ μὲν τὴν σὴν ἀρετὴν αὐξάνει, κοινώνει τοῖς φίλοις, ἃ δὲ τὴν γνώμην φαυλίζει, μήτε αὐτὸς μετέρχου, μήτε τοῖς φίλοις ἀνατίθη.

Mangey, 674.3, from Barocc. 143, ff. 77ᵛ 25 – 78ʳ 3 (no lemma; follows two Philo texts [f. 77ᵛ 10]: τοῦ Φίλωνος).
Harris, 102.8, from Mangey.

Removed by Früchtel as = Photius, *Epistle* 1.8.41 (*MPG* 102:669C3–5).

Fr. sp. 61

Πρότερον μέντοι ὁ νόμος τὰ ἐν οἷς εὐκολώτερον ὀλισθαίνομεν, οἷον τὸ μοιχεύειν, ἐπειδὴ τὸ πῦρ φυσικὸν καὶ ἔνδοθεν, καὶ τὸ φονεύειν, ἐπειδὴ μέγα θηρίον ὁ θυμός, δεύτερα τίθησι τὰ σπανιάκις συμβαίνοντα, λέγων μὴ κλέψῃς, μὴ ψευδομαρτυρήσῃς.

Cohn, *PCW* 5:xvi, n. 1, and 5:173, apparatus, from Vat. 1611, f. 245ᵛB 39–43 (follows a citation from *Spec Leg* 3.83–85).[127]

Removed as = Theophylact, *Enarratio in Evangelium Lucae*, on Luke 18:18–23 (*MPG* 123:1009D11–12, D14–1012A1, A5–7).[128] The Greek text is cited here as in Vat. 1611, which differs at several places from what Cohn reports. (Note further that while *PCW* 5:xvi, n. 1, correctly has συμβαίνοντα, *PCW* 5:173, apparatus, reads συμβάντα.) The manuscript, Vat. 1611, is the chief witness to the chain of Nicetas on Luke.[129]

---

[127]A Latin version is quoted by Wendland, *PCW* 2:xv, n. 2, with the comment: "quae Philonea esse mihi videntur; locum, unde sumpta sunt, non inveni." Cohn, giving the Greek in *PCW* 5:xvi, n. 1, says: "quae num Philonea sint equidem dubito."

[128]Vat. 1611 skips some of this section and makes some alterations; Theophylact reads:

Πρότερον ὁ νόμος τὰ ἐν οἷς εὐκολώτερον ὀλισθαίνομεν .
. . οἷον τὸ μοιχεύειν, ἐπειδὴ τὸ πῦρ καὶ φυσικὸν καὶ ἔνδοθεν, τὸ φονεύειν, ἐπειδὴ μέγα θηρίον ὁ θυμός· . . . ταῦτα
δὲ τὴν κλοπήν φημι καὶ τὴν ψευδομαρτυρίαν δεύτερα τί-
θησιν ὡς καὶ σπανιάκις ἀπατῶντα, καὶ ἐλαφρότερα.

[129]See Devreesse, "Chaînes," 1183–84; Goodhart and Goodenough, *Bibliography*, 169–71.

# 5

# THE SPURIOUS WORKS

Besides the spurious ascription of such brief fragments to Philo, there are also cases of the false ascription of entire works to Philo. Although some of these ascriptions have a certain foundation in ancient tradition, none appears to stand up to scrutiny, and all are generally rejected today.[1]

    1. Wisdom of Solomon. Already by the time of Jerome this work had been ascribed to Philo.[2]

    2. *Interpretatio Hebraicorum nominum.* This work is clearly very ancient, since Origen mentions it, Eusebius says it was assigned to Philo in his time, and Jerome discusses it.[3]

    3. *Liber antiquitatum biblicarum.* This book is found within the ancient Latin translation of Philo's works,[4] but is clearly spurious.[5]

---

[1]On the spurious works in general, see Schürer, *Geschichte* 3:687–95 (who includes *Vita Cont* and *Aet*); idem, *History* 3.2:868–70; and Cohn, "Einteilung," 425–26.

[2]Schürer, *Geschichte* 3:508; idem, *History* 3.1:573. Cf. the recent "Introduction" by David Winston, trans., *The Wisdom of Solomon* (Anchor Bible, vol. 43; Garden City, New York: Doubleday, 1979), 59–63, as well as Bruns, "Philo Christianus," 143, and Speyer, *Die literarische Fälschung*, 154 and 166.

[3]Schürer, *Geschichte* 3:693–95; idem, *History* 3.2:869–70; Cohn, "Einteilung," 426; idem, *PCW* 1:i–ii and liv, n. 1 (where an Armenian version is noted); Devreesse, *Les anciens commentateurs*, 9.

[4]See Cohn, "Einteilung," 426; idem, *PCW* 1:l–lii, 6:xv–xvii; Petit, *L'ancienne version* 1:7, n. 6; Speyer, *Die literarische Fälschung*, 41.

[5]See the "Introduction littéraire" by Charles Perrot and Pierre-Maurice Bogaert, with the collaboration of Daniel J. Harrington, eds. and trans., *Pseudo-Philon, Les Antiquités Bibliques*, vol. 2: *Introduction littéraire, commentaire et index* (SC, vol. 230; 1976), 10 (Harrington: "L'attribution à Philon est probablement due au fait que ce texte a été accidentellement transmis parmi d'authentiques oeuvres de Philon"), 66–74 (Bogaert on "La datation"), and 247–56 (bibliography). See also Schürer, *Geschichte* 3:384–86, 695; and idem, *History* 3.1:325–31, 3.2:870. Further references to the literature on this work can be found in Goodhart and Goodenough, *Bibliography*, 320–21 (nos.

The next two spurious works are products of Hellenistic Judaism preserved in the ancient Armenian translation:[6]

4. *De Jona*. This work is attributed to Philo in the Armenian manuscripts.[7]

5. *De Sampsone*. This work, transmitted anonymously among the works of Philo in Armenian, was attributed to Philo by Aucher.[8]

6. *De temporibus*. In 1498 Giovanni Nanni (or Ioannes Annius) published a collection purporting to contain various ancient works.[9] Provided with extensive commentaries on these works, the book went through many editions and attracted much attention.[10] But, as was eventually shown, the whole work, including the supposedly ancient texts, was the creation of Nanni himself.[11] Among the texts is a work attributed to Philo, and given simply

---

1601–3); Gerhard Delling and Malwine Maser, *Bibliographie zur jüdisch-hellenistischen und intertestamentarischen Literatur 1900–1970*, 2d ed. (TU, vol. 106; Berlin: Akademie-Verlag, 1975), 174–75 (nos. 3570–93); Radice, *Filone*, Index 1, p. 311 (s.v. *"LAB"*); and Louis H. Feldman, *Josephus and Modern Scholarship (1937–1980)* (Berlin and New York: Walter de Gruyter, 1984), 418–19. Frederick J. Murphy, "God in Pseudo-Philo," *JSJ* 19 (1988): 17, n. 34 (–18), has further references on the dating.

[6]On the spurious nature of these two works see Schürer, *Geschichte* 3: 693; idem, *History* 3.2:869; Cohn, "Einteilung," 425–26; idem, *PCW* 1:lii; Lewy, ed., *The Pseudo-Philonic "De Jona,"* pt. 1: *The Armenian Text with a Critical Introduction* (Studies and Documents, vol. 7; London: Christophers, 1936), 3 (of the introduction), n. 10; Siegert, *Predigten*, 2; and Terian, *Philonis Alexandrini de animalibus*, 4–5.

[7]See Aucher, *Paralipomena Armena*, 578, and Lewy, *"De Jona"*, 1 (of the text), apparatus.

[8]See *Paralipomena Armena*, 549, n. 1: "Huic soli orationi, etsi in ipsa sit serie sermonum Philonis, atque apud Glossarium caeterosque memorata, non erat praefixum nomen auctoris." However, a brief Greek fragment of the *De Sampsone* is preserved under Philo's name in a few manuscripts of the *Sacra parallela*; see the discussion of Fr. sp. 25 above. From this we can infer that the *De Sampsone* was already attributed to Philo at the time that the *Sacra parallela* was compiled.

[9]*Commentaria fratris Ioannis Annii Viterbensis ordinis praedicatorum Theologiae professoris super opera diuersorum auctorum de Antiquitatibus loquentium* (Rome: Eucharius Silber, 1498).

[10]See Goodhart and Goodenough, *Bibliography*, 319–20 (nos. 1587–96).

[11]See Pierre Louis Ginguené, "Annius de Viterbe," in *Biographie universelle, ancienne et moderne*, vol. 2 (Paris: Michaud Frères, 1811), 223–26

the title "De temporibus" or "Breuiarium de temporibus."[12] The contents of the two books of this work are briefly indicated by Nanni as follows:

> promittimus comentaria [sic] super duos libellos Breuiarii
> Philonis de temporibus: in quorum primo enumerat tem-
> pora ab Adam usque ad desolationem templi: & in secundo
> ab eadem desolatione usque ad suam etatem secula dige-
> rit.[13]

7. *De virtute.* In 1816 Mai edited, under the title Φίλωνος τοῦ Ἰου-δαίου περὶ ἀρετῆς καὶ τῶν ταύτης μορίων, *Philonis Iudaei de virtute eiusque partibus,*[14] a brief work which is attributed to Philo in Ambrosianus D 27 sup. In the manuscript the work is titled Φίλωνος ὅτι πᾶς ἄφρων δοῦλος ἐστίν,[15] which would thus seem to be the lost work which was the companion to *Quod Omn.*[16] And in fact *Quod Omn* follows this work in the Milan manuscript.[17] But Mai recognized that the manuscript's title did not suit the contents of the

---

(Goodhart and Goodenough, *Bibliography*, 319, cite him as "Ginguiné"); Bruce M. Metzger, *The Text of the New Testament: Its Transmission, Corruption, and Restoration*, 2d ed. (New York and Oxford: Oxford University Press, 1968), 156, and n. 2 (and references there); and Speyer, *Die literarische Fälschung*, 101, 319–20. Cf. also Fabricius and Harles, *Bibliotheca Graeca* 4: 743. On the other hand, Schürer (*Geschichte* 3:695; *History* 3.2:870) claims that Nanni probably printed the texts in good faith; see also *Geschichte* 1:182, n. 3 (from 181).

[12]Unfortunately, Nanni's pages are not numbered. The book is divided into lettered sections, and this "Breuiarium" appears on the pages of sections G and H (i.e., $G_{ii}r - H_{viii}r$).

[13]This is on the third of the pages lettered 'G' (i.e., $G_{ii}r$).

[14]Milan: Regiis Typis, 1816. There we find remarks on Philo (pp. i–lxxx), and then the work attributed to Philo (pp. 1–28). Then occurs another title page (*Porphyrii philosophi ad Marcellam*), and material on Porphyry (pp. iii–viii, 1–68). Thus, we in fact have two volumes bound as one.

[15]As noted by Mai, ii–iii (of the introductory material on Philo).

[16]See Schürer, *Geschichte* 3:675–76; idem, *History* 3.2:856; Cohn, *PCW* 6:iv–v. Indeed, in the catalogue by Aemidius Martini and Dominicus Bassi, *Catalogus codicum Graecorum bibliothecae Ambrosianae*, 2 vols. (Milan: U. Hoepli, 1906), 1:244, the manuscript's ascription is accepted: "Philonis (49 [i.e., f. 49]) quod omnis stultus servus est (edid. ex hoc cod. Mai, Philonis Iudaei, Porphyrii philos. etc. opera inedita. Mediolani, 1816; cfr. pp. II–IV)."

[17]See Mai, iii; Cohn, *PCW* 6:i, and n. 1.

work he found, and so he argued that the title was erroneous,[18] and proposed his own title as given above, based on a line in the treatise. Then, Désiré Raoul-Rochette, in his review of this edition,[19] accepted that the work was Philonic and justified Mai's title by referring to Eusebius's words (*Hist. eccl.* 2.6.3): ἐν δευτέρῳ συγγράμματι ὧν συνέγραψε [*sic*] περὶ ἀρετῶν. Raoul-Rochette then concluded:

> Le *premier*, auquel Eusèbe fait allusion, est ce traité [*Virt*] depuis long-temps connu et publié (*voy. tom. I* [i.e., II], *pag. 375 et seq.* de l'édition de Mangey), et dont parle plusieurs fois le même Eusèbe. Le *second* ne peut être que celui qu'a récemment découvert M. Mai.

Raoul-Rochette further claimed that the suggestion that this reference in Eusebius is to *Flacc* is unfounded, and notes that *Flacc*

> porte pour second titre: ἤτοι περὶ προνοίας, *ou de la providence*; titre sous lequel Eusèbe en fait mention en deux endroits de sa *Préparation évangélique*, VII, 21, VIII, 1, et qui paroît également dans tous les manuscrits de Philon consultés par Mangey.[20]

Of course, *Provid* had not yet been edited by Aucher, and so this identification of *Flacc* was perhaps plausible at the time, although Raoul-Rochette could have learned from Mai's own report here (xiii–xiv) that there were "De Providentia ad Alexandrum libri duo" among the unedited works in the Armenian version, and (xiv) that this work was cited by Eusebius at *Praep. ev.* 7.20–21. In any case, though, the interpretation of Eusebius's reference at *Hist. eccl.* 2.6.3 remains controversial.[21]

However, as it turned out, the work edited by Mai is ascribed in other manuscripts to Georgius Gemistus (Pletho), and in fact had already been

---

[18]Mai, ii–iv. Mai (iii) presents the following ingenious explanation of the title. The opening words of the work which follows in the manuscript are (*Quod Omn* 1): Ὁ μὲν πρότερος λόγος ἦν ἡμῖν, ὦ Θεόδοτε, περὶ τοῦ δοῦλον εἶναι πάντα φαῦλον. Now the previous treatise in this manuscript is in fact Mai's book, and so could be taken as the companion to *Quod Omn*. The title in the manuscript, which of course differs slightly from Philo's own words, was then taken from Sophronius's Greek translation of Jerome, *De vir. inl.* 11 (see the text in Cohn, *PCW* 1:ciii, ll. 3–4).

[19]*Journal des Savans* [*sic*] (1817): 227–38.

[20]Ibid., 233.

[21]See Schürer, *Geschichte* 3:681–82, *History* 3.2:862–63.

edited under the name of Gemistus.[22] Mai himself withdrew the claim of Philonic provenance by reissuing his 1816 book the same year with a new title page,[23] and by giving to the work itself the following title: "Γεωργίου Γεμίστου ἦ ὡς ἐν 'Αμβροσιάνῳ βιβλίῳ Φίλωνος περὶ ἀρετῆς καὶ τῶν ταύτης μορίων, *Georgii Gemisti sive ut scribitur in Ambrosiano codice Philonis de virtute eiusque partibus.*"[24] Nevertheless, Mai's original edition gave rise to Goodhart and Goodenough's citation of it simply as containing *Virt*, with no indication that the work is spurious.[25]

---

[22]A reprint appears in *MPG* 160:865–82, with the title ΠΕΡΙ ΑΡΕΤΩΝ. There the line from which Mai took his title is 880B1: Τοσαῦτα περὶ ἀρετῆς καὶ τῶν ταύτης μορίων κτλ.

[23]Πορφυρίου φιλοσόφου πρὸς Μαρκέλλαν, *Porphyrii philosophi ad Marcellam* (Milan: Regiis Typis, 1816). Here the material on Porphyry occupies the first part of the volume (pp. iii–viii, 1–68), followed by introductory remarks on Philo (pp. i–lxxx), and then the text formerly attributed to Philo (still on pp. 1–28). The rearrangement seems to have been somewhat hasty: on p. iii of the prefatory remarks to Porphyry (which in the first edition occurred after, but now occur before, the Philo material) we read: "idcirco et Philonis *de virtute* scriptum incognitum superius edidi . . . ." By the way, I have compared the copies of these two editions in the Bodleian Library, where the first edition is catalogued as "Auct. K. IV. 30," and the second edition is catalogued as "Fol. Δ. 194."

[24]Schürer, *Geschichte* 3:638, n. 11, says that Mai retracted the claim, and refers to "Leipziger Litteraturzeitung 1818, Nr. 276." This in fact refers to an anonymous review of Mai's *Philonis Judaei de Cophini festo et de colendis parentibus cum brevi scripto de Jona, Leipziger Literatur-Zeitung [sic]*, no. 276 (November 3, 1818): 2201–4. The reviewer goes into some detail on the history of Mai's editions involving the Milan manuscript, and on the work of Gemistus. Moreover, in his subsequent book, *Philo et Virgilii interpretes* (Milan: Regiis Typis, 1818), Mai says (p. xviii, n. 1): "Dum has locorum Philonis similitudines inter se congruentiasque vestigarem, obiter quoque notavi eiusdem Philonis locutiones sententiasque aliquot, quas Georgius Gemistus transtulisse videtur in libellum suum de virtutibus, quem libellum mediolanensia quidam codex (haud tamen probabili titulo) Philonis ipsi auctori tribuit." This admission is confirmed when we read on p. 83 (not numbered) of the same book a notice of the 1816 work with the following description: "Additur graecus Tractatus Gemisti editus de virtute cum nova interpretatione."

[25]*Bibliography*, 191 (no. 411). They also cite the review by Raoul-Rochette. Incidentally, although Schürer, *History* 3.2:870, includes this trea-

8. In 1942 Klara Stahlschmidt[26] claimed that a work (entitled περὶ θεοῦ) contained in *P.Berol.* inv. 17027 was probably to be attributed either to Philo or to a thinker closely related to him.[27] However, the papyrus is very fragmentary, and Stahlschmidt bolstered her case for Philonic authorship by filling in the lacunae with phrases from Philo's works. The evident circularity in this procedure, as well as her own citations of parallels to the papyrus from Hermetic writings, made her claim dubious. And the demonstration of the falsity of the claim was soon made by Kurt Aland,[28] who showed that one fragment of the papyrus agrees completely with a few lines from a Hermetic tractate, and accordingly concluded:

> Es handelt sich eben nicht um Philo, sondern um einen der zahlreichen hermetischen Traktate, von denen uns allerdings nur ein Teil erhalten ist.[29]

---

tise among the spurious works, the only reference given is to "n. 32," where (*History* 3.2:820), however, no mention is made of the spurious nature of the work published by Mai. On the other hand, Schürer, *Geschichte* 3:695, in connection with the spurious works, refers to "Anm. 11" (at 3:638), as cited in the preceding note. See also the comment by Pitra (*Analecta sacra* 2:310, n.) on Mai: "quum enim fere ab illo Judaeo sua analecta Mediolani auspicatus esset, haud bonis avibus incidit in fallax quoddam ἑρμαῖον, Philoni pro Plethone ascriptum."

[26]"Eine unbekannte Schrift Philons von Alexandrien (oder eines ihm nahestehenden Verfassers)," *Aeg* 22 (1942): 161–76. Stahlschmidt's view was supported by Luigi Alfonsi, "Sul περὶ θεοῦ del P. 17027 di Berlino," *Aeg* 23 (1943): 262–69. And Marcel Hombert, in his review of Stahlschmidt's article, *CE* 18 (1943): 306, says: "M^lle Stahlschmidt nous semble avoir tiré le maximum possible des débris, à première vue assez misérables, qui forment le papyrus de Berlin et elle a, avec beaucoup d'ingéniosité, proposé une série de restitutions qui, si elles restent très hypothétiques, sont du moins fort vraisemblables."

[27]Stahlschmidt claims that she can find no objections to Philonic authorship, but adds ("Eine Schrift," 174): "Es bleibt jedoch trotzdem die Möglichkeit bestehen, dass ein Philon nahestehender Philosoph, etwa ein Schüler, diese Schrift im Sinne des Meisters abfasste."

[28]"Eine neue Schrift Philos?" *TLZ* 68 (1943): 169–70. Hombert summarizes Aland's points in "Bulletin papyrologique XXI (1943 à 1946)," *REG* 61 (1948): 233.

[29]"Eine neue Schrift Philos?" 170. As far as I can determine, no reply has ever been offered to Aland's criticism of Stahlschmidt's claim.

Accordingly, this papyrus should not be considered Philonic, and thus should in no way join the two known papyri of Philo, the Coptos Papyrus and the Oxyrhynchus Papyrus. It must, moreover, be emphasized that in any case the work in the Berlin papyrus is not to be confused with the so-called *De Deo* found in Armenian,[30] which in fact had a different title, whereas Stahlschmidt's papyrus has the title clearly in the text. Nevertheless, the title in the papyrus has given rise to confusion with the *De Deo*.[31]

9. Anastasius Sinaita refers to the citation by Ammonius of Alexandria of a dialogue between Philo (called ἀπίστου Ἰουδαίου Φίλωνος τοῦ φιλοσόφου) and Mnason (mentioned in Acts 21:16), and the text of Anastasius is included by Cohn in his "Testimonia de Philone."[32] Furthermore, Elorduy

---

[30]See Siegert, *Philon*, 159, and our discussion of the *De Deo* below.

[31]This papyrus is cited by Joseph van Haelst, *Catalogue des papyrus littéraires juifs et chrétiens* (Paris: Publications de la Sorbonne, 1976), 252, no. 697, as: "Philon (?), De Deo." (Van Haelst does also cite Aland's article.) Likewise, Radice, *Filone*, 34 (no. 30; cf. nos. 31–32), says that Stahlschmidt ascribes the work "al trattato *De Deo* di F., o di un autore a lui vicino." However, Stahlschmidt does not, I believe, identify this work with the *De Deo*; see "Eine Schrift," 165:

> Unter den Schriften Philons v. Alexandrien, dem wir die vorliegenden Fragmente zuweisen möchten, ist bereits ein armenisches Bruchstück eines Kommentars zu *Genesis* 18, 2 bekannt, das in der lateinischen Uebersetzung bei Aucher den Titel *De Deo* trägt. Das Vorhandensein einer selbständigen Schrift περὶ θεοῦ ist daneben wohl möglich.

This seems to mean that it is possible that a complete treatise περὶ θεοῦ might well exist alongside ("daneben," but not identical with) the fragment printed by Aucher. Even Stahlschmidt's reconstruction of her περὶ θεοῦ seems to have nothing to do with the exegesis found in the Armenian *De Deo*.

This papyrus is also referred to (via the citation of Roger A. Pack, *The Greek and Latin Literary Texts from Greco-Roman Egypt*, 2d ed. [Ann Arbor: The University of Michigan Press, 1965], 79) in Schürer, *History* 3.2:823, n. 37: "listing an anonymous fragment of the fourth or fifth century which *may* be part of *Deus*." Since *Deus* is in fact *Quod deus sit immutabilis* (see ibid. 3.2:813), we have yet another confusion here. In fact, Pack cites this papyrus (no. 1346) as: "Philo: De Deo (or Hermetica?)," and refers to Aland's identification of the text with the Hermetica.

[32]See *PCW* 1:cviii–cix, taken there from *Viae dux* 14 (*MPG* 89:244D2–9), which is now edited as *Viae dux* 13.10 by Karl-Heinz Uthemann, *Anastasii*

has argued that the Ammonius involved is Ammonius Saccas,[33] and has even suggested that the dialogue might actually have taken place. Referring to Eusebius on Philo's contact with Peter in Rome,[34] Elorduy notes:

> Como es sabido, los especialistas en Filón suponen que éste vivió menos de lo que se infiere de Eusebio y otros textos cristianos. Pero es de advertir que la argumentación se basa en meras conjeturas.[35]

He then refers to the chief data on Philo's age, namely the chronological facts concerning the embassy to Gaius in A.D. 39, and says:

> Según los testimonios de Eusebio, Ammonio y Anastasio Sinaíta, habría que pensar que vivía todavía entre el 55 y el 65 de nuestra era. El estar en edad de no ser niños y poseer madurez de juicio el año 39, no era obstáculo para alargar la vida unos cuantos lustros: ambas cosas se podían decir perfectamente de San Pedro.[36]

Despite this possibility, however, such a dialogue should hardly be seen as more than mere legend.[37] Note that there also exists in some manuscripts

---

*Sinaitae opera: Viae dux* (Corpus Christianorum, Series Graeca, vol. 8; Turnhout: Brepols, Leuven University Press, 1981), 252, ll. 16–22. Furthermore, this passage (actually the wider context, *MPG* 89:244C1–D10 = Uthemann, 251, l. 1 – 252, l. 23), is cited from a Bodleian manuscript by Cramer, ed., *Catenae in Evangelia S. Lucae et S. Joannis ad fidem codd. mss.* (*Catenae Graecorum patrum in Novum Testamentum*, vol. 2; Oxford: University Press, 1841), v, to which Zahn (*Acta Joannis*, liv, n. 2) has referred as the "räthselhaften Andeutungen." Bruns, "The *Altercatio Jasonis et Papisci*, Philo, and Anastasius the Sinaite," *Theological Studies* 34 (1973): 290–92, translates the dialogue as found in Anastasius.

[33]Eleuterio Elorduy, *Ammonio Sakkas*, vol. 1: *La doctrina de la creación y del mal en Proclo y el Ps. Areopagita* (Estudios Onienses, series 1, vol. 7; Burgos: Sociedad Internacional Francisco Suarez, n.d. [1959]), 462; see generally 457–62 for a discussion of the reference in Anastasius to the dialogue. (Uthemann, ad *Viae dux* 13.10, l. 12, refers the reader to Elorduy.)

[34]*Hist. eccl.* 2.17.1; see Bruns, "Philo Christianus," 141.

[35]*Ammonio Sakkas*, 462.

[36]Ibid.

[37]Georg Heinrici, in his review of *PCW*, vol. 1, *TLZ* 22 (1897): 214, criticizes Cohn for including the passage from Anastasius, since the dialogue's "Beziehung auf den Alexandriner Philo dunkel ist." Heinrici refers to Adolf

a "dialogue between the Jews Papiscus and Philo and a Christian monk,"[38] and this (apparently later) dialogue may well bear some relationship to the dialogue cited by Anastasius. But the title of this later dialogue is reminiscent of a lost second-century dialogue between Jason (a Jewish Christian) and Papiscus (an Alexandrian Jew), which is entitled *Altercatio Jasonis et Papisci*.[39] Bruns has, in fact, suggested that the development was as follows:[40] i) an original dialogue between Jason and Papiscus; ii) the original dialogue with the addition of the name of Philo, who was the more famous Alexandrian Jew—this is the work cited by Anastasius (with "Jason" becoming "Mnason"); and iii) a new dialogue with the names of Papiscus and Philo but without the name of Jason (whose place is taken by a Christian monk).[41] None of this material has been generally considered as going back to Philo of

---

Harnack, *Geschichte der altchristlichen Litteratur bis Eusebius*, pt. 1: *Die Überlieferung und der Bestand*, 2 vols. (Leipzig: J. C. Hinrichs, 1893), 2:774, who says of this dialogue: "Philo soll natürlich der berühmte sein und Mnason der Act. 21, 16 genannte. Wann, wo und von wem der Dialog verfasst ist, wissen wir nicht—schwerlich im 2. Jahrh."

[38]See Bruns, *"Altercatio,"* 288–89; this dialogue was edited by A. C. McGiffert in a work which I have not seen (see Bruns, 289, n. 10). Harnack, *Geschichte* 2:860, also notes under Pseudo-Philonic texts: "Eine späte Ἀντιβολὴ Παπίσκου καὶ Φίλωνος Ἰουδαίων πρὸς μόναχόν [sic] τινα edirte McGiffert (New-York 1889)." (Bruns cites the place of publication as Marburg.) This is the dialogue to which Zahn, *Acta Joannis*, liv, n. 2, refers as existing in Marcianus 505, ff. 79–87: ἀντιβολὴ Παππίσκου καὶ Φίλωνος Ἰουδαίων, τῶν παρ' Ἑβραίοις σοφῶν πρὸς μοναχόν τινα Ἀναστάσιον περὶ πίστεως Χριστιανῶν καὶ νόμου Ἑβραίων.

[39]Bruns, *"Altercatio,"* 287–88. This dialogue is attributed by Maximus Confessor to Ariston of Pella; see Bruns, 287, and n. 3, as well as Schürer, *Geschichte* 1:63–65, and *History* 1:37–39. (Schürer includes references to yet other dialogues between Jews and Christians.)

[40]Bruns, *"Altercatio,"* 294.

[41]Zahn, *Acta Joannis*, liv, n. 2, had already commented on this dialogue: "Da ist also der aus dem alten Dialog des Aristo von Pella berühmte Jude Papiscus, nach der Vorrede des lateinischen Uebersetzers Celsus (Cypr. opp. ed. Hartel app. p. 128, 13) gleichfalls ein Alexandriner, mit seinem noch berühmteren Mitbürger und Glaubensgenossen Philo als Polemiker gegen das Christenthum zusammengestellt."

Alexandria, although the works do testify to the continuing belief that Philo had engaged in discussions with early Christians.[42]

10. As a final instance here we may note a conjecture which was put forward with respect to the treatise *De sublimitate* (Περὶ ὕψους). The anonymous author, in the past identified as Longinus, quotes (in 9.9) a combination of Gen 1:3, 9, 10, in a very favorable manner,[43] and betrays at various points in his work certain parallels to Philo's works. Norden has argued that the citation from an unnamed philosopher in chapter 44 comes from Philo, in fact either from a work of his which is now lost or even from Philo's own lips during his visit to Rome.[44] However, there seems to be no persuasive evidence for this conjecture.[45] Moreover, the remark νὴ Δία at 44.2 provides some evidence against the identification, given that we take this as having been said by the philosopher and not as having been added by Pseudo-Longinus (who also uses it at 11.2, 33.1, 35.4, and 43.1). Although Josephus once uses this expression (*Contra Apionem* 1.255), Philo never does.[46]

---

[42]Bruns ("*Altercatio*," 293–94) recalls that Anastasius elsewhere includes Philo among the writers of the Church (see chapter 1, note 2, above), and presumes that Anastasius thus must have thought that Philo was eventually converted by the Christian arguments. Similarly, Elorduy, *Ammonio Sakkas*, 462, refers to the early legends of Philo's conversion.

[43]See Schürer, *Geschichte* 3:631–32, *History* 3.1:702–3.

[44]Eduard Norden, *Das Genesiszitat in der Schrift vom Erhabenen*, *Abhandlungen der Deutschen Akademie der Wissenschaften zu Berlin*, Klasse für Sprachen, Literatur und Kunst, Jahrgang 1954, no. 1 (published 1955), reprinted in his *Kleine Schriften zum klassischen Altertum* (Berlin: Walter de Gruyter, 1966), 286–313. This identification is also defended by Augusto Rostagni, ed. and trans., *Anonimo, Del sublime* (Milan: Istituto Editoriale Italiano, 1947), vii–ix, xxix–xxxii.

[45]See generally the discussion by Menahem Stern, *Greek and Latin Authors on Jews and Judaism*, vol. 1: *From Herodotus to Plutarch* (Jerusalem: The Israel Academy of Sciences and Humanities, 1974), 361–65, along with a full bibliography. Stern comments that "this suggestion still cannot be proved" (363). See the further references cited in Radice, *Filone*, Index 5, p. 316, s.v. "Anonimo autore del Sublime," and also Feldman, *Josephus and Modern Scholarship*, 408–9.

[46]Cf. Stern, *Authors* 1:362, n. 8. Norden (*Genesiszitat*, 23 [= *Kleine Schriften*, 313], n. 25) had already commented that, just as Philo sometimes refers to Olympian gods, "so könnte er in der Konversation mit einem Helle-

In connection with the spurious works should be mentioned also the *De mundo*, which was the first "work" of Philo to be printed.[47] This is spurious only in so far as it is regarded as a separate book; actually it consists of excerpts from various genuine works of Philo.[48] A smaller version of this same phenomenon is the "book" *De mercede meretricis*, printed by Mangey as a separate work, but found by Wendland[49] to consist simply of *Sacr* 20–33 and *Spec Leg* 1.280–84.[50]

---

nen auch die ja ganz verblaßte Beteuerungsformel gebraucht haben; wenn nicht, so hat der Anonymus auch das stilisiert."

A further point of detail is found by Bernays, "Herennius' Metaphysik und Longinos," *Monatsberichte der königlichen Akademie der Wissenschaften zu Berlin* (1876): 61, n. 1 (reprinted in *Gesammelte Abhandlungen*, ed. H. Usener [Berlin: Wilhelm Hertz, 1885], 1:353, n. 2 [–354]), discussing the notion that the passage is an interpolation:

> In der That müsste doch die angebliche Interpolation zu Ehren der Bibel von einem Juden oder Christen ausgegangen sein, und ein solcher würde wohl nicht, wie es hier geschieht, neben γενέσθω φῶς, καὶ ἐγένετο auch die nirgends in der Bibel vorkommenden Worte γενέσθω γῆ, καὶ ἐγένετο als eine Stelle aus der Genesis citirt haben.

Schürer (*Geschichte* 3:631; *History* 3.1:702) cites this point approvingly. However, Konrat Ziegler, "Das Genesiscitat in der Schrift ΠΕΡΙ ΥΨΟΥΣ," *He* 50 (1915): 600, responds to Bernays by noting that incorrect citations are in fact very common, and gives the striking example of Eusebius, *Praep. ev.* 7.11.2: καὶ πάλιν· "εἶπεν ὁ θεός· γενηθήτω στερέωμα, καὶ ἐγένετο." By the way, Bernays thought that it was "äusserst unwahrscheinlich" that Longinus used Philo ("Herennius' Metaphysik," 62 [*Gesammelte Abhandlungen* 1:353–54]).

[47]In *Aristotelis opera*, vol. 2 (Venice: Aldus Manutius, 1497), 225–36. (In fact, this volume and the earlier vol. 1 [1495] do not have title pages as such, but they are generally catalogued under Aristotle, as they contain a number of his works. A photograph of the first page of this edition is found in Goodhart and Goodenough, *Bibliography*, facing p. 186.) Mangey printed the work in *Philonis opera* 2:601–24.

[48]Schürer, *Geschichte* 3:692–93; idem, *History* 3.2:868–69; Wendland, *PCW* 2:vi–ix; Cohn, *PCW* 5:xv; Cohn, *PCW* 6:xxxiv.

[49]*Fragmente*, 125–45.

[50]See Schürer, *Geschichte* 3:652, 668; idem, *History* 3.2:833–34, 849, 870; Cohn, *PCW* 1:lxxxvii–lxxxviii; and idem, *PCW* 5:xx.

Note too the brief passage from Isidore of Pelusium concerning Moses and the taskmasters, which is cited in *PCW* 1:cviii, with the comment: "locus

Of course, from time to time doubts have been raised about the authenticity of several other Philonic treatises.[51] In particular, serious arguments have been advanced to show that *Vita Cont* and *Aet* are not to be attributed to Philo, both of which were held to be "unecht" even by Schürer.[52] However, their place in the Philonic corpus seems secure at the present time.[53] *Provid* and *Anim* are also generally accepted as authentic.[54] And finally, there seems to be general agreement on the Philonic authorship of the

---

ab Isidoro allatus apud Philonem non exstat." I believe that Früchtel, "Neue Quellennachweise zu Isidoros von Pelusion," *PhWoch* 58 (1938): 765, is correct in seeing Isidore's citation as a composite of several phrases from *Vita Mos*; see my "Original Structure," 58.

[51]For example, on *Quod Omn* see the references in Schürer, *Geschichte* 2:655, n. 9 (–656), 3:675–76, especially n. 115 (–677); idem, *History* 3.2:856. As an extreme case, one may note that the authenticity of *Gaium* was challenged by Graetz (Schürer, *Geschichte* 3:683, and n. 136), and that the reprint of Bernays's *Über das Phokylideische Gedicht* in his *Gesammelte Abhandlungen* 1:244, n. 1, says: "In der sogenannten *legatio ad Gaium*, die sicherlich nicht von Philon . . . abgefasst ist . . . ." The wording here may be due to the editor, H. Usener (see p. vi), but in any case the "sicherlich" is remarkable.

[52]See Schürer, *Geschichte* 3:687–91 and 691–92, respectively. *Aet* was also rejected by Massebieau, "Le classement," 4.

[53]On *Vita Cont* see Massebieau, "Le classement," 59–65; Cohn, "Einteilung," 419–21; idem, *PCW* 6:x; F. H. Colson, *PLCL* 9 (1941): 107–8; and Schürer, *History* 3.2:856–58. On *Aet* see Cohn, "Einteilung," 389; idem, *PCW* 6:xxxi–xxxii; Colson, *PLCL* 9:172–77; David T. Runia, "Philo's *De aeternitate mundi*: The Problem of its Interpretation," *VC* 35 (1981): 105–51; and Schürer, *History* 3.2:858–59.

[54]Massebieau, "Le classement," 87–91 (doubts that Philo wrote *Provid* 1); Cohn, "Einteilung," 390–91; Schürer, *Geschichte* 3:683–85; idem, *History* 3.2:864–66; Wendland, *Philos Schrift über die Vorsehung: Ein Beitrag zur Geschichte der nacharistotelischen Philosophie* (Berlin: R. Gaertner, 1892), passim; Wilhelm Bousset, *Jüdisch-Christlicher Schulbetrieb in Alexandria und Rom: Literarische Untersuchungen zu Philo und Clemens von Alexandria, Justin und Irenäus* (Göttingen: Vandenhoeck & Ruprecht, 1915), 137–49; Terian, *Philonis Alexandrini de animalibus*, 28–34; and idem, "A Critical Introduction to Philo's Dialogues," in *Aufstieg und Niedergang der römischen Welt*, pt. 2: *Principat*, vol. 21, pt. 1, ed. Wolfgang Haase (Berlin and New York: Walter de Gruyter, 1984), especially 283–89.

Armenian fragment *De Deo*, which appears to be an excerpt from Philo's allegorical commentary on Gen 18:2.[55] As we have already noted, this title has caused some confusion. In fact, the title of the fragment in Armenian corresponds to: Περὶ τοῦ τὸν θεὸν ἐπ᾽ εὐεργεσίᾳ πῦρ ἀναλίσκον ὀνομά-ζεσθαι.[56] And it is from the first portion of this (the two Armenian words corresponding to περὶ τοῦ τὸν θεόν) that Aucher (somewhat arbitrarily) constructed his Latin title *De Deo*.

Naturally, questions of detail arise concerning possible glosses or cor-

---

[55]See the discussions by Massebieau, "Le classement," 29–31; Schürer, *Geschichte* 3:658; idem, *History* 3.2:839; Cohn, "Einteilung," 401; Adler, "Das philonische Fragment De deo," *MGWJ* 80 (1936): 163–70; and Terian, *Philonis Alexandrini de animalibus*, 4. Siegert, on the other hand, originally left open the question of authorship (*Predigten*, 2), and suggested (ibid., 8): "Vermutlich ist der Verfasser (das wäre die einfachste Hypothese) Leser Philons gewesen, ein zweiter Philon sozusagen." (Perhaps because of this comment, Radice, *Filone*, 311, puts this work under "Pseudo Filone.") However, Siegert, *Philon*, 2, has now retracted that position, and asserts (1) that "niemand als der alexandrinische Jude Philon der Verfasser dieses Textes sein kann."

[56]Siegert, *Philon*, 23; cf. idem, *Predigten*, 84, n. 887. Actually, the Armenian manuscripts have this title plus what corresponds to ἐν ὁράσει τῶν τριῶν παίδων, while C alone adds to that the equivalent of: τῇ πρὸς Ἀβραάμ, ὅτε ἐκάθιζε μεσημβρίας ἀναβλέψας δὲ τοῖς ὀφθαλμοῖς εἶδεν κτλ. This longest version is printed as part of the title in *Philon*, 23, while in *Predigten*, 84, the words which translate ἐν ὁράσει — εἶδεν κτλ. are separated as a subtitle. (On the manuscript variant, see *Predigten*, 84, n. 888, referring to Aucher, *Paralipomena Armena*, 613, n. 2.) Note also that in the earlier (possibly first) report of the contents of the Armenian version of Philo (by Johannes Zohrab, cited in Mai, Φίλωνος τοῦ Ἰουδαίου περὶ ἀρετῆς καὶ τῶν ταύτης μορίων, *Philonis Iudaei de virtute eiusque partibus*, x–xv of the prefatory remarks on Philo [present in both editions]), the title of *De Deo* is given (xiii) as "Quod Deus ob suam beneficentiam ignis consumens nominetur in visione trium puerorum," which clearly corresponds to the version as found in the manuscripts other than C. By the way, Siegert (*Philon*, 39) says of the Greek title: "Sie [die Überschrift] ist einer der stärksten Gräzismen des armenischen Textes—Beweis dafür, daß unser Textstück bereits auf einen griechischen (und nicht erst einen armenischen) Exzerptor zurückgeht." However, Siegert goes on to claim: "Der Titel unseres Fragments stammt von einem (christlichen?) griechischen Exzerptor, aber nicht von Philon selbst."

ruptions in the genuine works,[57] and there remain numerous fragments whose sources are uncertain, as noted in our Index locorum below. We may hope, of course, that at least some of these will yet be identified. But the complexity of the tradition which has preserved Philo's works, in part or in whole, in Greek or Armenian or Latin, guarantees that many questions will remain unanswered or controversial.

---

[57]See, for example, Wendland's claim (*Philos Schrift*, 11, n. 6 [-12]) that *Provid* 1.34 and *Quaes Ex* 2.117 have suffered Christian interpolations. However, Hadas-Lebel (*De providentia*, 154, n. 3 [-155]) opposes Wendland's view on *Provid* 1.34, while Marcus (without mentioning Wendland) brackets a portion of *Quaes Ex* 2.117 (see *Philo, Supplement* 2:168, n. i). On the other hand, Aucher (*Paralipomena Armena*, 545, n. 1) seems to think that the latter passage is genuine, and that all that remains for Philo to be a Christian is to add that Christ, the divine Word, is Jesus.

Incidentally, Speyer, *Die literarische Fälschung*, 237, n. 9, refers to the above passage of Wendland, as well as a later one (*Philos Schrift*, 95, n. 3), where Wendland cites Gomperz on Christian "Verfälschungen" to *Aet*, and Cumont on the preservation in the then recently discovered Coptos Papyrus of a text of Philo prior to Christian corrections.

APPENDIX

# INDEX LOCORUM

In his collection of fragments Früchtel included two tables, one for Mangey and one for Harris, giving identifications of previously printed Greek "fragments" of Philo. I have found Früchtel's tables to be very useful in my own studies of the Greek fragments, since they help to bring some order into the mass of texts to be considered. Obviously, much work has been duplicated over the years in the effort to find which of these texts occur in the printed works found in *PCW*, and which have already been identified within the *Quaestiones* or the other works preserved in Armenian. Moreover, correct identifications have from time to time been overlooked.

In the hope of minimizing such wasted effort in the future, I am including here tables for all the major collections of Greek fragments which have appeared so far, with their identifications as far as I have been able to determine them. In making these lists I have utilized Früchtel's original tables which covered only Mangey and Harris, but have completely revised even those tables. Cross-references to other collections are included in the third column, but in order to avoid undue complexity and duplication, the following guidelines have been observed. For the spurious fragments no references are given, since all of the occurrences in these sources are cited at the texts in chapter 4 above. And similarly no references are given for the glosses cited in chapter 2, pages 18–21, above. Otherwise, the tables are constructed so that the collection of Harris contains the fullest references. Thus, fragments in other collections which also occur in Harris are always referred to their locations in Harris, where all the remaining references are brought together. For those fragments which are not in Harris, the reference in Mangey or Lewy will provide the fullest information.

The fragments which have been identified as occurring within *PCW* are generally placed by the editors at their correct locations; I have noted with '(†)' those which are not, although in some (but not all) of these cases, related texts are cited in *PCW* from other sources. The fragments which have been identified as occurring within the *Quaestiones* are generally placed by subsequent editors at their correct locations; here I have noted with '(†)' those which are not found in Petit's edition. The source of the correct identification (if any) of each fragment is noted with an asterisk ('*') before the name of the identifier, or, if the fragment is correctly identified in the edition currently being indexed, by an asterisk after the '=' and before the identification itself.

Besides the additional collections of fragments, I have also indexed several of the principal sources of such collections: the *Sacra parallela*, Maximus, Antonius, and Johannes Georgides. In dealing with these four sources, I have tried to cite each text which meets at least one of the following criteria: a) is ascribed to Philo in the source indexed; b) is ascribed to Philo in one of the other sources indexed here; c) is printed somewhere as a Philo fragment; d) is in fact from Philo. (These criteria are listed in the order of difficulty of actually applying them.) There are, of course, some further texts in these sources which are ascribed to Philo in one or more of the manuscripts; but I have not tried to include those. Cross-references are included in the third column only for the unidentified fragments and for the fragments of the *Quaestiones* which are not found in Petit's edition. In these cases the guidelines for the references are the same as for the collections. And I have noted with '(†)' those texts which occur in *PCW* but are not cited by the editors, and those fragments of the *Quaestiones* which are not found in Petit's edition.

The method of citation of texts is as follows: When the author supplies numbers for the texts, those are cited. In the case of Mangey and Harris, where the texts are not numbered, those on each page are separately numbered here. E.g., 'Harris 70.5' refers to the fifth fragment on p. 70. (Since Harris shifts between one and two columns and also occasionally cites some Greek other than a Philo fragment, there may sometimes be a little confusion as to how to number; the Greek cited will provide a guide.) Mai's edition is cited by page and column. Texts from the two series of unidentified fragments of *Quaes Gen* and *Quaes Ex* which are printed by Marcus and Petit are cited as 'QG' and 'QE' respectively, and by the editor's number. Furthermore, sometimes what is printed as one text should be divided; the parts of the larger text are then denoted by an appended 'a,' 'b,' etc. References to identified fragments of the *Quaestiones* which are correctly located in Aucher 1826, Harris (pp. 12–68), Marcus, or Petit, omit further specification, since the texts occur in sequence and are thus readily found. References to identified fragments of *Provid* which are correctly located in Aucher 1822 also omit further specification. References to *PCW* for identified texts from the works edited in *PCW* are, unless there is further specification, to the apparatus of the cited passage. Other references follow the standard conventions. The following works are indexed here, and cross-references to them use simply the name (and for Aucher the date) in the left column:

1. *Sacra parallela*      Cited from Lequien's edition.
2. Maximus          Cited from Combefis's edition.
3. Antonius         Cited from Gessner's edition.

| | |
|---|---|
| 4. Johannes Georgides | Cited from Boissonade's edition. |
| 5. Mangey | *Philonis Judaei opera* (1742). |
| 6. Aucher 1822, Aucher 1826 | *Philonis Judaei sermones tres* (1822), *Philonis Judaei paralipomena Armena* (1826). |
| 7. Mai | *Scriptorum veterum nova collectio*, vol. 7 (1833). |
| 8. Tischendorf | *Anecdota sacra et profana* (1855 and 1861), and *Philonea* (1868). (Cross-references are always to the latter work.) |
| 9. Pitra | *Analecta sacra*, vol. 2 (1884). |
| 10. Harris | *Fragments* (1886). |
| 11. Wendland | *Fragmente* (1891). |
| 12. *PCW* | *PCW* (1896–1915). |
| 13. Lewy | "Neue Philontexte" (1932). |
| 14. Marcus | *PLCL Supplement*, vol. 2 (1953). |
| 15. Petit | *Quaestiones: Fragmenta Graeca* (1979). |

Occasional cross-references are also made to the following:

| | |
|---|---|
| Cramer 1837 | *Anecdota Graeca*, vol. 4 (1837). |
| Cramer 1843 | *Catenae Graecorum patrum in Novum Testamentum*, vol. 7: *Catenae in Sancti Pauli epistolas ad Timotheum, Titum, Philemona et ad Hebraeos* (Oxford: University Press, 1843). |
| Massebieau | "Le classement" (1889), 22, n. 3. |
| Wendland 1892 | *Philos Schrift über die Vorsehung.* |
| Bréhier | *Les idées philosophiques* (1908), 7, n. 2. |
| Früchtel 1937 | "Griechische Fragmente zu Philons Quaestiones in Genesin et in Exodum," *ZAW* 55 [N.F. 14] (1937): 108–15. |
| Früchtel 1938 | "Neue Quellennachweise." |
| Früchtel MS | "Philonis Alexandrini fragmenta Graece servata." |
| Junod | "Les fragments grecs" (1982). |
| Royse 1984 | "Further Greek Fragments." |

The fragments of the *Quaestiones* which were located by Früchtel in his MS are discussed in the last article above; some supplemental information may be found below in the section on Petit's edition.

In the light of the history of the inquiries into these spurious texts, I can hardly be confident that these indexes, which take us into what Pitra called the "labyrinthum omnium Philonis operum,"[1] are free from errors and omissions. But I trust that, at least, they will provide some guidance through these collections. By the way, peculiarities of accent, minor printing errors, and the like have now and then been silently corrected here.

_____

[1]*Analecta sacra* 2:310, n.

## 1. *SACRA PARALLELA*

The texts are cited first by page in Lequien's edition of 1712 (*Johannis Damasceni opera* 2:278–790), and then by column and line in the edition in *MPG* 95:1040–1588, 96:9–544 (which also includes the Lequien pagination).

First, Lequien prints selections from Vat. 1236.

| | | | |
|---|---|---|---|
| 301 (1080C2–6) | πάντα — πανταχοῦ | = | *Leg All* 3.4 |
| 301 (1080C6–7) | ἔκθεσμος — παρορᾶν | = | *Quod Det* 61 |
| 304 (1085D5–6) | εἰ ζητεῖς — ἀναζήτει | = | *Leg All* 3.47 |
| 309 (1097B2–4) | πνευματικαὶ — μεταμορφούμενοι | = | *Quaes Gen* 1.92 |
| 314 (1108D1–12) | κατὰ — παραιρεῖσθαι | = | *Op* 103 |
| 314 (1108D12–9A13) | ἰατρὸς — γέρων | = | *Op* 105 |
| 314 (1109B1–5) | δυνατὸν — γεννᾶν | = | *Quaes Gen* 2.5 (b) |
| 326 (1136B1–9) | κυρίως — ἀβέβαιον | = | *Quod Det* 136 |
| 326 (1136B10–C3) | πάντων μέν — κύριον | = | unidentified (Harris 6.1) |
| 341 (1169C12–D1) | φοβηθῶμεν — σώματος | = | Fr. sp. 28 |
| 341 (1169D2–4) | νόμος — ἀορασίας | = | *Quaes Gen* 4.40 |
| 341 (1169D5–7) | εἰ βούλει — θεοῦ | = | unidentified (Harris 77.2) |
| 343 (1176A1–5) | ἔνιοι — ἐναπέθετο | = | *Quaes Ex* 1.7 (b) |
| 343 (1176A6–11) | ὅταν ἄνθρωπος — ᾅδου | = | Fr. sp. 49 |
| 349 (1188A3–4) | οὐ τὸ — κολάσεως | = | Fr. sp. 26 |
| 349 (1188A5–11) | οὐκ ἔστι — θεόν | = | unidentified (Harris 10.1) |
| 349 (1188A12–B1) | ὁ νοῦς — ἀψευδέστατος | = | *Post* 59 |
| 356 (1204B3–4) | εἰρήνη — πολέμου | = | *Spec Leg* 4.221 |
| 357 (1205C6–7) | λάλει ἃ δεῖ — μὴ δεῖ | = | Fr. sp. 41 |
| 359 (1209A7–10) | ὁ μαθὼν — ἄρχεσθαι | = | *Quaes Gen* 3.30 (b) |
| 359 (1209A11) | τὸ ὑποτάττεσθαι — ὠφελιμώτατον | = | *Quaes Gen* 3.30 (a) |
| 359 (1209C6–8) | ὦ πόσα — φόβοι | = | *Gaium* 17 |
| 362–63 (1217B3–5) | τῶν φαύλων — πένητες | = | unidentified (Harris 69.1) |

| | | | |
|---|---|---|---|
| 363 (1217B5–8) | στενοχωρεῖται — διάγειν | = | *Quaes Gen* 4.33 (a) |
| 363 (1217B9–10) | μεῖζον — ζημιωθέντι | = | *Quaes Gen* 4.179 |
| 363 (1217B11) | νόσου — ἀπαιδευσία | = | *Ebr* 141 |
| 363 (1217B12–C1) | ἀμήχανον — παιδευθῆναι | = | *Vita Mos* 1.62 |
| 365 (1224B12–C1) | ὁ σπουδαῖος — ἀθανασίας | = | *Virt* 9 |
| 367 (1228C14–D5) | οὐ πᾶς δόλος — ἴδιον | = | *Quaes Gen* 4.228 |
| 367 (1229A3–4) | ἃ πρέσβεις — ἀναφοράν | = | *Gaium* 369 |
| 370 (1233C4–6) | ἀμήχανον — σκότος | = | Fr. sp. 30 |
| 372 (1240B11–14) | μακαρία — γινομένοις | = | *Quaes Gen* 3.38 (b) |
| 376 (1245D9–48A2) | ὁ σοφὸς — ἐντύχῃ | = | *Quaes Gen* 4.47 (a) |
| 378 (1252A3) | τὴν αἰδῶ — πολλοῖς | = | *Gaium* 36 |
| 378 (1252D10–53A2) | ὁ φαῦλος — τείνει | = | *Virt* 9 |
| 379 (1253D6–9) | αἰσχροὶ — προχειρότατοι | = | *Flacc* 34 |
| 382 (1260C2–4) | ἀμήχανον — σκότος | = | Fr. sp. 30 |
| 396 (1292C2–4) | τῶν μὲν — θεοφιλής | = | *Quaes Gen* 4.76 (a) |
| 397 (1293C1–2) | τὰ μὴ σὺν — κόσμια | = | *Leg All* 3.158 |
| 397 (1293C3–4) | χωρὶς θεωρίας — καλόν | = | *Praem* 51 (†) |
| 404 (1308C9–10) | ἀνθεῖται — μαραίνονται | = | *Somn* 1.11 (see pp. 45–46 above) |
| 404 (1308C11–D4) | ὁ ἀληθείᾳ — παιδευθέντας | = | *Abr* 271 |
| 404 (1308D4) | ἀκύμαντος λιμὴν πολιά | = | Fr. sp. 47 |
| 404 (1308D4–5) | σώματος — παθῶν | = | unidentified (Harris 97.12) |
| 405 (1312A5–6) | ἡ συνεχὴς — ἀμελετησία | = | *Sacr* 86 |
| 405 (1312A6–7) | καὶ πάλιν — τριβή | = | unidentified (Harris 79.1b) |
| 405 (1312A7–8) | μελέτη τροφὸς ἐπιστήμης | = | unidentified (Harris 69.3) |
| 407 (1313C14–D3) | τὰ κατὰ — δυναμένων | = | *Op* 124 |
| 418 (1340A4–5) | πλοῦτος — ὑπηρέτης | = | Fr. sp. 5 |
| 427 (1357C12–D3) | ἀξίως — τούτους | = | *Leg All* 3.10 |
| 434 (1373C4–5) | οἱ λεγόμενοι — ὀνομάζονται | = | *Cher* 83 |
| 434 (1373C5–8) | κύριος — ἡγεμών | = | *Mut* 22 |
| 435 (1376A12–B1) | παιδείας — ἀμήχανον | = | *Post* 97 |
| 435 (1376B2–5) | οὐχ ὡς — δυνάμεως | = | *Quaes Gen* 4.104 |
| 435 (1376B6–11) | ἐπίστησον — σοφίας | = | unidentified (Harris 98.1) |
| 436 (1377B5–8) | διάβολοι — ἀλλότριοι | = | unidentified (Harris 98.2) |

| | | | |
|---|---|---|---|
| 436 (1377B9–C1) | τί ἂν γένοιτο — γένηται | = | unidentified (Harris 98.3) |
| 438 (1381B9–11) | κακίας — ἐπεισέρχεται | = | *Sacr* 135 |
| 438 (1381B11–C1) | εἴ τις πάσας — τυγχάνοι | = | unidentified (Harris 79.3) |
| 448 (1401D8–9) | οὐδεὶς — δεσπότῃ | = | *Gaium* 233 |
| 448 (1404C10–12) | πέφυκεν — ἔχουσα | = | *Post* 24–25 |
| 481 (1473C10–D4) | μείζονα — πτωχεύσαντας | = | unidentified (Harris 75.4) |
| 481 (1473D6–7) | λεία ὁδὸς — γίνεται | = | Fr. sp. 43 |
| 481 (1473D14–15) | πλούτου — ἐπικουρίᾳ | = | *Jos* 144 |
| 502 (1520D6–7) | πλούτου — ἐπικουρίᾳ | = | *Jos* 144 |
| 506 (1529B10–14) | ὁ τῶν — πραγμάτων | = | *Quaes Ex* 2.55 (b) |
| 507 (1532A1–2) | φιλοῦσι — τίκτεσθαι | = | unidentified (Harris 109.9) |
| 509 (1536A10–11) | χαίρειν — ἀνθρώπινον | = | *Quaes Gen* 4.52 (b) |
| 518 (1556C3–4) | ἄτοπόν ἐστι — τιμαί | = | Fr. sp. 40 |
| 518 (1556C5–7) | νόμος — ἀορασίας | = | *Quaes Gen* 4.40 |
| 520 (1560B6–10) | ὡς τὸ — δικαιοσύνης | = | *Quaes Gen* 4.64 |
| 520 (1560C1–4) | τῷ μὲν — δικαστηρίῳ | = | *Flacc* 7 |
| 521 (1561D5–6) | ἔχουσιν — μεμφθῆναι | = | unidentified (Lewy 82.25) |
| 531 (1584B6–12) | γίνεται — δυσθήρατον | = | *Ebr* 174 |
| 533 (9B10–11) | οὐ θέμις — ἀμυήτοις | = | unidentified (Harris 69.4a) |
| 551 (49C6–9) | ἄξιον — ἀναπέμπουσι | = | *Gaium* 47 |
| 556 (60D9) | ἰσότης πηγὴ δικαιοσύνης | = | *Gaium* 85 (†) |
| 556 (60D10–11) | τὸ νέμειν — ἀδικίας | = | *Anim* 100 |
| 557 (61C1–6) | ἀγαθὸς — ἐμποιεῖ | = | *Quaes Ex* 2.25 (d) |
| 563 (76A6–7) | λάλει ἃ δεῖ — μὴ δεῖ | = | Fr. sp. 41 |
| 563 (76A7) | χρόνου φείδεσθαι καλόν | = | *Vita Cont* 16 |
| 564 (77C9–10) | οὐκ ἂν — κολακεία | = | *Leg All* 3.182 (†) |
| 564 (77C11–12) | τὰς τῶν — πλεῖστοι | = | *Gaium* 140 |
| 565 (77D1–3) | μὴ τοῖς — βλάπτοντας | = | unidentified (Lewy 80.17) |
| 567 (84B6) | τὸ ὑποτάσσεσθαι — ὠφελιμώτατον | = | *Quaes Gen* 3.30 (a) |
| 567 (84B7–8) | οὐδεὶς — δεσπότῃ | = | *Gaium* 233 (†) |
| 569 (88C3–4) | τὸ νέμειν — ἀδικίας | = | *Anim* 100 |
| 570 (89B13–14) | οὐχ ἡ — εἰλικρίνεια | = | unidentified (see p. 40, no. 3, above) |

| | | | |
|---|---|---|---|
| 575–76 (101C8–12) | μείζονα — πτωχεύσαντας | = | unidentified (Harris 75.4) |
| 576 (104B5–7) | οἱ λάλοι — ἄξια | = | *Quaes Ex* 2.118 |
| 597 (148C9–D1) | ὅταν ἄνθρωπος — ᾅδου | = | Fr. sp. 49 |
| 613 (181C6–9) | ὁ σπουδαῖος — ἀθανασίας | = | *Virt* 9 (†) |
| 613 (184B1–2) | τὸ ζητεῖν — ἀνυσιμώτατον | = | *Anim* 6 |
| 613 (184B3–6) | ὁ πεινῶν — οἰκίας | = | *Quaes Ex* 2.13 (b) |
| 613 (184B7–8) | τὸ εἰδέναι — δικαιοσύνης | = | unidentified (Harris 80.5) |
| 629 (216D3–5) | οἴησις — ἀνέχεται | = | *Quaes Gen* 3.48 |
| 629 (216D6) | οἴησις ἀκάθαρτον φύσει ἐστίν | = | *Leg All* 1.52 (†) |
| 630 (220B5–7) | μηδενὶ συμφορὰν — εὑρεθῇς | = | unidentified (Harris 98.5) |
| 637 (236A9–11) | ὅπερ — θεός | = | *Provid* 2.15 |
| 657 (280C7) | τὸ ὑποτάσσεσθαι — ὠφέλιμον | = | *Quaes Gen* 3.30 (a) |
| 658–59 (284B11–C4) | ἀναιδὲς — σώματι | = | *Quaes Gen* 4.99 |
| 663 (293A3–4) | τοῖς — οἷόν τε | = | *Leg All* 3.10 (†) |
| 663 (293A5–6) | γονέας τίμα — φυσικός | = | unidentified (Harris 110.7) |
| 674 (317C8–10) | ὄντως — κακοπάθεια | = | Fr. sp. 37 |
| 675 (321A9–12) | μακαρία — γενομένοις | = | *Quaes Gen* 3.38 (b) |
| 679 (329A8–10) | μέγα τῷ — συμφορᾶς | = | Fr. sp. 38 |
| 681 (333B7–9) | αἱ πάντων — δυνάμεις | = | unidentified (Harris 98.6) |
| 683 (337C12–13) | χρήσιμον — σωφρονίζεσθαι | = | *Flacc* 154 |
| 683 (337D1–4) | ἡ κόλασις — παθεῖν | = | *Gaium* 7 |
| 688 (348C6) | ἐσταλμένον — ἀγαθόν | = | *Ebr* 26 |
| 688 (349B1–3) | τῷ στρατιώτῃ — φυλάττειν | = | *Flacc* 5 |
| 692 (357A3–5) | βλαβεραὶ — εἴδωλα | = | *Fuga* 14 |
| 693 (360C7) | ἀπὸ ἑνὸς — πόλις | = | Fr. sp. 21 |
| 693 (360D1) | οὐκ ἔστιν — ψυχῆς | = | Fr. sp. 22 |
| 693 (360D7–8) | τὸ εἰδέναι — δικαιοσύνης | = | unidentified (Harris 80.5) |
| 693 (361A4–5) | μόνος — δεσπότας | = | *Post* 138 |
| 693 (361A6) | πᾶς σοφὸς θεοῦ φίλος | = | *Heres* 21 (see p. 5 above) |

| | | | |
|---|---|---|---|
| 693 (361A7–13) | τῷ ὄντι — μετιών | = | *Abr* 272, 274 |
| 693 (361B1–2) | τὸ ζητεῖν — ἀνυσιμώτατον | = | *Anim* 6 |
| 701 (377D6) | τέκνων — πατέρων | = | Fr. sp. 34 |
| 704 (384A1–3) | οἴησις — ἀνέχεται | = | *Quaes Gen* 3.48 |
| 704 (384A4) | οἴησις ἀκάθαρτον φύσει | = | *Leg All* 1.52 |
| 710 (397A9–10) | θεοῦ — ἐπάγειν | = | *Leg All* 3.105 |
| 710 (397A11–13) | οὐδὲ — ἐπανόρθωσιν | = | *Leg All* 3.106 |
| 711 (400B1) | χαλεπὸν — φύσει | = | *Sacr* 114 (†) |
| 711 (400B2–6) | ὥσπερ τὸ — πάντα | = | unidentified (Harris 99.4) |
| 711 (400C3) | φήμης οὐδὲν ὠκύτερον | = | *Gaium* 18 |
| 713 (401D13–14) | ἄτοπόν ἐστι — γίνεσθαι | = | Fr. sp. 40 |
| 715 (408D5–6) | οὐκ ἂν — κολακεία | = | *Leg All* 3.182 |
| 716 (409C3–4) | τὸ — κατεσκωμμένον | = | unidentified[2] |
| 721 (420D5–21A5) | οἱ ἑαυτῶν — θεοφιλής | = | unidentified (Harris 71.1) |
| 730 (441A5–7) | ἄνθρωποι — ἀρχή | = | *Praem* 69 |

Next, Lequien prints selections from Ber. 46.

| | | | |
|---|---|---|---|
| 748 (468D11–69A8) | τί ἐστιν — προσενεμήθη | = | *Quaes Gen* 1.51 |
| 748 (469A13–B9) | ἤγαγεν — προσέταττεν | = | *Quaes Gen* 1.21 |
| 748 (469B9–C6) | ἀνδρὸς — εὐκλείας | = | *Quaes Gen* 1.20 |
| 748 (469C6–10) | καὶ — γέννησιν | = | *Quaes Gen* 1.28 |
| 748 (469C11–D1) | διό φησιν — ἥδεσθαι | = | *Quaes Gen* 1.29 |
| 748 (469D5–8) | ἄβατος — ἐπιψαῦσαι | = | *Quaes Ex* 2.45 (b) |
| 748–49 (469D8–72A12) | ἀμήχανον — ὄψεται | = | unidentified (Harris 72.3a) |
| 749 (472A12–B6) | αἱ φιλοσοφίαι — διώσασθαι | = | unidentified (Harris 72.3b) |
| 749 (472B6–12) | δεῖ τὸν — προθέσεως | = | unidentified (Harris 72.3c) |
| 749 (472B12–C1) | ἀδυνατήσει — μαρμαρυγῶν | = | unidentified (Harris 72.3d) |
| 749 (472C1–5) | οὐχ — ἀναλώσῃ | = | *Quaes Ex* 2.28 |
| 749 (473A6–8) | ὥσπερ κίονες — γένος | = | unidentified (Harris 69.5) |

---

[2]This is assigned here to Basil, but in Antonius (Gessner 35) to Philo.

| | | | |
|---|---|---|---|
| 750 (473C2–76A2) | ἐάν τις — ὠφέλειαν | = | *Somn* 1.177, 176 (Harris 69.6) |
| 750 (476A6–12) | πέφυκεν — πραγμάτων | = | *Post* 24–25 (†) |
| 751 (476B11–13) | φοβηθῶμεν — νόσος | = | Fr. sp. 28 |
| 751 (476C1–C5) | ἡ φορὰ — τυφλουμένην | = | unidentified (Harris 73.1) |
| 751 (476C6–7) | οὐδὲν — ἀδικία | = | *Quaes Gen* 1.100 (a) |
| 751 (476C12–D2) | τὸ μὴ — ἔχοντες | = | *Quaes Gen* 1.65 |
| 752 (477C3–6) | περιέχει — πεπλήρωκεν | = | unidentified (Harris 73.5) |
| 754 (481C11–13) | παρ' ἐνίοις — ἀκοῇ | = | *Quaes Ex* 2.9 (b) |
| 754 (484A9–10) | ὁ σοφὸς — ἐπιτύχῃ | = | *Quaes Gen* 4.47 (a) |
| 754 (484A11–B2) | οὕτως — λέγεται | = | *Quaes Gen* 4.74 |
| 754 (484B3–5) | ὁ σοφὸς — ζωήν | = | *Ebr* 100 |
| 772 (505D11–13) | πνευματικὴ — μεταμορφούμενοι | = | *Quaes Gen* 1.92 |
| 772 (505D14–8A2) | αἱ τοῦ θεοῦ — ἐφιέμεναι | = | *Quaes Ex* 2.65 |
| 774 (512A12–B5) | ὥσπερ — τελευτῶσα | = | *Quaes Ex* 2.26 |
| 774 (512B6–12) | αἱ περὶ τῶν — ἀλήθειαν | = | unidentified (Harris 73.2) |
| 774 (512B13–C1) | τὸ ἐμμελὲς — πειρωμένους | = | *Quaes Ex* 2.38 (b) |
| 774 (512C1–3) | ὁ τοῦ σοφοῦ — κάλλος | = | *Quaes Ex* 2.44 |
| 774 (512C5–12) | τοὺς ἐντυγχάνοντας — συνᾴδουσιν | = | unidentified (Harris 73.4) |
| 774 (512C13–D8) | ἀτόπως — στερούμενα | = | *Quaes Gen* 3.3 (a) |
| 774 (512D9–11) | νόμος — ἀορασίας | = | *Quaes Gen* 4.40 |
| 775 (513C8–12) | οὐδὲν οὔτε — θεῷ | = | *Quaes Ex* 2.105 |
| 775–76 (513D2–16A2) | τῶν — ἐπιστήμονα | = | *Quaes Gen* 4.76 (a), (b) |
| 776 (516A3–5) | νεότης — γίνεται | = | *Gaium* 190 |
| 776 (516D1–5) | ἀνθρώποις — ἐχθρῶν | = | *Quod Deus* 27 |
| 776–77 (516D9–17A7) | ὁ μὲν Κάϊν — δεκάσιν | = | *Quaes Gen* 1.77 |
| 777 (517A7) | ἣν γνωσιμαχῶν — ἑαυτοῦ | = | gloss to *Quaes Gen* 1.77 (see p. 18 above) |
| 777 (517A8–11) | τὸ ἐπαισθάνεσθαι — ἀνδρός | = | unidentified (Harris 70.1) |
| 777 (517B4–6) | λέγεται — ἄρσεν | = | *Quaes Ex* 1.7 (a) |
| 777 (517B7–9) | ἀσθενέστεραι — καταλαβεῖν | = | *Gaium* 319 |

## 2. MAXIMUS

The texts are cited first by page in Combefis's edition of 1675 (*S. Maximi Confessoris* 2:528–689), and then by column and line in the edition in *MPG* 91:721–1018 (which also includes the Combefis pagination).

| | | | |
|---|---|---|---|
| 530 (725C4–6) | τοῦ φαύλου — μαχόμενα | = | unidentified (Harris 100.8, first part) |
| 530–31 (725C7–9) | κακίας — ἐπεισέρχεται | = | *Sacr* 135 |
| 548 (757C11–12) | φίλον — δύνηται | = | *Quaes Gen* 1.17 (a) |
| 548 (757D1–2) | ἐκ χρυσοῦ — ἐστιν | = | Fr. sp. 8 |
| 548 (757D3–4) | σκεύη μὲν — παλαιοτέρα | = | Fr. sp. 9 |
| 548 (757D5–6) | οἱ μὲν — φύονται | = | Fr. sp. 10 |
| 548 (757D7–8) | πολλοὶ — πλουτοῦντας | = | Fr. sp. 11 |
| 548 (760A1–2) | πολλοὶ — ἕκαστον | = | Fr. sp. 12 |
| 548 (760A3–4) | φεύγειν — διάθεσις | = | Fr. sp. 13 |
| 554–55 (769C1–6) | τοιοῦτος — ἀντιλάβωμεν | = | Fr. sp. 52 |
| 556 (773A12–13) | οὐδὲν — εὐφημία | = | *Quaes Ex* 2.6 (b) |
| 556 (773A14–B6) | πλέον ἀγάπα — σκοπόν | = | Fr. sp. 54 |
| 556 (773B7–8) | ἡ χάρις — φαίνεται | = | Fr. sp. 17 |
| 559 (777D4–80A1) | ὁ μὲν θεὸς — ἀναξίους | = | Fr. sp. 55 |
| 561 (781C5–12) | τῇ μὲν — ἁπλότητα | = | Fr. sp. 51 |
| 565 (789B1) | νόσος — κολακεία | = | *Leg All* 3.182 (†) |
| 565 (789B1–3) | τὰς τῶν — πλεῖστοι | = | *Gaium* 140 (†) |
| 567 (792C5–9) | ἀποστρέφου — κρείττονα | = | Fr. sp. 50 |
| 568 (793D7–8) | πλούτου — ἐπικουρίᾳ | = | *Jos* 144 |
| 568 (796A1–3) | αἱ μὲν — καλόν | = | *Vita Cont* 16 |
| 568 (796A4–8) | μείζονα — πτωχεύσαντας | = | unidentified (Harris 75.4) |
| 574 (805A8–11) | ὁ σπουδαῖος — ἀθανασίας | = | *Virt* 9 |
| 580 (817A4–5) | μήτε — ἀπαιδαγώγητον | = | Fr. sp. 35 |
| 582 (820A10–11) | οὐκ ἔστιν — ψυχῆς | = | Fr. sp. 22 |
| 583 (821C3–4) | τὸ εἰδέναι — δικαιοσύνης | = | unidentified (Harris 80.5) |
| 584 (821C9–11) | ἀνάγκη — διασῴζεσθαι | = | *Leg All* 1.73 |
| 584 (821C12–13) | ἀμήχανον — παιδευθῆναι | = | *Vita Mos* 1.62 |
| 588 (832A3–4) | χαίρειν — ἀνθρώπινον | = | *Quaes Gen* 4.52 (b) |

| | | | |
|---|---|---|---|
| 588 (832A5–6) | οὐ μὴ — ἀπαιδαγώγητον | = | Fr. sp. 35 |
| 588 (832A7–8) | μεγίστη — κείμενον | = | Fr. sp. 36 |
| 588–89 (832A9–10) | πληγὴ — κακοπάθεια | = | Fr. sp. 37 |
| 589 (832A11–12) | μεγίστη — ἀνακτησομένου | = | unidentified (see pp. 32–33 above) |
| 589 (832B1–3) | μέγα τῷ — συμφορᾶς | = | Fr. sp. 38 |
| 599 (852B1–3) | ὁ σοφὸς — ἐπιτύχῃ | = | Quaes Gen 4.47 (a) |
| 599 (852B4–6) | σοφὸς — ζωήν | = | Ebr 100 |
| 603 (860A11–14) | ἀξίως — τούτους | = | Leg All 3.10 |
| 610 (869C7–9) | τῷ μὲν — ἔχει | = | Flacc 7 |
| 610 (869C10–72A2) | φοβηθῶμεν — σώματος | = | Fr. sp. 28 |
| 612 (873D6–76A2) | ἐγκρατείας — θανάτῳ | = | Gaium 14 |
| 612 (876A3–5) | ἡ τρυφή — ἀφαιρεῖται | = | Pseudo-Plutarch (see p. 44, no. 2, above) |
| 615 (881A9–13) | εἰκότως — ὁλοκλήρου | = | unidentified (Harris 7.3) |
| 616 (881B5–6) | ὁ γὰρ ὕπνος — χρόνον | = | Fr. sp. 29 |
| 616 (881B12–13) | οἱ ἡμερήσιοι — σημαίνουσιν | = | Fr. sp. 1 |
| 620 (889C3–5) | ὁ μὲν — μακαριότητα | = | Vita Mos 2.184 |
| 621 (889D1–2) | ἄτοπόν ἐστι — τιμαί | = | Fr. sp. 40 |
| 623 (896B8–9) | τῶν πολιτικῶν — ἔχοντα | = | unidentified (Harris 7.2, first part) |
| 631 (912B6–7) | ὑπὸ γυναικὸς — ἐσχάτη | = | Fr. sp. 2 |
| 632 (912C1–4) | αὕτη — ἀρετή | = | Fr. sp. 18 |
| 633 (916A9–12) | ἀναισχυντία — ἀσυνκαθέτως [sic] | = | Leg All 2.65 |
| 633 (916A13–B3) | ἀναιδὲς — σώματι | = | Quaes Gen 4.99 |
| 633 (916B8–9) | τὸ μὴ — ὑπερβολή | = | Fr. sp. 7 |
| 635 (917B11–12) | ὁ ἀληθείᾳ — θεωρεῖται | = | Abr 271 |
| 635 (917C1–3) | τὸ ἔντιμον — ἔσεσθαι | = | Fr. sp. 42 |
| 635 (917C4–5) | ἀνθεῖ — περαίνονται | = | Somn 1.11 (see pp. 45–46 above) |
| 642 (932A11–B4) | οὐκ ἔστι — θεόν | = | unidentified (Harris 10.1) |
| 642 (932B5–6) | οὐ τὸ — κολάσεως | = | Fr. sp. 26 |
| 646 (937C2–5) | ὁ μαθὼν — ἄρχεσθαι | = | Quaes Gen 3.30 (b) |
| 647 (940B10–11) | λάλει ἃ δεῖ — μὴ δεῖ | = | Fr. sp. 41 |
| 658 (960C14–D1) | τὰ καλὰ — ἀναλάμπει | = | Vita Mos 2.27 |
| 660–61 (965A13–B3) | οὐχ — δικαιοσύνης | = | Quaes Gen 4.64 |

| | | | |
|---|---|---|---|
| 662 (968C12–13) | τὸ εἰδέναι — δικαιοσύνης | = | unidentified (Harris 80.5) |
| 669 (980C9–11) | οὐχ ἡ — εἰλικρίνεια | = | unidentified (see p. 40, no. 3, above) |
| 670 (984A10–12) | πέφυκεν — ἔχουσα | = | *Post* 24–25 |
| 670 (984A13–14) | μεῖζον — ζημιωθέντι | = | *Quaes Gen* 4.179 |
| 670 (984B1–3) | πέφυκεν — εἶναι | = | *Post* 24 |
| 670 (984B4–5) | οὔτε — εὐλαβεῖσθαι | = | Fr. sp. 14 |
| 670 (984B10–11) | οἱ ἐλαφροὶ — εἰσίν | = | Fr. sp. 15 |
| 670 (984B12–14) | κακόσιτος — φάρμακον | = | Fr. sp. 16 |
| 674 (989C15–D3) | ἐγχρονίζον — συναυξάνοντα | = | *Dec* 137 |
| 674 (989D4–5) | μηδαμῶς — ποιεῖ | = | unidentified (Harris 88.2, 105.4) |
| 681 (1004B6–10) | συγγνώμην — ἀπαλλαγή | = | Fr. sp. 56 |
| 685 (1012A1–3) | εἰ βούλει — ἐπιτίμα | = | Fr. sp. 53 |
| 686 (1012D5–6) | οἱ ἑαυτῶν — ἐπιτηδεύουσιν | = | unidentified (Harris 71.1, first part) |
| 689 (1017A5) | ἀπὸ ἑνὸς — πόλις | = | Fr. sp. 21 |

# 3. ANTONIUS

The texts are cited first by page in Gessner's editio princeps of 1546 (*Sententiarum*, 1–162), and then by column and line in the edition in *MPG* 136:765–1244.

| | | | |
|---|---|---|---|
| 3 (773B5–8) | ἡ ἀληθὴς — κόσμῳ | = | *Vita Mos* 2.108 (†) |
| 8 (788C10–11) | μεγίστη — κείμενον | = | Fr. sp. 36 |
| 8 (789A1–2) | ἐλπίς — προσδοκία | = | *Quaes Gen* 1.79 |
| 8 (789A3–5) | ἐλπίδα — δράσαντες | = | *Praem* 72 (†) |
| 10 (793C1–3) | κακίας — ἐπεισέρχεται | = | *Sacr* 135 |
| 10 (793C4–5) | ἀρεταὶ μόναι — | = | unidentified |
| | ἐπίστανται | | (Harris 109.7b) |
| 10 (793C6–7) | ἡ θεωρία — περιμάχητος | = | *Leg All* 1.58 |
| 11 (797B13–C2) | φρόνησις — δεσπότας | = | *Post* 138 (+ gloss) |
| 13 (801D11–12) | τὰ μὴ σὺν — κόσμια | = | *Leg All* 3.158 |
| 13 (801D13–14) | χωρὶς θεωρίας — καλόν | = | *Praem* 51 (†) |
| 13 (801D14–15) | ἐπιστήμη — πάντων | = | unidentified |
| | | | (Harris 78.8) |
| 13 (804A1–2) | ἀκερδὴς — μετάμελος | = | unidentified |
| | | | (Harris 100.4) |
| 16 (812C8–9) | δεσμὸς — μετάγουσαι | = | *Gaium* 72 |
| 19 (824A12–14) | φοβηθῶμεν — σώματος | = | Fr. sp. 28 |
| 19 (824B4–5) | δοκεῖ μὲν — ἔστιν | = | *Quaes Gen* 1.41 (b) |
| | | | (†) (Mangey |
| | | | 674.1) |
| 19 (824B6) | φεῦγε — παρακαλεῖ | = | unidentified |
| | | | (Harris 110.4) |
| 20 (824D8–10) | πολύχουν — ἀγαθόν | = | *Ebr* 26 (†) |
| 22 (832C5–8) | τὸ μὲν — ἀγνοήσαντος | = | *Virt* 177 |
| 22 (832C9–11) | τοῖς — ἐπανόρθωσιν | = | *Leg All* 3.106 (†) |
| 26 (844A9–10) | ἀλήθεια — δύναμις | = | *Ebr* 6 |
| 27 (845A11–12) | τὸ μὴ — πίστιν | = | *Ebr* 188 |
| 27 (845A13–B2) | ψεῦδος — ὑπάρχοντος | = | Fr. sp. 46 |
| 28 (849A6–7) | φίλον — δύνηται | = | *Quaes Gen* 1.17 (a) |
| 28 (849B1–2) | σκεύη μὲν — παλαιοτέρα | = | Fr. sp. 9 |
| 28 (849B3–4) | πολλοὶ — πλουτοῦντας | = | Fr. sp. 11 |

| 29 (852C13–D1) | ἐκ χρυσοῦ — ἐστιν | = Fr. sp. 8 |
| 30 (853A11) | φεύγειν — διάθεσις | = Fr. sp. 13 |

At this point there is a discrepancy between Gessner and MPG 136. In Gessner the sections A.κϛ´ (περὶ ἀγάπης, pp. 30–31) and B.ξζ´ (περὶ ἀγάπης καὶ εἰρήνης καὶ ὁμονοίας καὶ εἰρηνοποιῶν, pp. 130–32) have some (but not nearly all) material in common, and consequently in MPG the texts from B.ξζ´ are subsumed under A.κϛ´, and B.ξζ´ itself is omitted (cf. MPG 136: 1161–62, n. 1). Thus, the three Philo texts in Gessner's B.ξζ´ appear in MPG within A.κϛ´. They are found in this index at Gessner, p. 132, although they occur in MPG at 861.

| 35 (872D1–5) | τοιοῦτος — ἀντιλάβωμεν | = Fr. sp. 52 |
| 35 (lemma Φίλωνος; not in MPG)[3] | τὸ φιλότιμον εὐκλεές· καὶ τὸ μὴ τοιοῦτον κατεσκωμμένον | = unidentified[4] |
| 38 (881A4–7) | ὁ σπουδαῖος — ἀθανασίας | = Virt 9 (†) |
| 38 (881A8–9) | ἡ αὐτάρκεια — βίον | = Quaes Ex 1.6 (b) (†) (Harris 101.10, first part) |
| 38 (881A10–11) | ἀσκητέον — μακροτάτω | = Fr. sp. 3 |
| 38 (884B9–10) | πλούτου — ἐπικουρία | = Jos 144 |
| 39 (885A6–7) | πλοῦτος — ὑπηρέτης | = Fr. sp. 5 |
| 40 (889A1–2) | πλοῦτος — ὑπηρέτης | = Fr. sp. 5 |
| 41 (892D5–9) | μείζονα — πτωχεύσαντας | = unidentified (Harris 75.4) |
| 46 (908B13–14) | ἐγκρατείας — θανάτῳ | = Gaium 14 |
| 48 (913C6–7) | ἐγκρατείας — θανάτῳ | = Gaium 14 |
| 51 (920D7–11) | εἰκότως — ὁλοκλήρου | = unidentified (Harris 7.3) |
| 51 (920D12–13) | ὁ ὕπνος — χρόνον | = Fr. sp. 29 |

---

[3]In Gessner the preceding text is ἄξιον — πτωχεύσας (= 873D1–5), which is Γρηγ. νύσσης in Gessner, but without a lemma in MPG, thus being subsumed under the texts which begin with the third preceding text from it (ἄκουε — ἐνδεέσιν [873B9–C6]), which has the lemma ὁ ἅγιος Βασί. (Basilii). All of this ends the chapter A.κη´ in both editions. Thus, the MPG edition has lost the Philo text and its lemma, as well as the preceding lemma.

[4]This text has not been included in Philo collections, although it has the lemma Φίλωνος. It is assigned to Basil in the Sacra parallela (Lequien 716).

| | | | |
|---|---|---|---|
| 51 (920D14–15) | ὕπνος ἐστὶ — ἀργία | = | Fr. sp. 57 |
| 51 (921A1–5) | εἷς μὲν — βούλεται | = | Fr. sp. 58 |
| 51 (921A6–8) | ὥσπερ — ἰάσασθαι | = | Fr. sp. 59 |
| 51 (921A9–11) | ἡμερήσιοι — σημαίνουσιν | = | Fr. sp. 1 |
| 55 (932C7–8) | οὐκ ἔστιν — ψυχῆς | = | Fr. sp. 22 |
| 56 (933C6–7) | ἀμήχανον — παιδευθῆναι | = | *Vita Mos* 1.62 |
| 56 (933C8–10) | ὥσπερ — φύσεως | = | *Somn* 1.176 |
| 56 (933D5–6) | τὸ εἰδέναι — δικαιοσύνης | = | unidentified (Harris 80.5) |
| 58 (941A4) | νόσος — κολακεία | = | *Leg All* 3.182 (†) |
| 58 (941A5–6) | τὰς τῶν — πλεῖστοι | = | *Gaium* 140 (†) |
| 59 (941D11–44A3) | ἀποστρέφου — κρείττονα | = | Fr. sp. 50 |
| — (968A1–4)⁵ | ὁ μαθὼν — ἄρχεσθαι | = | *Quaes Gen* 3.30 (b) |
| 67 (972C7–8) | οὐχ ἡ — εἰλικρίνεια | = | unidentified (see p. 40, no. 3, above) |
| 70 (981A12)⁶ | ἀλγεῖν — ἀπαιδαγώγητον | = | Fr. sp. 35 |
| 70 (981B1–2) | μεγίστη — κείμενον | = | Fr. sp. 36 |
| 70 (981B3–4) | πληγὴ — κακοπάθεια | = | Fr. sp. 37 |
| 70 (981B5–6) | μεγίστη — ἀνακτησομένου | = | unidentified (see pp. 32–33 above) |
| 70 (981B7–9) | μέγα τῷ — συμφορᾶς | = | Fr. sp. 38 |
| 74 (996A1–2)⁷ | ᾧ μὴ ἐφεδρεύει — λέλυται | = | unidentified (Harris 102.2) |
| 77 (1004B7–11) | ὁ μὲν θεὸς — αἰτήσεις | = | Fr. sp. 55 |
| 77 (1004B12–13) | τύραννος — εἰρήνης | = | *Leg All* 3.81 |
| 77 (1004C1–5) | βασιλεῦ — εὐεργετεῖν | = | *Gaium* 50 |

---

⁵This text occurs in chapter A.ξα΄ in *MPG*. In Gessner, A.ξα΄ has only four texts (p. 65), which appear in *MPG* as 961D13–15, 964A1–2, 964A3 (δόξαν — κληρονομήσουσι only), and 964A11–12. The *MPG* edition has supplemented this meager material with additions from Maximus, chapter μς΄ (περὶ δόξης), and among the texts added was this one from Philo. Of course, since this text is not in Antonius, Petit does not cite it from Antonius.

⁶This is the first text in chapter A.ο΄, which is mutilated at the beginning. *MPG* omits the Greek of this first text entirely (apparently because of the missing first few words), but does include its Latin translation.

⁷The lemma (Φίλωνος) in Gessner is at the end of the preceding line owing to a textual note in the left margin to the preceding text (which is Γρηγορ. νύσσης in Gessner). In *MPG* this Φίλωνος is missed, and so this text is subsumed under Gregory.

| 77 (1004C6–7) | τί ἂν — ἄμεινον | = | *Gaium* 287 |
| 80 (1012B8–C1)[8] | τῇ μὲν — ἁπλότητα | = | Fr. sp. 51 |
| 80 (1012B6–7)[9] | νεότης — γίνεται | = | *Gaium* 190 |
| 86 (1029A1–2) | ἄτοπόν ἐστι — τιμαί | = | Fr. sp. 40 |
| 87 (1032D8–10) | ἀνάγκη — διασώζεσθαι | = | *Leg All* 1.73 |
| 87 (1032D11–14) | μέχρι μὲν — φρονεῖν | = | unidentified (Harris 7.2, second part) |
| 87 (1033A1–2) | τῶν πολιτικῶν — ἔχοντα | = | unidentified (Harris 7.2, first part) |
| 87 (1033A3–6) | ὅταν — ἀνερεθίζεσθαι | = | *Flacc* 17 |
| 88 (1037B1–2) | ἄτοπον — ἐξισοῦντας | = | *Spec Leg* 4.55 (†) |
| 88 (1037B3–4) | ὅταν — σιωπᾶν | = | *Gaium* 360 (†) |
| 90 (1041C5–6) | τὸ νέμειν — ἀδικίας | = | *Anim* 100 |
| 91 (1044C1–5) | ὅπερ — ἀθανατίζουσιν | = | *Spec Leg* 2.225 |
| 91 (1044D1–8)[10] | πατρὸς — ἀπέτεκεν | = | *Ebr* 30 |
| 92 (1049B5–6) | τοῖς — οἷόν τε | = | *Leg All* 3.10 (†) |
| 93 (1049D4–5) | μὴ δοξάζου — αὐτῶν | = | Fr. sp. 23 |
| 93 (1049D6–7) | οἱ γονέων — ἀνθρώπους | = | *Dec* 110 |
| 93 (1052B1) | τέκνων — πατέρων | = | Fr. sp. 34 |
| 93 (1052B2) | εὔπαιδες — ἐπιστήμονες | = | *Quaes Ex* 2.19 (b) (†) (Mangey 673.5b) |
| 94 (1056B1–2) | ὁ ἀληθείᾳ — θεωρεῖται | = | *Abr* 271 |
| 94 (1056B3–8) | μετὰ τὸν — καλόν | = | *Praem* 51 |
| 94 (1056B9–10) | ἀνθεῖ — μαραίνονται | = | *Somn* 1.11 (†) (see pp. 45–46 above) |
| 95 (1057B2–5) | τοὺς — παιδευθέντας | = | *Abr* 271 |
| 95 (1057B6–8) | μέχρι — νήπιοι | = | *Gaium* 1 |
| 97 (1061D3–4) | νεότης — γίνεται | = | *Gaium* 190 |
| 97 (1061D5–6) | νεότης — κακοπραγεῖ | = | Fr. sp. 19 |
| 97 (1064B3–5) | καὶ — νουθετοῦνται | = | *Quod Deus* 64 |
| 97 (1064B6–7) | οἱ λεγόμενοι — ὀνομάζονται | = | *Cher* 83 |
| 97 (1064B8–10) | κύριος — ἡγεμών | = | *Mut* 22 |
| 98 (1065D1–4) | μέγιστον — κατορθοῦν | = | *Heres* 9 |
| 98 (1068B11–12) | οὐδεὶς — δεσπότῃ | = | *Gaium* 233 |

---

[8]This is the text which in Gessner is ascribed to Agapetus.

[9]On the dislocation of this text, see p. 121, n. 110, above.

[10]I can find no explanation of the peculiar lemma, "Virtutes Philonis," in *MPG*; Gessner has Φίλωνος.

| 100 (1072D8–9) | οὐδὲν — εὐφημία | = | *Quaes Ex* 2.6 (b) |
| 101 (1073C1–3) | τοιοῦτον — εὐεργετήσασιν | = | *Gaium* 60 (†) |
| 102 (1077D8–11) | φιλάνθρωπος — βλάπτειν | = | *Quaes Gen* 4.193 |
| 102 (1077D12–13) | τοῖς — ὠφεληθήσονται | = | *Gaium* 245 |
| 102 (1077D14–80A2) | ἄνδρες — πολιτείας | = | *Quaes Ex* 1.21 |
| 102 (1080A3–5) | τὸ καλὸν — γνωρίσματα | = | *Vita Mos* 1.59 (†) |
| 104 (1084B6–11) | τοῦ φαύλου — πολέμιος | = | unidentified (Harris 100.8) |
| 104 (1084B12–C3) | τὸν φαῦλον — βίον | = | *Mut* 169 |
| 104 (1084C4–6) | ἀβέβαιοι — πασχόντων | = | *Flacc* 109 |
| 105 (1088A7–8) | λέγεται — ἄρρεν | = | *Quaes Ex* 1.7 (a) |
| 105 (1088A9–11) | ἀσθενέστεραι — καταλαβεῖν | = | *Gaium* 319 |
| 105 (1088A12–B2) | ἡ Φίλωνος — ἀρετή | = | Fr. sp. 18 |
| 107 (1089D12) | ὑπὸ γυναικὸς — ἐσχάτη | = | Fr. sp. 2 |
| 107 (1089D13–92A2) | δεινὸν — γίνεται | = | *Gaium* 39 |
| 107 (1092A3–4) | φίλαυτον — ἀνδρός | = | *Hyp* |
| 108 (1093C7–8) | καλὸν — ἐλπίδα | = | *Dec* 113 |
| 109 (1096D6–8) | βλαβεραὶ — εἴδωλα | = | *Fuga* 14 |
| 109 (1096D9–10) | οὐ ποιεῖ — συνδιατριβή | = | Fr. sp. 4 |
| 111 (1101D13) | ὠμῆς — κακία | = | *Provid* 2.31 |
| 111 (1105A7) | ἐπιχαιρεκακία ἀλλότριον σοφῶν | = | unidentified[11] |
| 112 (1105B8) | ἀπὸ ἑνὸς — πόλις | = | Fr. sp. 21 |
| 112 (1105C6–12) | ἐγὼ — δωρουμένου | = | *Sacr* 124 |
| 112 (1105C13–15) | εὐδαιμονιστέον — τοιούτου | = | unidentified (Mangey 671.1) |
| 112 (1105D1–6) | ἕνεκα — ὠφελεῖν | = | *Quaes Gen* 3.8 |
| 112 (1105D7–9) | ἄνδρες — πολιτείας | = | *Quaes Ex* 1.21 |
| 115 (1116B1–C3) | ἀνώμαλον — καθελών | = | *Somn* 1.150–52 |
| 116 (1117D6–10) | ἔνιοι — ἀντεπέθετο | = | *Quaes Ex* 1.7 (b) |
| 116 (1117D11–20A3) | πολλοὶ — ἑκάστην | = | *Leg All* 1.89 (†) |
| 116 (1120A4–6) | ἤδη — νόσον | = | *Quaes Gen* 1.85 |
| 117 (1124A5–8) | ἀρχὴν — συνιστάμενον | = | *Sacr* 35 |
| 117 (1124A9–10) | θνητῷ — δεδώρηται | = | *Sacr* 40 |
| 118 (1124A11–12) | αὕτη — ὑπολαμβάνειν | = | *Post* 158 |

---

[11]This text has not been included in the collections of Philo fragments, although it has the lemma Φίλωνος.

| | | | |
|---|---|---|---|
| 118 (1124A13–B1) | ὁ μὲν — μακαριότητα | = | *Vita Mos* 2.184 |
| 118 (1124B2–3) | τὰ πλεῖστα — περιγίνεσθαι | = | *Congr* 162 |
| 119 (1128B14–C2) | πόνος — ἀπεχθάνονται | = | *Mut* 170 |
| 119 (1128C3–5) | ἡ συνεχὴς — ἐξέλυσαν | = | *Sacr* 86 |
| 119 (1128C6–7) | ἡ ἐξ ἔθους — ἐπίβουλον | = | *Flacc* 41 (†)[12] |
| 123 (1137C4–8) | συγγνώμην — ἀπαλλαγή | = | Fr. sp. 56 |
| 125 (1145A12) | συγγνώμη — γεννᾶν | = | *Quaes Gen* 1.82 (†) (Mangey 672.3) |
| 126 (1149A9–10) | οὐδὲν — εὐφημία | = | *Quaes Ex* 2.6 (b) |
| 128 (1153A14–B1) | οὐδενὶ — ἐστι | = | *Mut* 170 |
| 128 (1153B2–3) | περισσὸς — ὁμόνοια ᾖ | = | Fr. sp. 24 |
| 128 (1156A9) | τὴν αἰδῶ — πολλοῖς | = | *Gaium* 36 (†) |
| 129 (1156D2–3) | ὅρκος — ἀμφισβητουμένου | = | *Dec* 86 (†)[13] |
| 129 (1156D4) | ὅρκον περίφευγε καὶ δικαίως ὀμνύειν | = | unidentified[14] |
| 129 (1157C8) | ἐκ πολυορκίας — φύεται | = | *Dec* 92 |
| 129 (1157C9–10) | φασί τινες — ὑπονοεῖται | = | *Dec* 84 |
| 129 (1157C11–D2) | μαρτυρία — ἀνοσιώτατον | = | *Dec* 86 |
| 129 (1157D3–6) | τὸν ὀμνύντα — τιμωρίας | = | *Spec Leg* 2.253 |
| 132 (861B5–6)[15] | εἰρήνη — πολέμου | = | *Spec Leg* 4.221 (†) |
| 132 (861B7) | εἰρήνη — φύεται | = | *Gaium* 68 |
| 132 (861B8–9) | τὸ μέγιστον — δῶρον | = | *Vita Mos* 1.304 (†) |
| 134 (1165B13–14) | οὔτε — εὐλαβεῖσθαι | = | Fr. sp. 14 |
| 135 (1168D3–4) | λάλει ἃ δεῖ — μὴ δεῖ | = | Fr. sp. 41 |

---

[12]This text is not cited in *PCW* 6, but it is cited in *PCW* 3 in the apparatus to *Mut* 170 (see p. 5 above).

[13]Philo has quite similar phrases also at *Leg All* 3.205, *Sacr* 91, and *Spec Leg* 2.10, and on the last phrase *PCW* cites this text from Antonius. But a fuller excerpt from *Dec* 86 occurs in Antonius (four texts later in this list) and also in Ber. 46 (see *PCW*). It is more reasonable to suppose that the present text is a shorter version of the fuller text, than that two excerpts were made independently of almost the same phrase from two of Philo's works. (See also Harris 97.1 and 110.3.)

[14]This text has not been included in the collections of Philo fragments, although it follows without a lemma a genuine Philo text.

[15]On the position of this and the following two texts, see the comment above after Gessner 30.

| | | | |
|---|---|---|---|
| 135 (1169D1–3) | ἀναισχυντία — ἀσυγκαταθέτως | = | *Leg All* 2.65 |
| 135 (1169D8) | τὸ μὴ — ὑπερβολή | = | Fr. sp. 7 |
| 137 (1173C13–D2) | θυμῷ μάλιστα — σῶμα | = | *Quaes Ex* 2.115 (†) (Harris 110.6) |
| 139 (1180B11–14) | τὸν καρτερίας — ἀτυφίας | = | unidentified (Harris 102.4) |
| 139 (1180C1–4) | εἰ δόξαις — ἐκτραχηλισθείς | = | unidentified (Harris 102.5) |
| 140 (1184B12–15) | φασί τινες — ἡττᾶσθαι | = | unidentified (Harris 7.4) |
| 140 (1184C1–2) | τῶν πολιτικῶν — ἔχοντα | = | unidentified (Harris 7.2, first part) |
| 140 (1184C3–5) | τίς τιμῆς — παράπαν | = | *Ebr* 57 (†) |
| 141 (1188A1–2) | οἱ ἑαυτῶν — ἐπιτηδεύουσιν | = | unidentified (Harris 71.1, first part) |
| 143 (1192A3–4) | ὁ σοφὸς — ἐπιτύχῃ | = | *Quaes Gen* 4.47 (a) |
| 143 (1192A4–6) | σοφὸς — ζωήν | = | *Ebr* 100 (†) |
| 143 (1192A7–10) | ἔστι — συνέρχεσθαι | = | *Mut* 37 (†) |
| 144 (1193B7–8) | πέφυκεν — εἶναι | = | *Post* 24 (†) |
| 144 (1193C3–7) | ὁ φαῦλος — ἀτιμότατον | = | *Quaes Gen* 4.47 (b) |
| 144 (1193C8–9) | δυσεύρετον — καλόν | = | *Fuga* 153 |
| 145–46 (1200A1–3) | ἐγχρονίζον — συναυξάνοντα | = | *Dec* 137 (†) |
| 146 (1200A4–5) | μηδαμῶς — ποιεῖ | = | unidentified (Harris 88.2, 105.4) |
| 149 (1208B14–15) | οἷς — κατορθοῦσιν | = | *Flacc* 1 |
| 149 (1209C2–4) | οὐχ ἡ — ἀκραιφνής | = | unidentified (see p. 40, no. 3, above) |
| 150 (1209C11–D2) | ἐπειδήπερ — θεός | = | *Cher* 98 |
| 150 (1209D3–5) | οἶκος — βασιλείῳ | = | *Praem* 123 |
| 150 (1209D6–8) | ὀφθαλμοῖς — μέλλοντα | = | *Gaium* 2 |
| 151 (1213A9–14) | αἱ συνεχεῖς — νοῦν | = | *Leg All* 3.16–17 |
| 151 (1213A15–B3) | τῷ μὲν — δικαστηρίῳ | = | *Flacc* 7 |
| 151 (1213B4–5) | τῷ ἔνδον — ἀλίσκεται | = | *Quaes Ex* 2.13 (c) (†) (Harris 109.12) |
| 154 (1224C3) | τὸ — ὠφελιμώτατον | = | *Quaes Gen* 3.30 (a) |
| 154 (1224C4–8) | ἄπειρα — ἀμήχανον | = | *Mut* 49 (†) |
| 155 (1225A5–9) | ἀναιδὲς — σώματι | = | *Quaes Gen* 4.99 |

# 4. JOHANNES GEORGIDES

The texts are cited first by page in Boissonnade's edition of 1829 (*Anecdota Graeca e codicibus regiis* 1:1–108) and then by column and line in the edition in *MPG* 117:1057–1164 (which also includes the Boissonade pagination).

| | | | |
|---|---|---|---|
| 14 (1072A10–11) | βέλτιον — ἡσυχία | = | *Vita Mos* 1.285 |
| 17 (1073C8–10) | βλαβεραὶ — εἴδωλα | = | *Fuga* 14 |
| 26 (1084C1–2) | δυσεύρετον — καλόν | = | *Fuga* 153 |
| 27 (1084C3–4) | δυσεκρίζωτος — πολλῷ | = | unidentified (Harris 105.5) |
| 34 (1092B11) | ἐκ πολυλογίας — φύεται | = | *Dec* 92 |
| 39 (1097A7) | ἡ ἐξ ἔθους — ἐπίβουλον | = | *Flacc* 41 (†) |
| 41 (1097C6–7) | ἡ χάρις — φαίνεται | = | Fr. sp. 17 |
| 47 (1104D1–5A1) | θεοῦ — ἐπάγειν | = | *Leg All* 3.105 |
| 47 (1105A1–3) | οὐδὲ — ἐπανόρθωσιν | = | *Leg All* 3.106 |
| 49 (1105C1–2) | καλὸν — ἐλπίδα | = | *Dec* 113 |
| 57 (1113C10–11) | μεγίστη — κείμενον | = | Fr. sp. 36 |
| 59 (1116C12–14) | μή σε — πράγματα | = | unidentified (Harris 108.1) |
| 59 (1116C15–D2) | μακαρία — γινομένοις | = | *Quaes Gen* 3.38 (b) |
| 79 (1136B5–7) | σοφιστείας — ἀποδοχῆς | = | *Provid* 2.51 |
| 82 (1140A9–10) | σκεύη τὰ — παλαιοτέρα | = | Fr. sp. 9 |
| 84 (1141A3–4) | τὰ μὴ συλλόγων — κόσμια | = | *Leg All* 3.158 |
| 84 (1141A5–6) | τοῖς — οἷόν τε | = | *Leg All* 3.10 (†) |
| 98 (1153B8–9) | χωρὶς θεωρίας — καλόν | = | *Praem* 51 (†) |
| 98 (1153B9–10) | ἐπιστήμη — καλόν | = | unidentified (Harris 78.8) |
| 104 (1160A12–13) | ᾧ μὴ ἐφεδρεύει — λέλυται | = | unidentified (Harris 102.2) |
| 104 (1160B5) | ὠμῆς — κακία | = | *Provid* 2.31 |

## 5. MANGEY

Thomas Mangey's edition of Philo, *Philonis Judaei opera* (1742), included an extensive collection of Greek fragments at 2:625–80.

625–47:  From Eusebius, *Praeparatio Evangelica*:

| 625.1 | διὰ τί ὡς — ἐξομοιοῦσθαι | = | *Quaes Gen* 2.62 (*Aucher 1826) |
|---|---|---|---|
| 625.2 | περὶ δὲ τοῦ — φύσει | = | *Provid* 2.50–51 (*Aucher 1822; Harris 75.8) |
| 626.1 | τὸν μὲν παλαιὸν — πολυανδρίαν | = | *Hyp* (cf. Harris 76) |
| 627.1 | ἀνήρ γε μὴν — πεισθῆναι | = | *Hyp* (cf. Harris 76) |
| 628.1 | ἆρά τι τούτων — ἀπανταχοῦ | = | *Hyp* (cf. Harris 76) |
| 630.1 | ὅλην δὲ ἡμέραν — λόγος | = | *Hyp* (cf. Harris 76) |
| 632.1 | μυρίους δὲ τῶν — σεμνοποιοῦσι | = | *Apol* (cf. Harris 76) |
| 634.1 | πρόνοιαν εἶναι — ταπεινοί | = | *Provid* 2.3 (*Aucher 1822; Harris 75.6) |
| 634.2 | οὐ τύραννος — εἰσόμεθα | = | *Provid* 2.15–33 (*Aucher 1822; Harris 75.7) |
| 642.1 | ἀνέμων καὶ — πραγμάτων | = | *Provid* 2.99–112 (*Aucher 1822; Harris 75.9) |

648–60:  "Ex Johannis Damasceni Sacris Parallelis":

| 648.1 | πάντων μέν — κύριον | = | unidentified (Harris 6.1) |
|---|---|---|---|
| 648.2 | εἰ βούλει — θεοῦ | = | unidentified (Harris 77.2) |
| 648.3 | ἔνιοι — ἐναπέθετο | = | *Quaes Ex* 1.7 (b) (*Harris) |
| 648.4 | ὅταν ἄνθρωπος — ᾅδου | = | Fr. sp. 49 |
| 649.1 | οὐκ ἔστι — θεόν | = | unidentified (Harris 10.1) |
| 649.2 | ὁ νοῦς — ἀψευδέστατος | = | *Post* 59 (*Harris 78.1) |
| 649.3 | ὁ μαθὼν — ἄρχεσθαι | = | *Quaes Gen* 3.30 (b) (*Aucher 1826, 443a) |
| 649.4 | ὦ πόσα — φόβοι | = | *Gaium* 17 (*Harris 78.3) |
| 649.5a | τῶν φαύλων — πένητες | = | unidentified (Harris 69.1) |
| 649.5b | στενοχωρεῖται — διάγειν | = | *Quaes Gen* 4.33 (a) (*Harris) |

| | | | |
|---|---|---|---|
| 649.6 | μεῖζον — ζημιωθέντι | = | *Quaes Gen* 4.179 (Harris 69.2) |
| 649.7 | νόσου — ἀπαιδευσία | = | *Ebr* 141 (Harris 78.5) |
| 649.8 | οὐ πᾶς δόλος — ἴδιον | = | *Quaes Gen* 4.228 (*Aucher 1826; not in Harris or Marcus) |
| 649.9 | ἀμήχανον — σκότος | = | Fr. sp. 30 |
| 650.1 | μακαρία — γινομένοις | = | *Quaes Gen* 3.38 (b) (Harris 97.10) |
| 650.2 | ὁ σοφὸς — ἐντύχῃ | = | *Quaes Gen* 4.47 (a) (*Harris) |
| 650.3 | αἰσχροὶ — προχειρότατοι | = | *Flacc* 34 (Harris 10.2) |
| 650.4 | τὰ μὴ σὺν — κόσμια | = | *Leg All* 3.158 (*Harris 78.6) |
| 650.5 | ἀκύμαντος λιμὴν πολιά | = | Fr. sp. 47 |
| 650.6 | σώματος — παθῶν | = | unidentified (Harris 97.12) |
| 650.7a | ἡ συνεχὴς — ἀμελετησία | = | *Sacr* 86 (*Harris 79.1a) |
| 650.7b | καὶ πάλιν — τριβή | = | unidentified (Harris 79.1b) |
| 650.8 | μελέτη τροφὸς ἐπιστήμης | = | unidentified (Harris 69.3) |
| 650.9 | διάβολοι — ἀλλότριοι | = | unidentified (Harris 98.2) |
| 650.10 | τί ἂν γένοιτο — γένηται | = | unidentified (Harris 98.3) |
| 650.11 | εἴ τις πάσας — τυγχάνοι | = | unidentified (Harris 79.3) |
| 651.1 | ὡς τὸ ἑκουσίως — δικαιοσύνης | = | *Quaes Gen* 4.64 (*Aucher 1826, 443a) |
| 651.2 | οὐ θέμις — ἀμυήτοις | = | unidentified (Mangey 658.4a; Harris 69.4a) |
| 651.3 | ἄξιον — ἀναπέμπουσι | = | *Gaium* 47 (Harris 98.4) |
| 651.4 | τὸ νέμειν — ἀδικίας | = | *Anim* 100 (*Harris 11.4) |
| 651.5 | ἀγαθὸς — ἐμποιεῖ | = | *Quaes Ex* 2.25 (d) (*Aucher 1826) |
| 651.6 | λάλει ἃ δεῖ — ἃ μὴ δεῖ | = | Fr. sp. 41 |
| 651.7 | χρόνου φείδεσθαι καλόν | = | *Vita Cont* 16 (Harris 79.6) |
| 651.8 | οἱ λάλοι — οὐκ ἄξια | = | *Quaes Ex* 2.118 (*Harris) |
| 651.9 | τὸ ζητεῖν — ἀνυσιμώτατον | = | *Anim* 6 (*Harris 11.2) |
| 651.10 | ὁ πεινῶν — οἰκίας | = | *Quaes Ex* 2.13 (b) (*Harris) |
| 651.11 | τὸ εἰδέναι — δικαιοσύνης | = | unidentified (Harris 80.5) |
| 652.1 | μηδενὶ συμφορὰν — εὑρεθῇς | = | unidentified (Harris 98.5) |
| 652.2 | τὸ ὑποτάσσεσθαι — ὠφέλιμον | = | *Quaes Gen* 3.30 (a) (*Harris) |
| 652.3 | ἀναιδὲς — σώματι | = | *Quaes Gen* 4.99 (*Aucher 1826, 443a) |
| 652.4 | αἱ πάντων — δυνάμεις | = | unidentified (Harris 98.6) |

| | | | |
|---|---|---|---|
| 656.5 | ὥσπερ οἱ — τελευτῶσα | = | *Quaes Ex* 2.26 (*Harris) |
| 656.6 | αἱ περὶ τῶν — ἀλήθειαν | = | unidentified (Harris 73.2) |
| 656.7a | τὸ ἐμμελὲς — πειρωμένους | = | *Quaes Ex* 2.38 (b) (Harris 73.3a) |
| 656.7b | ὁ τοῦ σοφοῦ — κάλλος | = | *Quaes Ex* 2.44 (Harris 73.3b) |
| 656.8 | τοὺς ἐντυγχάνοντας — συνᾴδουσιν | = | unidentified (Harris 73.4) |
| 657.1 | ἀτόπως — στερούμενα | = | *Quaes Gen* 3.3 (a) (*Harris) |
| 657.2 | νόμος ἔστω — ἀορασίας | = | *Quaes Gen* 4.40 (*Harris) |
| 657.3 | οὐδὲν οὔτε — θεῷ | = | *Quaes Ex* 2.105 (*Harris) |
| 657.4 | τῶν μὲν ἀφρόνων — ἐπιστήμονα | = | *Quaes Gen* 4.76 (a), (b) (*Harris) |
| 657.5 | ἀνθρώποις — ἐχθρῶν | = | *Quod Deus* 27 (Harris 69.8) |
| 658.1a | ὁ μὲν Κάϊν — δεκάσιν | = | *Quaes Gen* 1.77 (*Aucher 1826) |
| 658.1b | ἦν γνωσιμαχῶν — ἑαυτοῦ | = | gloss to *Quaes Gen* 1.77 (see p. 18 above) |
| 658.2 | τὸ ἐπαισθάνεσθαι — ἀνδρός | = | unidentified (Harris 70.1) |
| 658.3 | λέγεται — ἄρσεν | = | *Quaes Ex* 1.7 (a) (*Harris) |
| 658.4a | οὐ θέμις — ἀμυήτοις | = | unidentified (Mangey 651.2; Harris 69.4a) |
| 658.4b | ἄχρις ἂν — ἀμώμητα | = | unidentified (Harris 69.4b) |
| 658.4c | τοῖς ἀμυήτοις — τελετῆς | = | *Quaes Gen* 4.8 (c) (Harris 69.4c) |
| 658.5a | ἄτοπον ἐν μὲν — ἐκρίπτειν | = | unidentified (Harris 99.6) |
| 658.5b | οὐ πάντων — θέμις | = | unidentified (Harris 75.1) |
| 659.1 | ἐντὸς φέρει — ψυχῇ | = | unidentified (Harris 73.6) |
| 659.2 | τοῦ φαύλου — ἀνακέκραται | = | *Quaes Gen* 1.49 (†) (Harris 73.7) |
| 659.3 | ἐνίοις — παλινδρομοῦντες | = | *Quaes Ex* 2.40 (*Harris) |
| 659.4 | ἤδη τινὲς — νόσον | = | *Quaes Gen* 1.85 (*Harris) |
| 659.5 | τὸ ἐπιορκεῖν — ἀλυσιτελέστατον | = | unidentified (Harris 70.7) |
| 659.6 | φίλους — ἐγώ | = | *Quaes Gen* 1.17 (a), (b) (*Harris) |
| 660.1 | ὅταν οἱ — ὦσιν | = | *Quaes Ex* 1.1 (*Aucher 1826) |
| 660.2 | αἱ τοῦ θεοῦ — ἀπόλαυσιν | = | *Quaes Ex* 2.71 (Harris 73.8) |

660–70: "Johannes Monachus ineditus" ( = Ber. 46 and Coisl. 276):[16]

| 660.3 | σοὶ λέγεται — διαγγέλλῃ | = | *Heres* 105–6, 110 (*Harris 99.7) |
| 661.1 | τῶν πολιτικῶν — φρονεῖν | = | unidentified (Harris 7.2) |
| 661.2 | ἄνδρες — πολιτείας | = | *Quaes Ex* 1.21 (*Harris) |
| 661.3 | ἕνεκα μὲν — ὠφελεῖσθαι | = | *Quaes Gen* 3.8 (*Harris) |
| 661.4 | τόπος — περιπολοῦσιν | = | unidentified (Harris 100.1) |
| 661.5 | ἡ τῶν μελλόντων — ἀνθρώπῳ | = | *Heres* 261 (Harris 100.2a) |
| 661.6 | οὐ πάντα — γνώριμα | = | *Op* 61 (*Harris 81.7) |
| 661.7 | τὸ τέλος — μόνος | = | unidentified (Harris 100.2b) |
| 661.8 | βελτίων — ἡσυχία | = | *Vita Mos* 1.285 (*Harris 82.1) |
| 661.9 | οὐ ποιήσετε — αἴτιον | = | unidentified (Harris 100.3) |
| 662.1 | οἱ ἑαυτῶν — θεοφιλής | = | unidentified (Harris 71.1) |
| 662.2 | μυρία γε — νοῦν | = | unidentified (Harris 73.9) |
| 662.3 | οὐδεὶς αὐχήσει — ἀλογιστίᾳ | = | *Quaes Ex* 2.37 (*Harris) |
| 662.4 | ὥσπερ κίονες — γένος | = | unidentified (Mangey 655.1; Harris 69.5) |
| 662.5 | ἀδύνατον οἶμαι — δοκῇ | = | Fr. sp. 31 |
| 662.6 | ἀκερδὴς — μετάμελος | = | unidentified (Harris 100.4) |
| 662.7 | ὁ καλὸς — δόγμασιν | = | *Quaes Gen* 2.41 (Harris 100.5) |
| 663.1 | ἐὰν ἄρτι — αἴτιον | = | *Quaes Ex* 2.25 (b), (c) (*Harris) |
| 663.2a | ἡ τυχοῦσα — γέννημα | = | *Leg All* 3.89 (Harris 100.6) |
| 663.2b | ἴσον — τεινόμενον | = | *Quaes Gen* 2.54 (c), (d) (*Harris) |
| 663.3 | οἱ ἄνανδροι — γίνονται | = | *Praem* 5 (Harris 100.7) |
| 663.4 | ἡ ἐν τῷ φαύλῳ — φονώντων | = | *Quaes Gen* 2.12 (c) (*Harris) |
| 663.5 | τοῦ φαύλου — πολέμιος | = | unidentified (Harris 100.8) |
| 664.1 | ἀνελεύθερον — ἔχον | = | unidentified (Harris 100.9) |
| 664.2 | οἱ ὑπηρέται — θεοῦ | = | unidentified (Harris 100.10) |
| 664.3 | ἄσπονδος — ἀπειλεῖν | = | unidentified (Harris 100.11) |
| 664.4 | σωτήριον — οὐρανοῦ | = | *Quaes Gen* 1.98 (†) (Harris 101.1) |
| 664.5 | καλόν ἐστιν — μνήμην | = | unidentified (Harris 101.2) |

[16]See pp. 27–28, nn. 8–9, above.

| 664.6 | ψυχὴ πᾶσα — εὐφροσύνης | = | *Quaes Ex* 2.15 (b) (Harris 101.3) |
|---|---|---|---|
| 664.7 | μακρὰν — ἐπακολουθοῦντα | = | unidentified (Harris 101.4) |
| 665.1 | ἀνδρείας ἐστὶ — θάρσος | = | Fr. sp. 6 |
| 665.2 | ὥσπερ τῶν — ἰσότητος | = | unidentified (Harris 101.5) |
| 665.3 | τὸ ἄνισον — ὠφέλειαν | = | unidentified (Harris 101.6) |
| 665.4 | τὸ ἔννομον — ὄντων | = | *Quaes Ex* 2.64 (Harris 101.7) |
| 665.5 | τὰ τῶν προτέρων — σωτήρια | = | unidentified (Harris 101.8) |
| 665.6 | αἱ αἰσθήσεις — σώζει | = | *Quaes Gen* 2.34 (a), (c) (*Harris) |
| 666.1 | ἐὰν πολὺς — τέλματος | = | unidentified (Harris 101.9) |
| 666.2 | ἡ αὐτάρκεια — καθαιρεῖν | = | *Quaes Ex* 1.6 (b) (†) (Harris 101.10) |
| 666.3 | ἀσκητέον — μακροτάτω | = | Fr. sp. 3 |
| 666.4 | ἡ ἀληθὴς — κόσμῳ | = | *Vita Mos* 2.108 (†) (Harris 101.12) |
| 666.5 | ἀβέβαιοι — πάσχοντες | = | *Flacc* 109 (Harris 101.13) |
| 666.6 | τίς ἐξαμαρτὼν — ἐλέγχῃ | = | unidentified (Harris 102.1) |
| 666.7 | ἐπειδὴ πρὸς — ὁδηγίαν | = | unidentified (Harris 70.2) |
| 666.8 | τῷ μὴ ἐφεδρεύει — λέλυται | = | unidentified (Harris 102.2) |
| 667.1 | ἐν θεῷ — μεμαθημένως | = | unidentified (Harris 70.3) |
| 667.2 | φυσικώτατα — ὑπονόστησιν | = | *Quaes Gen* 4.100 (Harris 102.3) |
| 667.3 | τῆς καρτερίας — ἀτυφίας | = | unidentified (Harris 102.4) |
| 667.4 | ἐὰν δόξαις — ἐκτραχηλισθῇς | = | unidentified (Harris 102.5) |
| 667.5 | ὁ ὕπνος — ὑπεκλέλυνται | = | *Quaes Gen* 1.24 (*Harris) |
| 667.6 | εἰκότως — ὁλοκλήρου | = | unidentified (Harris 7.3) |
| 667.7 | τοῦ προθύμως — αἰώνιος | = | unidentified (Harris 10.3) |
| 668.1 | φασί τινες — ἡττᾶσθαι | = | unidentified (Harris 7.4) |
| 668.2 | οἴησις ἀκάθαρτον φύσει | = | *Leg All* 1.52 (Mangey 652.10; *Harris 81.2) |
| 668.3 | τὸ εὐχαριστεῖν — εἰσηγουμένη | = | *Quaes Gen* 1.64 (b), (c), (d) (*Aucher 1826) |
| 668.4 | πέφυκε τοῖς — φθόνος | = | Fr. sp. 25 |
| 668.5 | τὰ τέλεια — περιγίνεσθαι | = | *Congr* 162 (*PCW) |
| 668.6 | ἄτοπόν ἐστι — τιμαί | = | Fr. sp. 40 |
| 668.7 | τί ἐστιν — αἵματι | = | *Quaes Gen* 2.59 (*Aucher 1826) |
| 668.8 | τῆς εὐδαιμονίας — θεοῦ | = | unidentified (Harris 8.3) |
| 669.1 | ἀμήχανον — σώζει | = | *Quaes Gen* 2.34 (b), (c) (Harris 70.4) |

| | | | |
|---|---|---|---|
| 669.2 | βουληθεὶς — βίον | = | *Heres* 112–13 (*Harris 102.6) |
| 669.3 | μία ἀνάπαυσις — πράξεων | = | unidentified (Harris 73.10) |
| 669.4 | πέρας εὐδαιμονίας — στῆναι | = | unidentified (Harris 74.1) |
| 669.5 | οἱ ἀστέρες — ἐξαιρέτοις | = | *Quaes Ex* 2.55 (a) (*Harris) |
| 669.6 | ἔνιοι νομίζουσι — γῆς | = | *Quaes Gen* 1.93 (*Aucher 1826) |
| 669.7 | οὔτε ἐνδοιασμὸς — ἐστιν | = | *Quaes Gen* 1.55 (a) (*Aucher 1826) |
| 670.1 | ὁ μὴ ἐκ προαιρέσεως — ἀπαρχή | = | *Quaes Ex* 2.50 (b) (*Harris) |
| 670.2 | ἀεὶ φθάνουσι — προγενέσθαι | = | *Quaes Gen* 1.89 (*Harris) |

670–74: "Ex Antonio":[17]

| | | | |
|---|---|---|---|
| 670.3a | ἀρεταὶ μόναι — ἐπίστανται | = | unidentified (Harris 109.7b) |
| 670.3b | ἡ θεωρία — περιμάχητος | = | *Leg All* 1.58 (*Harris 95.3) |
| 670.4 | εἰ βούλει — ἐπιτίμα | = | Fr. sp. 53 |
| 670.5 | συγγνώμην — ἀπαλλαγή | = | Fr. sp. 56 |
| 670.6 | φιλάνθρωπος — βλάπτειν | = | *Quaes Gen* 4.193 (*Harris) |
| 670.7 | καλὸν τότε — γνωρίσματα | = | *Vita Mos* 1.59 |
| 670.8 | καλὸν ἀεὶ — ἐλπίδα | = | *Dec* 113 (†) (*Harris 88.1) |
| 671.1 | εὐδαιμονιστέον — τοιούτου | = | unidentified[18] |
| 671.2 | οἷς ἰσχὺς — κατορθοῦσι | = | *Flacc* 1 |
| 671.3a | βλαβεραὶ — εἴδωλα | = | *Fuga* 14 (Mangey 652.7; *Harris 81.1) |
| 671.3b | οὐ ποιεῖ — συνδιατριβή | = | Fr. sp. 4 |
| 671.4a | οὔτε — εὐλαβεῖσθαι | = | Fr. sp. 14 |
| 671.4b | οἱ ἐλαφροὶ — εἰσίν | = | Fr. sp. 15 |
| 671.5a | χωρὶς θεωρίας — καλόν | = | *Praem* 51 (*Harris 78.7, 94.4, 96.1 [last part]) |
| 671.5b | ἐπιστήμη — πάντων | = | unidentified (Harris 78.8) |
| 671.5c | περισσὸς — ὁμόνοια ᾗ | = | Fr. sp. 24 |
| 671.6a | ὁ φαῦλος — ἀτιμότατον | = | *Quaes Gen* 4.47 (b) (*Harris) |
| 671.6b | δυσεύρετον — καλόν | = | *Fuga* 153 (*Harris 97.6) |
| 671.7 | οὐδὲν οὕτως — εὐφημία | = | *Quaes Ex* 2.6 (b) (*Harris) |
| 671.8 | τὸ μὴ — πίστιν | = | *Ebr* 188 |
| 671.9 | ἀποστρέφου — κρείττονα | = | Fr. sp. 50 |

---

[17]See pp. 30–32 above.
[18]Früchtel's MS assigns to *Sacr* 124, but the resemblance seems remote.

| 671.10 | τὸ μέγιστον — ἔργον | = | *Vita Mos* 1.304 (†) |
| | | | (Harris 108.6) |
| 672.1 | τοιοῦτος — ἀντιλάβωμεν | = | Fr. sp. 52 |
| 672.2a | ὕπνος ἐστὶ — ἀργία | = | Fr. sp. 57 |
| 672.2b | εἷς μὲν — βούλεται | = | Fr. sp. 58 |
| 672.2c | ὥσπερ — ἰάσασθαι | = | Fr. sp. 59 |
| 672.3 | συγγνώμη — γεννᾶν | = | *Quaes Gen* 1.82 (†) |
| | | | (*Früchtel 1937, |
| | | | 112–13; Royse 1984, |
| | | | 149–50) |
| 672.4 | ἀναισχυντία — ἀσυγκαταθέτως | = | *Leg All* 2.65 (*Mangey 692; |
| | | | Harris 95.2) |
| 672.5a | ἐπειδήπερ — θεός | = | *Cher* 98 (*Harris 97.7) |
| 672.5b | οἶκος θεοῦ — βασιλείῳ | = | *Praem* 123 (*Harris 97.8) |
| 672.5c | ὀφθαλμοῖς — μέλλοντα | = | *Gaium* 2 (*Harris 97.9) |
| 672.6 | τὸν ὀμνύντα — τιμωρίας | = | *Spec Leg* 2.253 |
| | | | (*Harris 97.5) |
| 672.7 | τὰ κἂν — ἀναλάμπει | = | *Vita Mos* 2.27 (*Harris 89.1) |
| 673.1 | τῇ μὲν — ἁπλότητα | = | Fr. sp. 51 |
| 673.2 | καὶ — νουθετοῦνται | = | *Quod Deus* 64 |
| 673.3 | μέγιστον — κατορθοῦν | = | *Heres* 9 (*Harris 96.2) |
| 673.4 | ἡ Φίλωνος — ἀρετή | = | Fr. sp. 18 |
| 673.5a | τέκνων — πατέρων | = | Fr. sp. 34 |
| 673.5b | εὔπαιδες — ἐπιστήμονες | = | *Quaes Ex* 2.19 (b) (†) |
| | | | (Lewy 82.24; *Royse |
| | | | 1984, 151) |
| 673.6a | ἐκ χρυσοῦ — ἐστιν | = | Fr. sp. 8 |
| 673.6b | σκεύη μὲν — παλαιοτέρα | = | Fr. sp. 9 |
| 673.6c | οἱ μὲν — φύονται | = | Fr. sp. 10 |
| 673.6d | πολλοὶ — πλουτοῦντας | = | Fr. sp. 11 |
| 673.6e | πολλοὶ — ἕκαστον | = | Fr. sp. 12 |
| 673.7 | νεότης — κακοπραγεῖ | = | Fr. sp. 19 |
| 673.8 | οὐ τὸ — κολάσεως | = | Fr. sp. 26 |
| 673.9 | ἐλπίδα — δράσαντες | = | *Praem* 72 (†) |
| 674.1 | δοκεῖ μὲν — ἔστι | = | *Quaes Gen* 1.41 (b) (†) |
| | | | (*Wendland 140, n. 1; |
| | | | Früchtel 1937, 113, n. 1; |
| | | | Royse 1984, 149) |

674: "Ex Anonymi Collectione Florilegâ. [sic] MS. Barocc. Nº 143. in
Bibliotheca Bodleiana Oxonii":[19]

| 674.2 | ἡ πρὸς τοὺς — ποιεῖσθαι | = | unidentified (Harris 102.7) |
| 674.3 | τῶν ἀπορρήτων — ἀνατίθη | = | Fr. sp. 60 |
| 674.4 | ὁ τῶν ἀνθρώπων — πνευμάτων | = | Quaes Ex 2.55 (b) (*Harris) |
| 674.5 | φοβηθῶμεν — σώματος | = | Fr. sp. 28 |
| 674.6 | στενοχωρεῖται — διαβαίνειν | = | Quaes Gen 4.33 (a) (*Harris) |
| 674.7 | τὴν εὐταξίαν — γνωρίζομεν | = | unidentified (Harris 102.9) |
| 674.8 | ἐγχρονίζον — αὐξάνοντα | = | Dec 137 (*Harris 82.2) |

675–80: "Ex Catenâ Inedita Cod. Reg. Nº 1825. in Bibliotheca Regis
Christianissimi" ( = Par. 128):

| 675.1 | διὰ τί ἄνθρωπον — γέγονε | = | Quaes Gen 1.94 (Aucher 1826 cites on Quaes Gen 2.9; *Harris [cites also on Quaes Gen 2.9]) |
| 675.2a | οὐδὲν — τιμωρία | = | Quaes Gen 3.52 (*Harris) |
| 675.2b | οὐκ ἐπειδὴ — πληρουμένου | = | gloss to Quaes Gen 3.52 (see p. 20 above) |
| 675.3 | διὰ τί ἐξῆλθεν — ἐχόντων | = | Quaes Gen 4.51 (a) (*Aucher 1826) |
| 675.4 | κατάσκοποι — αὐτῶν | = | Quaes Gen 4.195.7* (*Harris) |
| 676.1 | αὗται αἱ — μετῴκησαν | = | gloss to Quaes Gen 4.195.7* (see p. 20 above) |
| 676.2 | οὐ διὰ τὸν — μετάνοιαν | = | Quaes Gen 4.195.8* (*Harris) |
| 676.3 | δυοῖν — κακοδαιμονέστατος | = | Quaes Gen 4.198 (*Aucher 1826) |
| 676.4a | ἄξιον καὶ — ἄξω | = | Quaes Gen 4.202 (a) (*Aucher 1826) |
| 676.4b | ἐθάρρει μὲν — θεοῦ | = | gloss to Quaes Gen 4.202 (see p. 20 above) |

---

[19]See p. 30 above.

| | | | |
|---|---|---|---|
| 676.5 | οὐκ ἐπὶ τῷ — πάτερ | = | *Quaes Gen* 4.227 |
| | | | (*Aucher 1826) |
| 676.6 | ἀλλ᾽ εἴ γε — σπουδαῖος | = | *Quaes Gen* 4.228 |
| | | | (*Aucher 1826) |
| 677.1 | τί ἐστι — δεόμενα | = | *Quaes Ex* 2.1 |
| | | | (*Aucher 1826) |
| 677.2 | ἐμφανέστατα — ὑπογράφεται | = | *Quaes Ex* 2.2 |
| | | | (*Aucher 1826) |
| 677.3 | χήραν — ἀναπληροῦσθαι | = | *Quaes Ex* 2.3 (a) |
| | | | (*Aucher 1826) |
| 677.4 | μάταιόν φησιν — ἀκοῇ | = | *Quaes Ex* 2.9 (a), (b) |
| | | | (*Aucher 1826) |
| 678.1 | πενία — ἐστι | = | *Quaes Ex* 2.10 (a), (b) |
| | | | (*Harris) |
| 678.2 | ἀντὶ τοῦ — ἔγγονα | = | *Quaes Ex* 2.14 (*Harris) |
| 678.3 | τὸ αἶμα — ὅσιον | = | *Quaes Ex* 2.14 (*Harris) |
| 678.4 | φωνὴν θεοῦ — καθαιρεῖν | = | *Quaes Ex* 2.16 (*Harris) |
| 678.5 | στῆλαί εἰσι — καλοῖς | = | *Quaes Ex* 2.17 |
| | | | (*Aucher 1826) |
| 679.1 | σύμβολον — παράπαν | = | *Quaes Ex* 2.24 (b) |
| | | | (*Aucher 1826) |
| 679.2 | ταῦτα μὲν — Βηρσαβεέ | = | gloss to *Quaes Ex* 2.25 (b) |
| | | | (see p. 21 above) |
| 679.3 | τὸ μὲν ῥητὸν — διαφωνεῖν | = | *Quaes Ex* 2.38 (a) |
| | | | (*Aucher 1826) |
| 679.4 | τοὺς ἐβδομήκοντα — ἀπελείφθη | = | gloss on Exod 24:11 |
| | | | (see p. 21 above) |
| 679.5 | ἐναργέστατα — νομοθετεῖσθαι | = | *Quaes Ex* 2.45 (a) |
| | | | (*Aucher 1826) |
| 679.6 | τὸ δὲ εἶδος — διάνοιαν | = | *Quaes Ex* 2.47 |
| | | | (*Aucher 1826) |
| 680.1 | ὅτι ἔμελλε — ἀχάριστον | = | *Quaes Ex* 2.49 (a) |
| | | | (*Aucher 1826) |

## 6. AUCHER

In Aucher's 1822 edition of the Armenian version of *Provid* and *Anim*, *Philonis Judaei sermones tres*, he includes the excerpts from *Provid* found in Eusebius, as well as one fragment (at 75, n. 2) from the *Sacra parallela* which had been printed by Mangey. No Greek fragment of *Anim* is given.

| | | |
|---|---|---|
| 45–46 | πρόνοιαν εἶναι — ταπεινοί | = *Provid* 2.3 (Mangey 634.1; Harris 75.6) |
| 53–72 | οὐ τύραννος — εἰσόμεθα | = *Provid* 2.15–33 (Mangey 634.2; Harris 75.7) |
| 75, n. 2 | οὐ θέμις — ἀμυήτοις | = unidentified (assigned to *Provid* 2.40; Mangey 651.2 [ = Mangey 658.4a, not cited by Aucher]; Harris 69.4a) |
| 80–82 | περὶ δὲ τοῦ — φύσει | = *Provid* 2.50–51 (Mangey 625.2; Harris 75.8) |
| 107–20 | ἀνέμων καὶ — πραγμάτων | = *Provid* 2.99–112 (Mangey 642.1; Harris 75.9) |

In Aucher's 1826 edition of the Armenian version of *Quaes Gen* and *Quaes Ex*, *Philonis Judaei paralipomena Armena*, he identifies fragments from thirty sections. These are (with the exception of *Quaes Gen* 1.94 [taken from Mangey 675.1, and identified as *Quaes Gen* 2.9]) placed correctly, and so no index is needed; note that four texts are printed on the unnumbered page following p. 443, which I call p. 443a, and are referred to their correct locations. A list of the texts which Aucher located is given in my "Further Greek Fragments," 143, n. 2.

# 7. MAI

Mai's 1833 edition, *Scriptorum veterum nova collectio* 7:74–109, prints some of the texts found in Vat. 1553, including many from Philo. These are listed by their location (page and column there) along with their place in the reprint in *MPG* 86.2:2017–2100.

| | | | |
|---|---|---|---|
| 95b (2061D2–64B6) | ἰδοὺ δέδωκα — γενητοῦ | = | unidentified (Harris 8.1) |
| 96a (2064C3–10) | κυρίως — ἀβέβαιον | = | *Quod Det* 136 (*Harris 82.3) |
| 96b (2065B9–11) | πολλὰ ἀσωμένοις — ἐστι | = | unidentified (Harris 74.2) |
| 98b (2069D1–3) | ἀμήχανον — σκότος | = | Fr. sp. 30 |
| 98b (2072B4–5) | πᾶσα ἡ — ξένων | = | *Quaes Gen* 3.7 (*Harris 29 [but has '§ 3' instead of '§ 7']) |
| 99a (2072D1) | μελέτη τροφός ἐστιν ἐπιστήμης | = | unidentified (Harris 69.3) |
| 99b (2073B1–3) | παιδείας — ἀμήχανον | = | *Post* 97 (*Harris 82.4) |
| 99b (2073B3–C2) | εὐήθεις — δίδωσιν | = | *Post* 141 (*Harris 82.5) |
| 99b (2073C4–7) | οὐχ ὡς — δυνάμεως | = | *Quaes Gen* 4.104 (*Harris) |
| 99b (2073C7–9) | ἀκοῦσαι — πρᾶξαι | = | *Quaes Gen* 4.110 (a) (*Harris) |
| 99b (2073C11–13) | διδάσκουσι — ἀπαγγέλλοντες | = | *Anim* 7 (*Harris 11.3) |
| 100a (2073D2–6) | ἐπίστησον — προέσθαι | = | unidentified (Harris 98.1) |
| 100a (2073D8–76A7) | ἐὰν τοῦ — ἐμποιεῖ | = | *Quaes Ex* 2.25 (b), (c), (d) (*Harris) |
| 100a (2076B6–12) | πέφυκεν — πραγμάτων | = | *Post* 24–25 (*Harris 72.2) |

| 100b (2076C1–4) | τὸ τῶν φαύλων — ἑαυταῖς | = unidentified (Harris 74.3) |
|---|---|---|
| 100b (2076D14–77A3) | τὰ αὐτὰ — πλεονεξίαν | = *Quaes Gen* 4.211 (Harris 70.5) |
| 101a (2077A13–14) | τὰ βουλήματα — ζώντων | = unidentified (Harris 74.4) |
| 101b (2080A3–B1) | εἰώθασιν — καιροί | = unidentified (Harris 70.6) |
| 101b (2080B4–11) | οἱ ἐν ταῖς — τίθενται | = *Quaes Gen* 4.43 (*Harris) |
| 102a (2080C2–3) | δόξα — ἀβέβαιος | = *Quaes Ex* 2.107 (*Harris) |
| 102a (2080C9–10) | χαίρειν — ἀνθρώπινον | = *Quaes Gen* 4.52 (b) (*Aucher 1826, 443a) |
| 102a (2080D7–9) | καθάπερ — ἀκούσια | = *Post* 11 (Harris 103.1) |
| 102a (2080D12–81A3) | ὡς τὸ — δικαιοσύνης | = *Quaes Gen* 4.64 (*Aucher 1826, 443a) |
| 102a (2081A6–8) | τρεπτοὶ — ὑπολαμβάνομεν | = unidentified (Harris 71.2) |
| 102b (2081A12–14) | ἐν νυκτὶ βουλή· — ἀπόλιπος | = unidentified (Lewy 80.16) |
| 102b (2081D1–2) | τὸ νέμειν — ἀδικίας | = *Anim* 100 (*Harris 11.4 [Mai not cited]) |
| 103a (2081D7–11) | μεταδοτέον — συγχύσεως | = *Spec Leg* 1.120 (*Harris 83.1a) |
| 103a (2081D13–14) | τὰ ὅμοια — κακῶν | = *Spec Leg* 1.121 (*Harris 83.1b) |
| 103a (2084A9–10) | τὴν καρδίαν — γραφή | = *Quaes Ex* 2.50 (a) (*Harris) |
| 103a (2084A14) | τὸ ὑποτάττεσθαι — ὠφελιμώτατον | = *Quaes Gen* 3.30 (a) (*Harris) |
| 103b (2084C7–8) | συγκρύπτεται — δοκιμώτατον | = *Quaes Gen* 3.3 (b) (†) (Harris 71.3) |
| 104a (2085A8–12) | μείζονα — πτωχεύσαντας | = unidentified (Harris 75.4) |
| 104a (2085A15–B2) | διττὸν τὸ — πίπτει | = *Quaes Gen* 2.68 (b) (*Harris) |

| | | | |
|---|---|---|---|
| 104b (2085D14–88A4) | οὐ δυναμένου — γονεῖς | = | *Quaes Ex* 2.3 (a) (*Harris) |
| 105a (2088D1) | οἴησις ἀκάθαρτον φυσᾷ [*sic*] | = | *Leg All* 1.52 (*Harris 81.2 [Mai not cited]) |
| 105b (2089B1–6) | τοὺς ἄρξαντας — πέρας | = | unidentified (Harris 71.4) |
| 105b (2089B9–14) | ἀγονίαν — διαμονήν | = | *Quaes Ex* 2.19 (a) (*Harris) |
| 105b (2089C3–10) | τὸ μὲν — παρθενίας | = | unidentified (Harris 74.5) |
| 105b (2089C13–14) | οὐχ ἧττον — ἐργάζεται | = | unidentified (Lewy 76.4) |
| 106a (2089D11–92A5) | ἄξιον ἀποδέχεσθαι — ἴσον | = | *Quaes Gen* 4.102 (a), (b), (c) (*Harris) |
| 106a (2092A7–12) | ὑπερβολαὶ — ἄγαν | = | *Quaes Ex* 1.6 (a) (*Harris) |
| 106a (2092A14–B2) | τὰ μέτρα — θρασύτητα | = | unidentified (Harris 74.6) |
| 106a (2092B12–C3) | ἡ εὐφυΐα — περικόπτειν | = | unidentified (Harris 74.7 [cites as 108]) |
| 106b (2092D1–3) | οὐ πάντα — ὀνομάτων | = | *Quaes Gen* 4.67 (*Harris) |
| 106b (2092D3–11) | τὸ δὲ — δύνανται | = | *Quaes Gen* 4.69 (*Harris) |
| 106b (2092D13–93A10) | ὥσπερ τὰς — ὑβριστής | = | *Quaes Gen* 4.204 (*Harris) |
| 106b (2093A10–B1) | λεγέτω καὶ — δρωμένων | = | *Quaes Gen* 4.206 (b) (*Harris) |
| 107a (2093B3–C5) | προσήκει — ὑπολαμβάνοντες | = | unidentified (Harris 8.2) |
| 107a (2093C9–12) | ἐν ᾗ μὲν — ὑπείληπται | = | *Quod Det* 4 (*Harris 83.3) |
| 107a (2093D2–3) | φίλων καὶ — πταίσματα | = | *Provid* 2.15 (*Harris 71.5 and n. 1) |
| 107a (2093D6–9) | ὁ εὐλαβέστερος — κακοπαθῇ | = | unidentified (Harris 71.6) |
| 107b (2096A3–4) | βασιλεὺς — εἰσηγητής | = | *Leg All* 3.79 (*Harris 83.4) |

## 8. TISCHENDORF

Tischendorf first published fragments of Philo in his *Anecdota sacra et profana* (1855), 171–74, which were reprinted in the second edition of that work (1861) without change. Although, as noted earlier (see p. 29, n. 19 [– p. 30] above), this publication has usually been ignored, it provides a fuller collection than his later book (1868), along with more details on the mysterious manuscript from which the extracts were taken.

Note that for these texts, since they are never cited anywhere else in the Philo literature, I have made cross-references merely to Tischendorf's 1868 edition or, for the unidentified texts not printed in 1868, to Harris.

171–74:

| | | |
|---|---|---|
| 171.1 | αἱ ἐκ — καλόν | = *Vita Cont* 16 ( = 1868, 152.1) |
| 171.2 | τὰ καλὰ κἂν — ἀναλάμπει | = *Vita Mos* 2.27 ( = 1868, 152.2) |
| 171.3 | μεῖζον — ζημιωθέντι | = *Quaes Gen* 4.179 ( = 1868, 152.3) |
| 172.4 | ἐγχρονίζον — συναυξάνοντα | = *Dec* 137 ( = 1868, 152.4) |
| 172.5 | οὐχ ὡς τὸ — δικαιοσύνης | = *Quaes Gen* 4.64 |
| 172.6 | οἱ ἑαυτῶν — ἐπιτηδεύουσιν | = unidentified (Harris 71.1, first part) |
| 172.7 | τοῦ φαύλου — μαχόμενα | = unidentified ( = 1868, 153.6) |
| 172.8 | φρόνησις — δεσπότας | = *Post* 138 ( + gloss) |
| 172.9 | φίλον ἡγητέον — δύνηται | = *Quaes Gen* 1.17 (a) |
| 172.10 | τοιοῦτος — ἀντιλάβωμεν | = Fr. sp. 52 ( = 1868, 153.5) |
| 172.11 | οὐδὲν οὕτως — εὐφημία | = *Quaes Ex* 2.6 (b) |
| 172.12 | ἀποστρέφου — κρείττονα | = Fr. sp. 50 |
| 172.13 | πλούτου — ἐπικουρία | = *Jos* 144 |
| 172.14 | ὁ σπουδαῖος — ἀθανασίας | = *Virt* 9 |
| 172.15 | ἀμήχανον — παιδευθῆναι | = *Vita Mos* 1.62 |
| 172.16 | ἀξίως οὐδεὶς — τούτους | = *Leg All* 3.10 |
| 172.17 | οἱ γονεῖς — ἀθανατίζουσιν | = *Spec Leg* 2.225 |
| 173.18 | τὸν ὀμνύντα — οὐδέποτε | = *Spec Leg* 2.253 |
| 173.19 | τίνα ἕτερον — δυνάμενον | = *Dec* 112 |
| 173.20 | τῷ μὲν — ἔχει | = *Flacc* 7 |

| | | |
|---|---|---|
| 173.21 | φοβηθῶμεν — σώματος | = Fr. sp. 28 |
| 173.22 | εἰκότως — ὁλοκλήρου | = unidentified (Harris 7.3) |
| 173.23 | ὁ μὲν τὸν — μακαριότητα | = *Vita Mos 2.184 |
| 173.24 | ἀναιδὲς βλέμμα — σώματι | = Quaes Gen 4.99 |
| | | ( = 1868, 154.7) |
| 173.25 | οὐκ ἔστιν — θεόν | = unidentified ( = 1868, 154.8) |
| 174.26 | οἱ ἄνθρωποι — ἀρχή | = *Praem 69 |
| 174.27 | ἡ Φίλωνος — ἀρετή | = Fr. sp. 18 |
| 174.28 | τῶν πολιτικῶν — ἔχοντα | = unidentified (Harris 7.2, first part) |
| 174.29 | ἀναισχυντία — ἀσυγκαταθέτως | = Leg All 2.65 |
| 174.30 | ἀνάγκη ἀπειρία — διασῴζεσθαι | = *Leg All 1.73 |
| 174.31 | συγγνώμην — ἀπαλλαγή | = Fr. sp. 56 |
| 174.32 | ἄτοπον γὰρ — πονηρευομένων | = Spec Leg 4.55, 63 |
| | | ( = 1868, 155.12) |
| 174.33 | δοκεῖ γάρ — λογισμοῦ | = Spec Leg 3.194 |
| | | ( = 1868, 155.13) |
| 174.34 | ἐγκρατείας — θανάτῳ | = Gaium 14 |
| | | ( = 1868, 155.11) |
| 174.35 | κακίας ἔξοδος — εἰσέρχεται | = Sacr 135 |
| | | ( = 1868, 154.9) |
| 174.36 | ὁ ἀληθείᾳ — θεωρεῖται | = Abr 271 |
| 174.37 | ὁ μὲν θεὸς — ἀναξίους | = Fr. sp. 55 ( = 1868, 155.14) |
| 174.38 | πέφυκεν — ἔχουσα | = Post 24–25 |
| 174.39 | πέφυκεν — εἶναι | = Post 24 ( = 1868, 155.15) |
| 174.40 | πλέον ἀγάπα — σκοπόν | = Fr. sp. 54 ( = 1868, 155.16) |
| 174.41 | χαίρειν ἐπὶ — ἀνθρώπινον | = Quaes Gen 4.52 (b) |
| | | ( = 1868, 154.10) |

Tischendorf's edition of 1868, *Philonea*, besides presenting a superior text of *Sacr*, gives several fragments.

From Vaticanus 379:

| | | |
|---|---|---|
| 144–52 | τίνα τὰ Χερουβὶμ — κόσμον | = *Quaes Ex 2.62–68 (Harris 63–68) |

This long excerpt from *Quaes Ex* had been previously edited by Mai, *Classicorum auctorum e Vaticanis codicibus editorum*, vol. 4 (Rome: Typis Vaticanis, 1831), 430–41, and by Grossmann, *Philonis Iudaei anecdoton Graecum de cherubinis ad Exod. 25, 18* (Leipzig: Friedrich Fleischer, 1856), 5–8.

The identification of the text was made by Mai, and then independently by Tischendorf, who, like Harris, did not know of Mai's earlier edition, but communicated his discovery to Grossmann. The text is included by Marcus, but is not found in Petit's edition of the fragments (see *Quaestiones: Fragmenta Graeca*, 13, and 273, n. a), since it represents the "tradition directe" of the text of the *Quaestiones*.

From Vaticanus 746:

| | | |
|---|---|---|
| 152 | διατί — παρανόμημα | = *Vita Mos* 2.218 (*Harris 88.3) |

This brief text had been printed by Grossmann, *Philonis anecdoton*, 8.

152-55: "Philonis sententiae":

These are said (152, n.) to be "Ex codice Cahirino saeculi decimi." This manuscript has never been identified, but is clearly a florilegium deriving from Maximus (see p. 29, n. 19 [- p. 30] above). The texts presented are fewer than half of those printed in 1855 (and 1861); the order is not the same, and Tischendorf remarks in the preface (xx): "Repetitae sunt ex Anecdotis nostris sacris et profanis, ita quidem ut non repeteremus nisi quae ab editis Mangeianis notabiliter differrent aut nondum editae viderentur."

| | | |
|---|---|---|
| 152.1 | αἱ ἐκ — καλόν | = *Vita Cont* 16 (Harris 88.4) |
| 152.2 | τὰ καλὰ κᾶν — ἀναλάμπει | = *Vita Mos* 2.27 (*Harris 89.1) |
| 152.3 | μεῖζον — ζημιωθέντι | = *Quaes Gen* 4.179 (Harris 69.2) |
| 152.4 | ἐγχρονίζον — συναυξάνοντα | = *Dec* 137 (*Harris 82.2) |
| 153.5 | τοιοῦτος — ἀντιλάβωμεν | = Fr. sp. 52 |
| 153.6 | τοῦ φαύλου — μαχόμενα | = unidentified (Harris 100.8 [first part]) |
| 154.7 | ἀναιδὲς βλέμμα — σώματι | = *Quaes Gen* 4.99 (*Aucher 1826, 443a) |
| 154.8 | οὐκ ἔστιν — θεόν | = unidentified (Harris 10.1) |
| 154.9 | κακίας ἔξοδος — εἰσέρχεται | = *Sacr* 135 (*Harris 89.2) |
| 154.10 | χαίρειν ἐπὶ — ἀνθρώπινον | = *Quaes Gen* 4.52 (b) (*Aucher 1826, 443a) |
| 155.11 | ἐγκρατείας — θανάτῳ | = *Gaium* 14 (Harris 89.4) |
| 155.12 | ἄτοπον γὰρ — πονηρευομένων | = *Spec Leg* 4.55, 63 (*Harris 89.3) |

## 9. PITRA

In his *Analecta sacra* 2 (1884), Pitra prints fragments from Coisl. 276 and from several Vatican manuscripts. Of those printed on p. xxiii, the first two are from Coisl. 276, and the latter three are from Vat. Reg. 77.

xxiii:

| | | |
|---|---|---|
| xxiii.I | τῷ μὲν ᾿Αβραὰμ — σκότει | = *Quaes Gen* 4.30 (*Harris) |
| xxiii.II | αἱ τοῦ θεοῦ — ἐφιέμεναι | = *Quaes Ex* 2.65 (*Harris) |
| xxiii.III | ἐσχάρα ἄνθραξι — μάχης | = Fr. sp. 20 |
| xxiii.IV | τοῦ πυρὸς — ἀνακαίεται | = *Sobr* 43 (*Harris 84.1) |
| xxiii.V | τὴν — ἀποτίθεσθαι | = Fr. sp. 32 |

304–10: "Fragmenta Coisliniana" (from Coisl. 276):

| | | |
|---|---|---|
| 304.I | ἡ πρότασις — βεβαιοτάτου | = *Quaes Gen* 2.54 (a) (*Harris) |
| 305.II | ἴδιον θεοῦ — χειρός | = *Vita Mos* 1.174 (*Harris 84.3) |
| 305.III | οὐχ ὡς πέφυκεν — αὐτῶν | = *Op* 23 (*Harris 84.2) |
| 306.IV | θεοῦ ἴδιον — ἐπάγειν | = *Leg All* 3.105 (*Harris 84.4) |
| 306.V[20] | οὐδὲ τοῖς — ἐπανόρθωσιν | = *Leg All* 3.106 (*Harris 80.1) |
| 306.VI | ἀναζητοῦσιν — αὐτῆς | = *Post* 21 (*Harris 84.5) |
| 306.VII | τὸ σὺν θεῷ — φευκτόν | = *Cher* 24 (*Harris 84.6) |
| 306.VIII | οὐ πάντα — σταθμᾶται | = *Post* 142, 142–43, 145 (*Harris 84.7) |
| 307.IX | οὐκ ἐν χρόνῳ — χρόνου | = *Post* 14 (*Harris 85.1) |
| 307.X | τί οὖν — ἐγχειρήσεως | = unidentified (Harris 71.7) |

---

[20]Pitra adds (306, n.): "Lemma videtur elegantissimae Philonis homiliae in Jonam, servatae ab Armenis . . . ."

| 307.XI | ὡς ἀμέτοχος — θεός | = *Quaes Gen* 1.100 (c) (*Harris) |
|---|---|---|
| 307.XII | οὐ πάντων — θέμις | = unidentified (Harris 75.1) |
| 308.XIII | οὔτε πλοῦτον — ἀποστρέφεται | = *Quaes Ex* 2.99 (*Harris) |
| 308.XIV[21] | ψυχαὶ δέ — κηδεμονίας | =* *Quaes Ex* 2.3 (b) |
| 308.XV[22] | φθαρτὸν καλῶ — βίος | = unidentified (Harris 75.2) |
| 308.XVIa | ἄγευστον — σπανιώτατον | = *Sacr* 111 (*Harris 85.2) |
| 308.XVIb | ἀδύνατον — ἐνδεδεμένον | = *Mut* 36 (*Harris 85.3) |
| 309.XVII | ἀδύνατον οἶμαι — δοκῇ | = Fr. sp. 31 |
| 309.XVIII | οὐ δύναται — αὐτομολοῦμεν | = *Ebr* 56–58 (*Harris 85.4) |
| 309.XIX | οὐχ ἃ δοῦναι — δωρεάς | = *Mut* 218 (*Harris 85.5) |
| 309.XX | οὐ λήψῃ — παρήγγειλεν | = *Dec* 82–83 (*Harris 85.6) |
| 310.XXI | τίνας γὰρ — ἐλπίζομεν | = unidentified (Harris 11.1) |
| 310.XXII | οὐκ ἔστι — θεόν | = unidentified (Harris 10.1) |
| 310.XXIII | αὐτὸς πάντα — μόνος | = Fr. sp. 27 |

310–14: "Fragmenta Vaticana" (from various Vatican manuscripts):

| 310.Ia | ζητοῦσιν βρῶσιν — οὐρανοῖς | = Fr. sp. 33 |
|---|---|---|
| 310.Ib | ὥσπερ γὰρ — σκεδάννυσιν | = *Leg All* 1.46 (Harris 103.3b) |
| 310.Ic | καὶ τὰ τῶν παθῶν θηρία κοιμίζει | = gloss to *Leg All* 1.46 (Harris 103.3c) |
| 311.II | λέγω δὲ — ζῶσιν | = *Quod Omn* 4–5 (*Harris 87.1) |
| 311.IIIa | οὐ παντὸς — θεοφιλοῦς | = *Leg All* 2.79 (*Harris 87.2) |
| 311.IIIb | ἡδονῇ ἐναντίον — ἀρετή | = *Leg All* 2.79 (*Harris 87.3) |
| 311.IV | ὄντως ὑπὸ — εὐδαιμονήσει | = *Leg All* 2.101, 102 (*Harris 87.4) |
| 311.V | καὶ τὸ ῥητὸν — λαβόντων | = *Quaes Gen* 4.168 (*Harris) |

---

[21]Pitra (308, n.) identifies the page in Aucher (470) for *Quaes Ex* 2.3 (and cites some of the Latin), but refers to the section as "cap. 4," having seen that 2.4 begins at the bottom of that page.

[22]This text is ascribed to the last book of *Quaes Ex*; Pitra (308, n.) inexplicably says: "Etiam apud Armenos, quaestionum in Exodum sunt libri tres Philoniani."

| | | | |
|---|---|---|---|
| 312.VIa | ἐὰν ἄρτι — αἴτιον | = | *Quaes Ex* 2.25 (b), (c) (*Harris) |
| 312.VIb | πρὸς τούτοις — ἐχθρῷ | = | gloss to *Quaes Ex* 2.25 (a) (see p. 20 above) |
| 313.VII[23] | τὸ μὲν ῥητὸν — προσγενομένης | = | *Quaes Ex* 2.21 |
| 313.VIII | θεοπρεπῶς — δίκαιον | = | *Quaes Gen* 2.15 (b) (*Harris) |
| 313.IX[24] | αἱ μὲν γὰρ — ἐπιθυμιῶν | = | *Quaes Ex* 1.19 |
| 313.X | ἔτι ἐν τῷ — σωτήριον | = | *Sobr* 49–50 (*Harris 87.5) |
| 314.XI | δεῖ γὰρ — δῶρα | = | *Quaes Gen* 4.130 (*Harris) |

---

[23]Pitra (313, n.) refers to the page in Aucher (483) for this section.

[24]Pitra (313, n.) merely says: "Idem fere armenice exstat l. l." (i.e., 483 as on no. VII). I suppose that he thought that this was a close enough reference, although the Armenian is actually on p. 462.

## 10. HARRIS

Harris's edition, *Fragments* (1886), brought together most (but not all) of the previously printed fragments, added some further fragments, and for most of those he printed gave the correct locations either in the works preserved in Greek or in the Armenian version of Philo.

6–8: Fragments of the lost *Leg All* 4:

| | | | |
|---|---|---|---|
| 6.1 | πάντων μέν — κύριον | = | unidentified (Mangey 648.1; Petit QE no. 16) |
| 7.1 | ἀμήχανον — σκότος | = | Fr. sp. 30 |
| 7.2 | τῶν πολιτικῶν — φρονεῖν | = | unidentified (Mangey 661.1) |
| 7.3 | εἰκότως — ὁλοκλήρου | = | unidentified (Mangey 667.6) |
| 7.4 | φασί τινες — ἡττᾶσθαι | = | unidentified (Mangey 668.1) |
| 8.1 | ἰδοὺ δέδωκα — γενητοῦ | = | unidentified (Mai 95b; see p. 9, n. 42, above) |
| 8.2 | προσήκει — ὑπολαμβάνοντες | = | unidentified (Mai 107a) |
| 8.3 | τῆς εὐδαιμονίας — θεοῦ | = | unidentified (Mangey 668.8) |

9: Fragments of the lost portion of *Gig*:

| | | | |
|---|---|---|---|
| 9.1 | ἀδύνατον οἶμαι — δοκῇ | = | Fr. sp. 31 |
| 9.2 | ἀνδρείας ἐστὶ — θάρσος | = | Fr. sp. 6 |
| 9.3 | πέφυκε τοῖς — φθόνος | = | Fr. sp. 25 |
| 9.4 | τῆς ψυχῆς — δέξασθαι | = | *Quod Deus* 46–47 (Harris refers to *De mundo*; Harris 95.1; *Massebieau) |
| 9.5 | τῷ ἄριστα — ἐντυγχάνοντας | = | *Quod Deus* 61 (*PCW*) |

10: Fragments of the lost portion of *Flacc*:

| | | | |
|---|---|---|---|
| 10.1 | οὐκ ἔστι — θεόν | = | unidentified (Mangey 649.1; Tischendorf 154.8; Pitra 310.XXII; *PCW* 6:l) |

10.2    αἰσχροὶ — προχειρότατοι        = *Flacc* 34 (Mangey 650.3;
                                              *\*PCW*)

10–11: Fragments of the lost book περὶ εὐσεβείας:

10.3    τοῦ μὴ προθύμως — αἰώνιος      = unidentified (Mangey 667.7)
10.4    ὡς ἂν ἔχουσιν — ἐστι           = unidentified
11.1    τίνας γὰρ — ἐλπίζομεν          = unidentified (Pitra 310.XXI)

11: Fragments of *Anim*:

11.2    τὸ ζητεῖν — ἀνυσιμώτατον       = *\*Anim* 6 (Mangey 651.9)
11.3    διδάσκουσι — ἀπαγγέλλοντες     = *\*Anim* 7 (Mai 99b)
11.4    τὸ νέμειν — ἀδικίας            = *\*Anim* 100 (Mangey 651.4;
                                              Mai 102b [not cited])

12–46: Identified fragments of *Quaes Gen*

47–68: Identified fragments of *Quaes Ex*

69–72: Unidentified fragments of *Quaes Gen*:

69.1    τῶν φαύλων — πένητες           = unidentified (Mangey 649.5a;
                                              Marcus QG no. 1; Petit
                                              QG no. 11)
69.2    μεῖζον — ζημιωθέντι            = *Quaes Gen* 4.179 (Mangey
                                              649.6; Tischendorf
                                              152.3; *\*Bréhier; Früch-
                                              tel 1937, no. 1)
69.3    μελέτη τροφὸς ἐπιστήμης        = unidentified (Mangey 650.8;
                                              Mai 99a; Marcus QG
                                              no. 2; Petit QG no. 4)
69.4a   οὐ θέμις — ἀμυήτοις            = unidentified (Mangey 651.2,
                                              658.4a; Aucher 1822,
                                              75, n. 2 [assigns to
                                              *Provid* 2.40]; cited by
                                              Marcus as *Quaes Gen*
                                              4.8 [from Harris 69.4c];
                                              Petit 147, n. b, and QG
                                              no. 2a; see pp. 6–8
                                              above)

| 69.4b | ἄχρις ἂν — ἀμώμητα | = | unidentified (Mangey 658.4b; cited by Marcus as *Quaes Gen* 4.8 [from Harris 69.4c]; Petit 147, n. b, and QG no. 2b) |
| 69.4c | τοῖς ἀμυήτοις — τελετῆς | = | *Quaes Gen* 4.8 (c) (Mangey 658.4c; *Bréhier; Früchtel 1937, no. 2) |
| 69.5 | ὥσπερ κίονες — γένος | = | unidentified (Mangey 655.1, 662.4; Marcus QG no. 3; Petit QG no. 1) |
| 69.6 | ἐάν τις — ὠφέλειαν | = | *Somn* 1.177, 176 (Mangey 655.2; *PCW*; Früchtel 1937, 112; Marcus QG no. 4; Petit QE no. 28) |
| 69.7 | οὕτως γὰρ — λέγεται | = | *Quaes Gen* 4.74 (Mangey 656.1; *Früchtel 1937, no. 3) |
| 69.8 | ἀνθρώποις — ἐχθρῶν | = | *Quod Deus* 27 (Mangey 657.5; *PCW*; Früchtel 1937, 112; Marcus QG no. 5) |
| 70.1 | τὸ ἐπαισθάνεσθαι — ἀνδρός | = | unidentified (Mangey 658.2; Marcus QG no. 6; Petit QG no. 12) |
| 70.2 | ἐπειδὴ πρὸς — ὁδηγίαν | = | unidentified (Mangey 666.7; Marcus QG no. 7; Petit QG no. 15) |
| 70.3 | ἐν θεῷ — μεμαθημένως | = | unidentified (Mangey 667.1; Marcus QG no. 8; Petit QG no. 16) |
| 70.4 | ἀμήχανον — σῴζει | = | *Quaes Gen* 2.34 (b), (c) (Mangey 669.1; *Früchtel 1937, no. 4) |
| 70.5 | τὰ αὐτὰ — πλεονεξίαν | = | *Quaes Gen* 4.211 (Mai 100b; *Bréhier; Früchtel 1937, no. 5) |
| 70.6 | εἰώθασιν — καιροί | = | unidentified (Mai 101b; Marcus QG no. 9; Petit QG no. 5) |
| 70.7 | τὸ ἐπιορκεῖν — | = | unidentified (Mangey 659.5; |

|       | ἀλυσιτελέστατον | Marcus QG no. 10; Petit QG no. 14) |
|-------|----------------|-----------------------------------|
| 70.8  | οὐδὲν ἐναντίον — ἀδικία | = *Quaes Gen* 1.100 (a) (Mangey 655.4; *Früchtel 1937, no. 6) |
| 71.1  | οἱ ἑαυτῶν — θεοφιλής | = unidentified (Mangey 662.1; Mai 108b; Marcus QG no. 11; Petit QG no. 10; see p. 9, n. 41, above) |
| 71.2  | τρεπτοὶ — ὑπολαμβάνομεν | = unidentified (Mai 102a; Marcus QG no. 12; Petit QG no. 6) |
| 71.3  | συγκρύπτεται — δοκιμώτατον | = *Quaes Gen* 3.3 (b) (†) (Mai 103b; Marcus QG no. 13; Petit QG no. 7; *Früchtel MS; Royse 1984, 150) |
| 71.4  | τοὺς ἄρξαντας — πέρας | = unidentified (Mai 105b; Marcus QG no. 14; Petit QG no. 8) |
| 71.5  | φίλων καὶ — πταίσματα | = *Provid* 2.15 (Mai 107a; Wendland 1892, 88, no. 2; see Harris's n. 1) |
| 71.6  | ὁ εὐλαβέστερος — κακοπαθῇ | = unidentified (Mai 107a; Marcus QG no. 15; Petit QG no. 9) |
| 71.7  | τί οὖν — ἐγχειρήσεως | = unidentified (Pitra 307.X; Marcus QG no. 16; Petit QG no. 3) |
| 72.1  | τὰ γὰρ τοῦ — ἐστίν | = unidentified (Cramer 1843, 549 [Harris cites as 580]; Marcus QG no. 17; Petit QG no. 17; perhaps from *Quaes Gen* on Gen 14:20: see p. 21, and p. 34, n. 42, above) |
| 72.2  | πέφυκεν — πραγμάτων | = *Post* 24–25 (Mai 100a) |

72–75: Unidentified fragments of *Quaes Ex*:

|       |                          |   |                                                                                                                  |
|-------|--------------------------|---|------------------------------------------------------------------------------------------------------------------|
|       |                          |   | 55, n. 2; Marcus QE no. 8; Petit QE no. 33)                                                                       |
| 73.8  | αἱ τοῦ θεοῦ — ἀπόλαυσιν   | = | *Quaes Ex* 2.71 (Mangey 660.2; Marcus QE no. 9; *Früchtel MS; *Petit)                                            |
| 73.9  | μυρία γε — νοῦν           | = | unidentified (Mangey 662.2; Marcus QE no. 10; Petit QE no. 2)                                                     |
| 73.10 | μία ἀνάπαυσις — πράξεων   | = | unidentified (Mangey 669.3; Marcus QE no. 11a; Petit QE no. 11)                                                   |
| 74.1  | πέρας εὐδαιμονίας — στῆναι | = | unidentified (Mangey 669.4; Marcus QE no. 11b; Petit QE no. 12)                                                  |
| 74.2  | πολλὰ ἀσωμένοις — ἐστιν   | = | unidentified (Mai 96b; Marcus QE no. 12; Petit QE no. 17)                                                         |
| 74.3  | τὸ τῶν φαύλων — ἑαυταῖς   | = | unidentified (Mai 100b; Marcus QE no. 13; Petit QE no. 18)                                                        |
| 74.4  | τὰ βουλήματα — ζώντων     | = | unidentified (Mai 101a; Marcus QE no. 14; Petit QE no. 19)                                                        |
| 74.5  | τὸ μὲν — παρθενίας        | = | unidentified (Mai 105b; Marcus QE no. 15; Petit QE no. 22; perhaps from *Quaes Ex* on Exod 13:2: see p. 34, n. 42, above) |
| 74.6  | τὰ μέτρα — θρασύτητα      | = | unidentified (Mai 106a; Marcus QE no. 16; Petit QE no. 24)                                                        |
| 74.7  | ἡ εὐφυΐα — περικόπτειν    | = | unidentified (Mai 106a [Harris cites as 108]; Marcus QE no. 17; Petit QE no. 25)                                  |
| 74.8  | ὁ σοφιστικός — σημεῖα     | = | unidentified (Mai 108a [Harris cites as 106]; Marcus QE no. 18; Petit QE no. 26)                                  |

| 74.9 | ὅρασις παρὰ — εἰσδύεται | = unidentified (Mai 109b; Marcus QE no. 19; Petit QE no. 21) |
| 75.1 | οὐ πάντων — θέμις | = unidentified (Mangey 658.5b; Pitra 307.XII; Marcus QE no. 20; Petit QE no. 14) |
| 75.2 | φθαρτὸν καλῶ — βίος | = unidentified (Pitra 308.XV; Marcus QE no. 21; Petit QE no. 15) |
| 75.3 | μάταιον οὐδὲν — ζημίαι | = *Quaes Ex* 2.9 (a) (*Früchtel 1937, 109; Marcus QE no. 22) |

75: Unidentified fragments of the (supposed) *Quaestiones* on Leviticus:

| 75.4 | μείζονα — πτωχεύσαντας | = unidentified (Mai 104a) |
| 75.5 | ὡς δεινὸν — παραδοθέν | = unidentified (Mai 109a) |

75: References to the fragments of *Provid* in Eusebius (Greek not cited):

| 75.6 | πρόνοιαν εἶναι — ταπεινοί | = *Provid* 2.3 (Mangey 634.1; *Aucher 1822) |
| 75.7 | οὐ τύραννος — εἰσόμεθα | = *Provid* 2.15–33 (Mangey 634.2; *Aucher 1822) |
| 75.8 | περὶ δὲ τοῦ — φύσει | = *Provid* 2.50–51 (Mangey 625.2; *Aucher 1822) |
| 75.9 | ἀνέμων καὶ — πραγμάτων | = *Provid* 2.99–112 (Mangey 642.1; *Aucher 1822) |

76: Other fragments of *Provid*:

| 76.1 | ὠμῆς γὰρ — κακία | = *Provid* 2.31 (Mangey 642, n. x, cites; Wendland 1892, 88, no. 3) |
| 76.2 | ἀεὶ πρὸς — κρειττόνων | = *Provid* 2.39 (*Wendland 1892, 88, no. 5) |
| 76.3 | βασιλεῖ — πατρός | = *Provid* 2.15 (Mangey 635, n. b, cites; Wendland 1892, 88, no. 1) |

76–77:  Fragments of *Hyp* (and *Apol*):

| 76.4 | φίλαυτον γυνὴ — παραλῦσαι | = * *Hyp* |
|------|--------------------------|-----------|
| 76.5 | φίλαυτον γυνὴ — πράττειν | = * *Hyp* |
| 77.1 | οὐκ ἐπὶ φιλίας — χάριτος | = unidentified |

77–82:  Identified texts from the *Sacra parallela*:

| 77.2 | εἰ βούλει — θεοῦ | = unidentified (Mangey 648.2) |
|------|-----------------|------------------------------|
| 77.3 | φοβηθῶμεν — σώματος | = * Fr. sp. 28 |
| 77.4 | ὅταν ἄνθρωπος — ᾅδου | = Fr. sp. 49 |
| 78.1 | ὁ νοῦς — ἀψευδέστατος | = * *Post* 59 (Mangey 649.2) |
| 78.2 | εἰρήνη κἂν — πολέμου | = * *Spec Leg* 4.221 |
| 78.3 | ὦ πόσα — φόβοι | = * *Gaium* 17 (Mangey 649.4) |
| 78.4 | ἃ πρέσβεις — ἀναφοράν | = * *Gaium* 369 |
| 78.5 | νόσου — ἀπαιδευσία | = *Ebr* 141 (Harris refers to *Ebr* 12; Mangey 649.7; Wendland 20.1a [refers to *Ebr* 12]; *PCW*) |
| 78.6 | τὰ μὴ σὺν — κόσμια | = * *Leg All* 3.158 (Mangey 650.4) |
| 78.7 | χωρὶς θεωρίας — καλόν | = * *Praem* 51 (Mangey 671.5a; Harris 94.4, 96.1 [last part]) |
| 78.8 | ἐπιστήμη — καλόν | = unidentified (Mangey 671.5b) |
| 79.1a | ἡ συνεχὴς — ἀμελετησία | = * *Sacr* 86 (Mangey 650.7a) |
| 79.1b | καὶ πάλιν — τριβή | = unidentified (Mangey 650.7b; Lewy 82.22) |
| 79.2 | μυρίοι γοῦν — ἐξέλυσαν | = * *Sacr* 86 |
| 79.3 | εἴ τις πάσας — τυγχάνοι | = unidentified (Mangey 650.11) |
| 79.4 | τῷ μὲν — δικαστηρίῳ | = * *Flacc* 7 (Harris 94.7) |
| 79.5 | λάλει ἃ δεῖ — ἃ μὴ δεῖ | = * Fr. sp. 41 |
| 79.6 | χρόνου φείδεσθαι καλόν | = *Vita Cont* 16 (Mangey 651.7; *Tischendorf 152.1 [last part]; cf. Harris 88.4) |
| 79.7 | οὐκ ἂν εἴποι — κολακεία | = * *Leg All* 3.182 |
| 79.8 | τὰς τῶν — πλεῖστοι | = * *Gaium* 140 |
| 80.1 | τοῖς — ἐπανόρθωσιν | = * *Leg All* 3.106 (Pitra 306.V) |
| 80.2 | θεοῦ ἴδιον — ἐπάγειν | = * *Leg All* 3.105 (Harris 84.4) |

| 80.3 | τῷ ὄντι — μετιών | = *Abr 272, 274 |
| 80.4 | ἡ κόλασις — παθεῖν | = *Gaium 7 (Mangey 652.6) |
| 80.5 | τὸ εἰδέναι — δικαιοσύνης | = unidentified (Mangey 651.11; see p. 39, no. 1, above) |
| 81.1 | βλαβεραὶ — εἴδωλα | = *Fuga 14 (Mangey 652.7, 671.3a) |
| 81.2 | οἴησις ἀκάθαρτον φύσει | = *Leg All 1.52 (Mangey 652.10, 668.2; Mai 105a [not cited]) |
| 81.3 | χαλεπὸν — φύσει | = *Sacr 114 (†) |
| 81.4 | ἄτοπόν ἐστι — γίνεσθαι | = Fr. sp. 40 |
| 81.5 | νεότης — γίνεται | = *Gaium 190 |
| 81.6 | ἀσθενέστεραι — καταλαβεῖν | = *Gaium 319 |
| 81.7 | οὐ πάντα — γνώριμα | = *Op 61 (Mangey 661.6) |
| 82.1 | βέλτιον — ἡσυχία | = *Vita Mos 1.285 (Mangey 661.8) |

82: Identified text edited by Mangey from Barocc. 143:

| 82.2 | ἐγχρονίζον — αὐξάνοντα | = *Dec 137 (Mangey 674.8; Tischendorf 152.4) |

82–83: Identified texts edited by Mai:

| 82.3 | κυρίως — ἀβέβαιον | = *Quod Det 136 (Mai 96a) |
| 82.4 | παιδείας — ἀμήχανον | = *Post 97 (Mai 99b) |
| 82.5 | εὐήθεις — δίδωσιν | = *Post 141 (Mai 99b) |
| 83.1a | μεταδοτέον — συγχύσεως | = *Spec Leg 1.120 (Mai 103a) |
| 83.1b | τὰ ὅμοια — κακῶν | = *Spec Leg 1.121 (Mai 103a) |
| 83.2 | εἰ γὰρ ἴσον — κακῶν | = *Spec Leg 1.121 (not in Mai; follows Harris 83.1a in Par. 923) |
| 83.3 | ἐν ᾗ μὲν — ὑπείληπται | = *Quod Det 4 (Mai 107a) |
| 83.4 | βασιλεὺς — εἰσηγητής | = *Leg All 3.79 (Mai 107b) |
| 83.5 | πάνυ εὐήθεις — ὑφηγητήν | = *Post 152 (Mai 107b) |

83–88: Identified texts edited by Pitra:

| 83.6 | ἐσχάρα ἄνθραξι — μάχης | = *Fr. sp. 20 |
| 84.1 | τοῦ πυρὸς — ἀνακαίεται | = *Sobr 43 (Pitra xxiii.IV) |
| 84.2 | οὐχ ὡς πέφυκεν — αὐτῶν | = *Op 23 (Pitra 305.III) |

| | | |
|---|---|---|
| 84.3 | ἴδιον θεοῦ — χειρός | = *Vita Mos 1.174 (Pitra 305.II) |
| 84.4 | θεοῦ ἴδιον — ἐπάγειν | = *Leg All 3.105 (Pitra 306.IV; Harris 80.2) |
| 84.5 | ἀναζητοῦσιν — αὑτῆς | = *Post 21 (Pitra 306.VI) |
| 84.6 | τὸ σὺν θεῷ — φευκτόν | = *Cher 24 (Pitra 306.VII) |
| 84.7 | οὐ πάντα — σταθμᾶται | = *Post 142, 142–43, 145 (Pitra 306.VIII) |
| 85.1 | οὐκ ἐν χρόνῳ — χρόνου | = *Post 14 (Pitra 307.IX) |
| 85.2 | ἄγευστον — σπανιώτατον | = *Sacr 111 (Pitra 308.XVIa) |
| 85.3 | ἀδύνατον — ἐνδεδεμένον | = *Mut 36 (Pitra 308.XVIb) |
| 85.4 | οὐ δύναται — αὐτομολοῦμεν | = *Ebr 56–58 (Pitra 309.XVIII; Wendland 21.4a) |
| 85.5 | οὐχ ἃ δοῦναι — δωρεάς | = *Mut 218 (Pitra 309.XIX) |
| 85.6 | οὐ λήψῃ — παρήγγειλεν | = *Dec 82–83 (Pitra 309.XX) |
| 85.7 | αὐτὸς πάντα — μόνος | = *Fr. sp. 27 |
| 87.1 | λέγω δὲ — ζῶσιν | = *Quod Omn 4–5 (Pitra 311.II) |
| 87.2 | οὐ παντὸς — θεοφιλοῦς | = *Leg All 2.79 (Pitra 311.IIIa) |
| 87.3 | ἡδονῇ ἐναντίον — ἀρετή | = *Leg All 2.79 (Pitra 311.IIIb) |
| 87.4 | ὄντως ὑπὸ — εὐδαιμονήσει | = *Leg All 2.101, 102 (Pitra 311.IV) |
| 87.5 | ἔτι ἐν τῷ — σωτήριον | = *Sobr 49–50 (Pitra 313.X) |
| 87.6 | ἀμήχανον — παιδευθῆναι | = *Vita Mos 1.62 (Pitra 348 [ascribed to Clement]) |
| 88.1 | ὅσον δοκεῖ — ἐλπίδα | = *Dec 113 (Mangey 670.8; Pitra 349 [ascribed to Clement]) |
| 88.2 | μηδαμῶς — ποιεῖ | = unidentified (Pitra 349 [ascribed to Clement]; Harris 105.4; see p. 40, no. 2, above) |

88–89: Identified texts edited by Tischendorf (1868):

| | | |
|---|---|---|
| 88.3 | διατί — παρανόμημα | = *Vita Mos 2.218 (Tischendorf 152) |
| 88.4 | αἱ ἐκ — καλόν | = Vita Cont 16 (*Tischendorf 152.1; cf. Harris 79.6) |
| 89.1 | τὰ καλὰ κἂν — ἀναλάμπει | = *Vita Mos 2.27 (Mangey 672.7; Tischendorf 152.2) |

| 89.2 | κακίας ἔξοδος — εἰσέρχεται | = *Sacr* 135 (Tischendorf 154.9) |
| 89.3 | ἄτοπον γὰρ — πονηρευομένων | = *Spec Leg* 4.55, 63 (Tischen-dorf 155.12) |
| 89.4 | ἐγκρατείας — θανάτῳ | = *Gaium* 14 (*Tischendorf 155.11) |
| 89.5 | πέφυκεν — εἶναι | = *Post* 24 (Tischendorf 155.15) |

89–95: Further identified texts found in Par. 923:

| 89.6 | καλὸν οὐδὲν — ἐπινοίαις | = *Op* 28 |
| 89.7 | τὰ κατὰ γαστρὸς — δυναμένων | = *Op* 124 |
| 90.1 | τοῦ τεχνίτου — ἡμῶν | = *Op* 135 |
| 90.2 | ὁ δημιουργὸς — μίμημα | = *Op* 138, 139 |
| 90.3 | ὁ νοῦς — ἀσώματον | = *Leg All* 1.91 |
| 90.4 | σπάνιον — ἀναρίθμητον | = *Leg All* 1.102 |
| 90.5 | πάντα πεπλήρωκεν — πανταχοῦ | = *Leg All* 3.4 |
| 90.6 | ἀξίως γὰρ — τούτους | = *Leg All* 3.10 |
| 90.7 | εἰ ζητεῖς — ἀναζήτει | = *Leg All* 3.47 |
| 90.8 | ἡ χαρὰ — χαρά | = *Leg All* 3.86 |
| 91.1 | μόνος — δεσπότας | = *Post* 138 |
| 91.2 | ἐσταλμένον — ἀγαθόν | = *Ebr* 26 (Wendland 21.2b) |
| 91.3 | γίνεται θηρίον — εἶναι | = *Ebr* 174 (Wendland 21.7) |
| 91.4 | πότε ἄγει — ἐβασίλευσε | = *Heres* 6–7 |
| 91.5 | φησὶν ὁ νομοθέτης — τούτου | = *Heres* 56–58 |
| 91.6 | μυρίοι — καταχρησάμενοι | = *Heres* 105 |
| 92.1 | οἱ πιθανῶν — συνεπιγράφεται | = *Heres* 302, 303 |
| 92.2 | κύριος — ἡγεμών | = *Mut* 22 |
| 92.3 | τῷ Ἀβραὰμ — γενομένου | = *Mut* 39–40, 42, 45 |
| 92.4 | τοῦ κατ' ἀρετὴν — ζῆσαι | = *Mut* 213 |
| 92.5 | χαλεπὸν — βλαβερώτερον | = *Mut* 239–40, 243 |
| 92.6 | ἀνθεῖ πρὸς — μαραίνονται | = *Somn* 1.11 (see pp. 45–46 above) |
| 93.1 | ὁ ἀληθείᾳ — παιδευθέντας | = *Abr* 271 |
| 93.2 | πλούτου — ἐπικουρίᾳ | = *Jos* 144 |
| 93.3 | οἱ ξένοι — γραφέσθωσαν | = *Vita Mos* 1.35 |
| 93.4 | ὀλισθηραὶ — ἐνσφραγιζόμεναι | = *Vita Mos* 1.230 |
| 93.5 | τιμὴ τίς ἂν — τίμιον | = *Dec* 6 |
| 93.6 | πλάνος τις — παρεκαλύψαντο | = *Dec* 52–53 |
| 93.7 | ὁ ἑκάστῃ ψυχῇ — ἀπορρήξῃ | = *Dec* 87 |
| 94.1 | οἶδά τινας — ἀσέβειαν | = *Dec* 94 |
| 94.2 | ὁ φαῦλος — τείνει | = *Virt* 9 |

| 94.3 | ὁ σπουδαῖος — ἀθανασίας | = *Virt 9 |
| 94.4 | χωρὶς θεωρίας — καλόν | = *Praem 51 (Mangey 671.5a; Harris 78.7, 96.1 [last part]) |
| 94.5 | παντὸς — φαντασιούμενον | = *Praem 63 |
| 94.6 | οἷς ὁ ἀληθινὸς — κτῆσις | = *Praem 104–5 |
| 94.7 | τῷ μὲν — δικαστηρίῳ | = *Flacc 7 (Harris 79.4) |
| 94.8 | οὐδεὶς — δεσπότῃ | = *Gaium 233 |
| 94.9 | οὐκ ἀσφαλὲς — πράγματα | = Gaium 247 (Harris 109.4; *PCW) |
| 95.1 | τῆς ψυχῆς — δέξασθαι | = Quod Deus 46–47 (Harris refers to De mundo; Harris 9.4; *Massebieau) |

95: Identified text edited by Cramer (see under Fr. sp. 7 above):

| 95.2 | ἀναισχυντία — ἀσυγκαταθέτως | = Leg All 2.65 (Mangey 672.4; *Mangey 692 [not cited]; Cramer 1837, 254) |

95–97: Identified texts from Antonius:

| 95.3 | ἡ θεωρία — περιμάχητος | = *Leg All 1.58 (Mangey 670.3b) |
| 95.4 | δεσμὸς — μετάγουσαι | = *Gaium 72 |
| 95.5 | τὸ μὲν μηδὲν — ἔρχεται | = *Virt 177 |
| 95.6 | ὥσπερ — φύσεως | = *Somn 1.176 |
| 95.7 | βασιλεῦ — εὐεργετεῖν | = *Gaium 50 |
| 95.8 | ὅταν — ἀνερεθίζεσθαι | = *Flacc 17 |
| 95.9 | ὅπερ, οἶμαι — ἀθανατίζουσιν | = *Spec Leg 2.225 |
| 95.10 | οἱ γονέων — ἀνθρώπους | = *Dec 110 |
| 96.1 | μετὰ τὸν — καλόν | = *Praem 51 (last part is Harris 78.7, 94.4) |
| 96.2 | μέγιστον — κατορθοῦν | = *Heres 9 (Mangey 673.3) |
| 96.3 | τῶν φαύλων — βίον | = *Mut 169 |
| 96.4 | ἐγὼ οὖν — δωρούμενον | = *Sacr 124 |
| 96.5 | δεινὸν — γίνεται | = *Gaium 39 |
| 96.6 | ἀνώμαλον — καθελών | = *Somn 1.150–52 |
| 96.7 | ἀρχήν, εἰ δεῖ — δεδώρηται | = *Sacr 35, 40 |

96.8    ὁ μὲν — μακαριότητα           = *Vita Mos 2.184
97.1    ὅρκος — ἀμφισβητουμένου       = Dec 86 (†) (Harris cites as
                                           Leg All 3.205; PCW
                                           cites as Spec Leg 2.10;
                                           see the note on
                                           Antonius, Gessner 129
                                           [MPG 136:1156D2–3],
                                           above; cf. Harris 110.3)
97.2    ἐκ πολυορκίας — φύεται        = *Dec 92
97.3    φασί τινες — ὑπονοεῖται       = *Dec 84
97.4    μαρτυρία — ἀνοσιώτατον        = *Dec 86
97.5    τὸν ὀμνύντα — τιμωρίας        = *Spec Leg 2.253 (Mangey
                                           672.6)
97.6    δυσεύρετον — καλόν            = *Fuga 153 (Mangey 671.6b)
97.7    ἐπειδήπερ — θεός              = *Cher 98 (Mangey 672.5a)
97.8    οἶκος θεοῦ — βασιλείῳ         = *Praem 123 (Mangey 672.5b)
97.9    ὀφθαλμοῖς — μέλλοντα          = *Gaium 2 (Mangey 672.5c)

97–99: Remaining texts edited by Lequien from Vat. 1236:

97.10   μακαρία — γινομένοις         = Quaes Gen 3.38 (b) (Mangey
                                           650.1; *Früchtel 1937,
                                           no. 7)
97.11   ἀκύμαντος λιμὴν πολιά        = Fr. sp. 47
97.12   σώματος — παθῶν              = unidentified (Mangey 650.6;
                                           see p. 33 above)
98.1    ἐπίστησον — σοφίας           = unidentified (Mai 100a)
98.2    διάβολοι — ἀλλότριοι         = unidentified (Mangey 650.9)
98.3    τί ἂν γένοιτο — γένηται      = unidentified (Mangey
                                           650.10)
98.4    ἄξιον — ἀναπέμπουσι          = Gaium 47 (Mangey 651.3;
                                           *Wendland 1892, 67,
                                           n. 2)
98.5    μηδενὶ συμφορὰν — εὑρεθῇς     = unidentified (Mangey 652.1)
98.6    αἱ πάντων — δυνάμεις         = unidentified (Mangey 652.4;
                                           Wendland 24.10)
98.7a   χρήσιμον — σωφρονίζεσθαι     = Flacc 154 (Mangey 652.5;
                                           *PCW 6:lxxix)
98.7b   καὶ τοῖς ἑτέρων — σωφρονεῖν  = Spec Leg 4.223 (*PCW [cit-
                                           ing the same text from
                                           Escur. X. I. 13])

| 99.1 | τῷ στρατιώτῃ — φυλάττειν | = *Flacc* 5 (**PCW*) |
|------|------|------|
| 99.2 | πᾶς σοφὸς θεοῦ φίλος | = *Heres* 21 (Mangey 652.8; **PCW*; see p. 5 above) |
| 99.3 | οἴησις — ἀνέχεται | = *Quaes Gen* 3.48 (Mangey 652.9; *Früchtel 1937, no. 8) |
| 99.4 | ὥσπερ τὸ — πάντα | = unidentified (Mangey 652.11) |

99: Remaining texts edited by Lequien from Ber. 46:

| 99.5 | ὁ σοφὸς — ζωήν | = *Ebr* 100 (Mangey 656.2; **PCW*) |
|------|------|------|
| 99.6 | ἄτοπον ἐν μὲν — ἐκρίπτειν | = unidentified (Mangey 658.5a; Petit QE no. 13) |

99–102: Remaining texts edited by Mangey from Ber. 46:

| 99.7 | σοὶ λέγεται — διαγγέλλῃ | = * *Heres* 105–6, 110 (Mangey 660.3) |
|------|------|------|
| 100.1 | τόπος — περιπολοῦσιν | = unidentified (Mangey 661.4) |
| 100.2a | ἡ τῶν μελλόντων — ἀνθρώπῳ | = *Heres* 261 (Mangey 661.5; **PCW*) |
| 100.2b | τὸ τέλος — μόνος | = unidentified (Mangey 661.7) |
| 100.3 | οὐ ποιήσετε — αἴτιον | = unidentified (Mangey 661.9) |
| 100.4 | ἀκερδὴς — μετάμελος | = unidentified (Mangey 662.6) |
| 100.5 | ὁ καλὸς — δόγμασιν | = *Quaes Gen* 2.41 (Mangey 662.7; *Früchtel 1937, no. 9) |
| 100.6 | ἡ τυχοῦσα — γέννημα | = *Leg All* 3.89 (Mangey 663.2a; **PCW*) |
| 100.7 | οἱ ἄνανδροι — γίνονται | = *Praem* 5 (Mangey 663.3; **PCW*) |
| 100.8 | τοῦ φαύλου — πολέμιος | = unidentified (Mangey 663.5; first part = Tischendorf 153.6) |
| 100.9 | ἀνελεύθερον — ἔχον | = unidentified (Mangey 664.1) |
| 100.10 | οἱ ὑπηρέται — θεοῦ | = unidentified (Mangey 664.2; Petit QE no. 29) |
| 100.11 | ἄσπονδος — ἀπειλεῖν | = unidentified (Mangey 664.3; Petit QE no. 30) |

| 102.8 | τῶν ἀπορρήτων — ἀνατίθη | = Fr. sp. 60 |
| 102.9 | τὴν εὐταξίαν — γνωρίζομεν | = unidentified (Mangey 674.7) |

103: Remaining text edited by Mai from Vat. 1553:

| 103.1 | καθάπερ — ἀκούσια | = *Post* 11 (Mai 102a; *\*PCW*) |

103–4: Remaining texts edited by Pitra:

| 103.2 | τὴν — ἀποτίθεσθαι | = Fr. sp. 32 |
| 103.3a | ζητοῦσιν βρῶσιν — οὐρανοῖς | = Fr. sp. 33 |
| 103.3b | ὥσπερ γὰρ — σκεδάννυσιν | = *Leg All* 1.46 (Pitra 310.Ib; *\*PCW* 1:lix) |
| 103.3c | καὶ τὰ τῶν παθῶν θηρία κοιμίζει | = gloss to *Leg All* 1.46 (Pitra 310.Ic; *PCW* 1:lix, 1:72, app.; see under Fr. sp. 33 above) |
| 103.4 | πρὸς τούτοις — ἐχθρῷ | = gloss to *Quaes Ex* 2.25 (a) (see p. 20 above) |

104–5: Remaining texts edited by Tischendorf (1868):

| 104.1 | τοιοῦτος — ἀντιλάβωμεν | = Fr. sp. 52 |
| 104.2 | δοκεῖ γάρ — λογισμοῦ | = *Spec Leg* 3.194 (Tischendorf 155.13; *\*PCW*) |
| 104.3 | ὁ μὲν θεὸς — ἀναξίους | = Fr. sp. 55 |
| 105.1 | πλέον ἀγάπα — σκοπόν | = Fr. sp. 54 |

105: Remaining texts found in Par. 923:

| 105.2 | λεία ὁδὸς — γίνεται | = Fr. sp. 43 |
| 105.3 | κοινωνικὸν — ἄνθρωπος | = unidentified (*PCW* 3:163, app.; see p. 9, n. 41, above) |
| 105.4 | μηδαμῶς — ποιεῖ | = unidentified (Harris 88.2; see p. 40, no. 2, above) |
| 105.5 | δυσεκρίζωτος — χρόνῳ | = unidentified[25] |
| 105.6 | φιλοῦσιν — ἐξάπτουσιν | = unidentified |

---

[25]This text reads: δυσεκρίζωτος ἡ πλάνη ὅταν διαδράμη πολλῷ χρόνῳ. In his MS Früchtel assigned this to "Just. Mart. p. 441 ed. Ben.," which seems to refer to Pseudo-Justin's *Quaestiones et responsiones ad orthodoxos*, Resp. 1 (*MPG* 6:1249A9–10): μένειν ἀνεκρίζωτον τὴν πλάνην. But this is hardly a close parallel.

105.7    τίς ἔχει — γλωσσαλγίας        = unidentified (*PCW* 4:290,
                                                app.)

106:  Remaining texts edited by Cramer:

106.1    τὸ δὲ μάννα — διασῴζεσθαι      = unidentified (Cramer 1837,
                                                243; *PCW* 1:civ; per-
                                                haps from *Quaes Ex* on
                                                Exod 16:31:  see p. 34,
                                                n. 42, above)
106.2    τὸ μὴ — ὑπερβολή              = Fr. sp. 7

106–7:  Remaining texts found in Burneianus 34:

106.3    οὐκ ἐπειδὴ — προσαγορεύονται  = gloss to *Quaes Gen* 2.15 (see
                                                p. 19 above)
106.4    ἑβδόμη — ἑορτάζειν           = gloss to *Quaes Gen* 2.47 (see
                                                p. 19 above)
106.5    τόξον — ὑπερθήσομαι          = gloss to *Quaes Gen* 2.64 (see
                                                p. 19 above)

107:  Remaining texts found in the *Catena Lipsiensis*:

107.1    διδύμους — αὐτοῦ             = unidentified (see pp. 22–23
                                                above)
107.2    δῆλον δὲ — ἡμάρτανον         = gloss to *Quaes Gen* 1.100
                                                (see p. 19 above)
107.3    ἰδοὺ τοῦτο — τούτοις         = gloss to *Quaes Gen* 2.10 (see
                                                p. 19 above)
107.4    ἄγγελος ἦν — ἀποστείλω       = Fr. sp. 39

108:  Remaining texts from Johannes Georgides:

108.1    μή σε — πράγματα             = unidentified
108.2    σοφιστείας — ἀποδοχῆς        = *Provid* 2.51 (*Wendland
                                                1892, 88, no. 6)

108–10:  Remaining texts from Ber. 46:[26]

| 108.3 | ἐπειδὰν ἡγεμὼν — εἰσίν | = | *Vita Mos* 1.160–61 (*PCW*) |
|-------|------------------------|---|------------------------------|
| 108.4 | τὸ λέγειν — ἀτελές | = | *Quaes Ex* 2.110 (†) (*Früchtel 1938, 766; Petit QE no. 27; Royse 1984, 151–52) |
| 108.5 | τὸ περὶ θεὸν — ἀφορητότερον | = | *Spec Leg* 1.100 (*PCW*) |
| 108.6 | τὸ μέγιστον — δῶρον | = | *Vita Mos* 1.304 (†) (Mangey 671.10; *Früchtel MS) |
| 109.1 | ἀλήθεια — δύναμις | = | *Ebr* 6 (*PCW*) |
| 109.2 | ἀλήθεια αὐταρκέστατος ἔπαινος | = | *Flacc* 99 (†) (*PCW* 2:xxvi, n. 1, refers to *Plant* 128; *Früchtel MS; *Junod) |
| 109.3 | ὁ τῆς εἰρήνης — βίῳ | = | *Gaium* 147 (*PCW*) |
| 109.4 | οὐκ ἀσφαλὲς — πράγματα | = | *Gaium* 247 (Harris 94.9; *PCW*) |
| 109.5 | ὁ μηδέποτε — φίλοις | = | *Mut* 55 (*PCW* [+ gloss ?]) |
| 109.6 | νόμος οὗτος — τιμᾶν | = | *Leg All* 3.167 (*PCW*) |
| 109.7a | ἀρετὴ προηγούμενον — ἀρχαῖον | = | unidentified |
| 109.7b | ἀρεταὶ μόναι — ἐπίστανται | = | unidentified (Mangey 670.3a; Lewy 81.21) |
| 109.8 | ὅταν — σιωπᾶν | = | *Gaium* 360 (*PCW*) |
| 109.9 | φιλοῦσι — τίκτεσθαι | = | unidentified |
| 109.10 | τοῖς — δημιουργοῦσι | = | *Gaium* 195 (*PCW*) |
| 109.11 | ὦ διάνοια — θεοῦ | = | *Cher* 29 (*PCW*) |
| 109.12 | τῷ ἔνδον — ἁλίσκεται | = | *Quaes Ex* 2.13 (c) (†) (*Früchtel MS; Royse 1984, 151) |
| 109.13 | τοῖς — ὠφεληθήσονται | = | *Gaium* 245 (*PCW*) |
| 110.1 | πόνος — ἀπεχθάνονται | = | *Mut* 170 (*PCW*) |
| 110.2 | ἐνέχυρον — θεόν | = | unidentified (*PCW* 4:287–88, app.) |
| 110.3 | ἔστω οὖν — ἀμφισβητουμένου | = | unidentified[27] (latter part = Harris 97.1; *PCW* 4:287–88, app.) |

---

[26]On these see p. 37 (and nn. 52–53 [– p. 38]) above.

[27]Junod refers to *Sacr* 91.  But only the latter part of Harris 110.3 is found there, and that part (which = Harris 97.1) appears also at *Leg All* 3.205, *Dec* 86, and *Spec Leg* 2.10.  See also under Harris 97.1 above.

| 110.4 | φεύγετε — παρακαλεῖ | = | unidentified |
| 110.5 | οὐκ ἔστι τῶν — ἐᾷ | = | *Leg All* 3.160 (*\*PCW* 1: lxxxxiii) |
| 110.6 | θυμῷ μάλιστα — σῶμα | = | *Quaes Ex* 2.115 (†) (\*Royse 1984, 152) |
| 110.7 | γονέας τίμα — φυσικός | = | unidentified |
| 110.8 | οὐδενὶ — ἐστιν | = | *Mut* 170 (*\*PCW*) |
| 110.9 | ἀπὸ ἑνὸς — πόλις | = | Fr. sp. 21 |
| 110.10 | οὐκ ἔστιν — ψυχῆς | = | Fr. sp. 22 |
| 110.11 | τίς τιμῆς — παράπαν | = | *Ebr* 57 (\*Wendland 21.4b) |
| 110.12 | αὕτη — ὑπολαμβάνειν | = | *Post* 158 (*\*PCW*; cf. Petit 209–10 n. a [on *Quaes Gen* 4.210]) |

## 11. WENDLAND

Wendland's 1891 work, *Fragmente*, prints fragments of both the extant and the lost books περὶ μέθης, and also systematically gathers the fragments of the *Quaestiones* found in Procopius.

20–22: Fragments of the extant book περὶ μέθης:

| | | |
|---|---|---|
| 20.1a | νόσου — ἀπαιδευσία | = *Ebr* 141 (Harris 78.5 [refers to *Ebr* 12, followed by Wendland]; *PCW) |
| 20.1b | τοῦ ληρεῖν — ἀπαιδευσία | = *Ebr* 6 (†) (Wendland and PCW refer to *Ebr* 11) |
| 20.1c | ἀπαιδευσία — χρησομένοις | = *Ebr* 12 |
| 21.2a | τῷ ὄντι — ἀγαθόν | = *Ebr* 26 |
| 21.2b | ἐσταλμένον — ἀγαθόν | = *Ebr* 26 (*Harris 91.2) |
| 21.3 | τοῖς ἀσκηταῖς — ἐντυχεῖν | = *Ebr* 48–49 |
| 21.4a | οὐ δύναται — αὐτομολοῦμεν | = *Ebr* 56–58 (*Harris 85.4) |
| 21.4b | τίς τιμῆς — παράπαν | = *Ebr* 57 (Harris 110.11) |
| 21.5 | τὰ ἀκούσια — καταβαρούμενα | = *Ebr* 125 |
| 21.6 | ὁ ἰδὼν καὶ — ἐπιβουλεύεται | = *Ebr* 160 |
| 21.7 | γίνεται θηρίον — εἶναι | = *Ebr* 174 (*Harris 91.3) |
| 21.8a | οὐ μόνον — νομισθῆναι | = *Ebr* 176–77 |
| 21.8b | οὐ γὰρ — γεγηρακόσιν | = *Ebr* 179 |
| 22.9 | χαλεπὸν — ἐπαιρόμενος | = *Ebr* 162 |

22–25: "Citate aus dem verlorenen Buche περὶ μέθης":

| | | |
|---|---|---|
| 22.1 | τί γὰρ — χρῆται | = unidentified |
| 22.2 | ὥσπερ — ἐξαπιναῖος | = unidentified |
| 22.3 | τὰς ἐπηρείας — μεῖζον | = unidentified |
| 23.4 | ἐπίσταται — αἰσθάνονται | = unidentified |
| 23.5 | τίς οὐκ οἶδεν — δυνατά | = unidentified |
| 23.6 | πῶς οὐκ ἔστιν — ἔργα | = unidentified |
| 24.7 | ὥσπερ τῶν — ἰσότητος | = unidentified (Harris 101.5) |
| 24.8 | τὸ ἄνισον — ὠφέλειαν | = unidentified (Harris 101.6) |
| 24.9 | τὸ εὔνομον — ὄντων | = *Quaes Ex* 2.64 (Harris 101.7) |

| 24.10 | αἱ πάντων — δυνάμεις | = unidentified (Harris 98.6) |
| 25.11 | τῶν θείων — οἴσομεν | = *Ebr* 32 (*PCW*) |

29–105: "Philo und Procopius von Gaza":

Extracts from the *Quaestiones* found in Procopius; these are usually assigned to their correct locations, although Wendland's manner of citation does not always distinguish clearly between genuine fragments and other material. The following is a list of texts which have been referred to above or were missed by Marcus. I have not duplicated the remarks found in Petit, *Quaestiones: Fragmenta Graeca*, passim, on the misuse of the material from Procopius; see generally pp. 23–25 above.

| 36 | μήποτε ὡς ἵππος — δεῖται | = *Quaes Gen* 1.3 (not in Marcus; see p. 24 above) |
| 37, n. 1 | τινὲς ἀπὸ μιᾶς — δηλοῦν | = unidentified (see p. 22, n. 36, above) |
| 39 | σημεῖον δὲ — τεθυκότι | = *Quaes Gen* 1.63 (not in Marcus; see p. 24 above) |
| 40 | μία δὲ — πλημμελεῖν | = see p. 24, n. 44, above |
| 47 | ἐκ τούτου — ἔκτισεν | = gloss to *Quaes Gen* 1.94 (a) (see p. 18 above) |
| 47, n. 1 | ἀνθρωποπρεπῶς — ἔχει | = see p. 24, n. 44, above |
| 49 | ἑβδόμη — ἀριθμούμενον | = gloss to *Quaes Gen* 2.47 (see p. 19 above) |
| 51–52 | δῆλον δὲ — ἡμάρτανον | = gloss to *Quaes Gen* 1.100 (see p. 19 above) |
| 55–56 | καλῶς — σωτηρίας | = *Quaes Gen* 2.22 (cited as *Quaes Gen* 1.99, which Marcus follows; *Früchtel 1937, 112) |
| 61, n. 4 | νεώτερον — κακία | = *Quaes Gen* 2.74 (not in Marcus; *Petit; see p. 24, n. 44, above) |
| 86 | αὗται αἱ — μετῴκησαν | = gloss to *Quaes Gen* 4.195.7* (see p. 20 above) |
| 86 | ἐθάρρει μὲν — θεοῦ | = gloss to *Quaes Gen* 4.202 (see p. 20 above) |
| 100 | ἐθέλει δὲ — περιστοιχίζεται | = gloss to *Quaes Ex* 2.25 (a) (in part) (see p. 20 above) |

101, n. 2  ταῦτα μὲν — Βηρσαβεέ       = gloss to *Quaes Ex* 2.25 (b)
                                                    (see p. 21 above)

One further fragment printed by Wendland, which has often been over-looked, is:

140, n. 1  δοκεῖ μὲν — ἔστι       = *Quaes Gen* 1.41 (b) (†)
                                                    (Mangey 674.1; Früch-tel 1937, 113, n. 1;
                                                    Royse 1984, 149)

On this see further my "Two Problems in Philo's *Quaestiones*," *REA*, n.s. 16 (1982): 81–83. I subsequently found that Bousset, *Jüdisch-Christlicher Schulbetrieb*, 63, n. 3, and 72, n. 1, also refers to this text (citing Wendland).

## 12. *PCW*

Cohn, Wendland, and Reiter cite in their apparatus most of the excerpts in the florilegia which can be located in the works which they edited. Even though it was not part of their task to edit the fragments, they do occasionally refer to such texts, both genuine and spurious. The following list indicates the references in *PCW* which are of relevance here.

| | | | |
|---|---|---|---|
| 1:xxvii | reference to *Quaes Ex* 2.62–68 | = | see pp. 186–87 above |
| 1:lix | ζητοῦσιν βρῶσιν — οὐρανοῖς | = | Fr. sp. 33 |
| 1:lix | ὥσπερ γὰρ — σκεδάννυσιν | = | *Leg All* 1.46 (Harris 103.3b) |
| 1:lix | καὶ τὰ τῶν παθῶν θηρία κοιμίζει | = | gloss to *Leg All* 1.46 (Harris 103.3c; *PCW* 1:72, app.) |
| 1:lix | ἡ τῆς ἀρχῆς — γαλήνη | = | Fr. sp. 48 |
| 1:civ | τὸ μάννα — διασῴζεσθαι (from Basil) | = | unidentified (Harris 106.1) |
| 1:cvii–cviii | texts from Isidore of Pelusium | = | see Früchtel 1938, 764–66 (and p. 144, n. 50 [– p. 145] above) |
| 1:cviii–cix | Anastasius Sinaita, *Viae dux* 14 | = | see pp. 140–43 above |
| 1:72, app. | καὶ τὰ τῶν παθῶν θηρία κοιμίζει | = | gloss to *Leg All* 1.46 (Harris 103.3c; *PCW* 1:lix) |
| 2:xv, no. 1 | αἱ μὲν γὰρ — ἐπιθυμιῶν | = | *Quaes Ex* 1.19 (*Pitra 313.IX) |
| 2:xv, n. 2 | *primum — testimonium* | = | Latin version of Fr. sp. 61 |
| 2:xviii | τὴν — ἀποτίθεσθαι | = | Fr. sp. 32 |
| 2:xxvii, n. 1 | λόγου θεοῦ — ψυχῶν | = | *Ebr* 71 (†) (see pp. 4–5 above) |
| 3:163, app. | κοινωνικὸν — ἄνθρωπος | = | unidentified (Harris 105.3) |
| 4:287–88, app. | ἐνέχυρον — θεόν | = | unidentified (Harris 110.2) |

| | | | |
|---|---|---|---|
| 4:287–88, app. | ἔστω οὖν — ἀμφισβητουμένου | = | unidentified<br>(Harris 110.3) |
| 4:290, app. | τίς ἔχει — γλωσσαλγίας | = | unidentified<br>(Harris 105.7) |
| 5:xvi, n. 1 | πρότερον — ψευδομαρτυρήσῃς | = | Fr. sp. 61 |
| 5:173, app. | πρότερον — ψευδομαρτυρήσῃς | = | Fr. sp. 61 |
| 6:i, n. 1 | reference to work of Georgius<br>Gemistus (Pletho) | = | see pp. 136–38 above |
| 6:1 | οὐκ ἔστι — θεόν | = | unidentified<br>(Harris 10.1) |

## 13. LEWY

Lewy's edition of 1932, "Neue Philontexte," prints some new fragments of *Quaes Gen* and *Quaes Ex*, and also includes a few further fragments. Lewy comments (74, n. 3): "Die folgenden Texte sind nur eine Auswahl der Neufunde, alle schlecht bezeugten und zweifelhaften Fragmente sind weggelassen."

75–80: Fragments from the *Quaestiones*:

| | | |
|---|---|---|
| 75.1 | διὰ τί τὴν — γεγονότα | = *Quaes Gen* 1.1 |
| 75.2 | ἀποικίαν — τῶν νόμων | = *Quaes Gen* 1.27 |
| 75.3 | τί δ' ἐστιν — ἐγκατώρυξαν | = *Quaes Gen* 1.70 |
| 76.4 | οὐχ ἥττονα — ἐργάζεται | = unidentified (Mai 105b; not in Harris or Marcus; Petit QE no. 23) |
| 76.5 | τί ἐστιν — τῇ κτήσει | = *Quaes Gen* 2.10 |
| 77.6 | ἠθικώτατον — ἐστίν | = *Quaes Gen* 2.12 (d) |
| 77.7 | εὔλογον — δυνατόν | = *Quaes Gen* 2.17 (c) |
| 77.8 | πρότερον — λαχεῖν | = unidentified |
| 78.9 | πάγκαλον — πάθους | = *Quaes Gen* 4.33 (b) |
| 78.10 | ἐκ τοῦ — βαρύτατα | = *Quaes Gen* 4.51 (b), (c) |
| 79.11 | μετανενοήκασιν — ἀπότρεχε | = *Quaes Gen* 4.131 |
| 79.12 | διὰ τί λέγει — νόμου | = *Quaes Gen* 4.184 |
| 79.13 | διὰ τί ἃ — χάριτας | = *Quaes Gen* 4.191 (c), (d) |
| 79.14 | τῷ ἀγαθῷ — εὐφημία | = *Quaes Ex* 2.6 (b) |
| 80.15 | διὰ τί τὸν — ἰδίᾳ | = *Quaes Ex* 2.11 (a) |
| 80.16 | ἐν νυκτὶ βουλή· — ἀποπόμπιμον | = unidentified (Mai 102b; not in Harris or Marcus; Petit QE no. 20) |

80–81: Fragments from the lost portion of *Gaium*:

| | | |
|---|---|---|
| 80.17 | μὴ τοὺς — βλάπτοντας | = unidentified |
| 81.18 | καλὰ ἑκάστοις — πάθει | = unidentified |

81: Fragment from the lost portion of *Somn*:

| | | | |
|---|---|---|---|
| 81.19 | πρὸς τὰς — ἀνατυπούσης | = | Fr. sp. 45 |

81–84: Further fragments:

| | | | |
|---|---|---|---|
| 81.20 | ἀποστρέφου — κρείττονα | = | Fr. sp. 50 |
| 81.21 | ἀρεταὶ μόναι — ἐπίστανται | = | unidentified (Mangey 670.3a [not cited by Lewy]; Harris 109.7b [not cited by Lewy]) |
| 82.22 | αὔξει τὴν — τριβή | = | unidentified (Mangey 650.7b [not cited by Lewy]; Harris 79.1b [not cited by Lewy]) |
| 82.23 | εἰ βούλει — ἐπιτίμα | = | Fr. sp. 53 |
| 82.24 | εὔπαιδες — ἐπιστήμονες | = | *Quaes Ex* 2.19 (b) (†) (Mangey 673.5b [not cited by Lewy]) |
| 82.25 | ἔχουσιν — μεμφθῆναι | = | unidentified |
| 82.26 | οἱ οἰκέται — ὕβρις | = | unidentified |
| 82.27 | παρατηρητέον — ἐπιστήμην | = | unidentified (Früchtel discovered that this fragment overlaps a fragment in *P.Oxy.* 1356; see p. 3, n. 11, above) |
| 83.28 | τὸ δὲ — διαφαίνουσιν | = | unidentified |
| 83.29 | τὸ ἔντιμον — ἔσεσθαι | = | Fr. sp. 42 |
| 83.30 | τὸ δ᾿ εὐδαιμονεῖν — μέλη | = | unidentified |
| 83.31 | φησὶ Μωυσῆς — βούλεται | = | unidentified (Petit QG no. 13) |
| 84.32 | φιλόσοφος — ἐπιδεικνυμένη | = | unidentified |

## 14. MARCUS

As Appendix A, "Greek Fragments of the *Quaestiones*," to his *PLCL Supplement* 2:177–263, Marcus prints texts mostly as found in Harris and Wendland with a few additions and textual observations. The fragments of *Quaes Gen* 4.195.7*, 195.8*, and 195.9*, may be found in Marcus's Appendix B on the Latin version of the *Quaestiones*, 271–73. Most of these texts, of course, are located correctly. Listed below are those classified by Marcus as unidentified, as well as a few texts which have been referred to above. Here, as with Wendland, I have not duplicated the remarks found in Petit, *Quaestiones: Fragmenta Graeca*, passim, on the misuse of the material from Procopius; see generally pp. 23–25 above. It should be emphasized that Marcus's collection of the Greek fragments, apparently compiled in some haste from printed sources which themselves are not always reliable, and not based on any first-hand knowledge of the Greek manuscripts, should be viewed with considerable caution.

Misassigned texts or glosses:

| 190 | ἦν γνωσιμαχῶν — ἑαυτοῦ | = gloss to *Quaes Gen* 1.77 (see p. 18 above) |
| 191–92 | ἐκ τούτου — ἔκτισεν | = gloss to *Quaes Gen* 1.94 (a) (see p. 18 above) |
| 192 | καλῶς — σωτηρίας | = *Quaes Gen* 2.22 (Wendland 55–56 [cited as *Quaes Gen* 1.99, which Marcus follows]; *Früchtel 1937, 112) |

234–37: Unidentified fragments of *Quaes Gen*:

| 1 | τῶν φαύλων — πένητες | = unidentified (Harris 69.1) |
| 2 | μελέτη τροφὸς ἐπιστήμης | = unidentified (Harris 69.3) |
| 3 | ὥσπερ κίονες — γένος | = unidentified (Harris 69.5) |
| 4 | ἐάν τις — ὠφέλειαν | = *Somn* 1.177, 176 (Harris 69.6; cf. Royse 1984, 146, n. 20) |

| 5 | ἀνθρώποις — ἐχθρῶν | = | *Quod Deus* 27 (Harris 69.8; cf. Royse 1984, 146, n. 20) |
|---|---|---|---|
| 6 | τὸ ἐπαισθάνεσθαι — ἀνδρός | = | unidentified (Harris 70.1) |
| 7 | ἐπειδὴ πρὸς — ὁδηγίαν | = | unidentified (Harris 70.2) |
| 8 | ἐν θεῷ — μεμαθημένως | = | unidentified (Harris 70.3) |
| 9 | εἰώθασιν — καιροί | = | unidentified (Harris 70.6) |
| 10 | τὸ ἐπιορκεῖν — ἀλυσιτελέστατον | = | unidentified (Harris 70.7) |
| 11 | οἱ ἑαυτῶν — θεοφιλής | = | unidentified (Harris 71.1) |
| 12 | τρεπτοὶ — ὑπολαμβάνομεν | = | unidentified (Harris 71.2) |
| 13 | συγκρύπτεται — δοκιμώτατον | = | *Quaes Gen* 3.3 (b) (†) (Harris 71.3) |
| 14 | τοὺς ἄρξαντας — πέρας | = | unidentified (Harris 71.4) |
| 15 | ὁ εὐλαβέστερος — κακοπαθῇ | = | unidentified (Harris 71.6) |
| 16 | τί οὖν — ἐγχειρήσεως | = | unidentified (Harris 71.7) |
| 17 | τὰ γὰρ τοῦ — ἐστίν | = | unidentified (Harris 72.1) |

258–63: Unidentified fragments of *Quaes Ex*:

| 1a | ἀμήχανον — ὄψεται | = | unidentified (Harris 72.3a) |
|---|---|---|---|
| 1b | αἱ φιλοσοφίαι — διώσασθαι | = | unidentified (Harris 72.3b) |
| 1c | δεῖ τὸν — προθέσεως | = | unidentified (Harris 72.3c) |
| 1d | ἀδυνατήσει — μαρμαρυγῶν | = | unidentified (Harris 72.3d) |
| 2 | ἡ φορὰ — τυφλουμένην | = | unidentified (Harris 73.1) |
| 3 | αἱ περὶ τῶν — ἀλήθειαν | = | unidentified (Harris 73.2) |
| 4a | τὸ ἐμμελὲς — πειρωμένους | = | *Quaes Ex* 2.38 (b) (Harris 73.3a) |
| 4b | ὁ τοῦ σοφοῦ — κάλλος | = | *Quaes Ex* 2.44 (Harris 73.3b) |
| 5 | τοὺς ἐντυγχάνοντας — συνᾴδουσιν | = | unidentified (Harris 73.4) |
| 6 | περιέχει — πεπλήρωκεν | = | unidentified (Harris 73.5) |
| 7 | ἐντὸς φέρει — ψυχῇ | = | unidentified (Harris 73.6) |
| 8 | τοῦ φαύλου — ἀνακέκραται | = | *Quaes Gen* 1.49 (†) (Harris 73.7) |
| 9 | αἱ τοῦ θεοῦ — ἀπόλαυσιν | = | *Quaes Ex* 2.71 (Harris 73.8) |
| 10 | μυρία γε — νοῦν | = | unidentified (Harris 73.9) |
| 11a | μία ἀνάπαυσις — πράξεων | = | unidentified (Harris 73.10) |
| 11b | πέρας εὐδαιμονίας — στῆναι | = | unidentified (Harris 74.1) |
| 12 | πολλὰ ἀσωμένοις — ἐστιν | = | unidentified (Harris 74.2) |
| 13 | τὸ τῶν φαύλων — ἑαυταῖς | = | unidentified (Harris 74.3) |

| 14 | τὰ βουλήματα — ζώντων | = unidentified (Harris 74.4) |
| 15 | τὸ μὲν — παρθενίας | = unidentified (Harris 74.5) |
| 16 | τὰ μέτρα — θρασύτητα | = unidentified (Harris 74.6) |
| 17 | ἡ εὐφυΐα — περικόπτειν | = unidentified (Harris 74.7) |
| 18 | ὁ σοφιστικός — σημεῖα | = unidentified (Harris 74.8) |
| 19 | ὅρασις παρὰ — εἰσδύεται | = unidentified (Harris 74.9) |
| 20 | οὐ πάντων — θέμις | = unidentified (Harris 75.1) |
| 21 | φθαρτὸν καλῶ — βίος | = unidentified (Harris 75.2) |
| 22 | μάταιον οὐδὲν — ζημίαι | = *Quaes Ex* 2.9 (a) (Harris 75.3) |
| 23 | πρὸς τούτοις — ἐχθρῷ | = gloss to *Quaes Ex* 2.25 (a) (see p. 20 above) |

267–75: "Additions in the Old Latin Version":

272, n. c  σωτηρίαν τὴν — ἔχοντες    = gloss to *Quaes Gen* 4.195.8* (see p. 20 above)

## 15. PETIT

In her *Quaestiones: Fragmenta Graeca* (1978), Petit improves greatly on her predecessors by presenting a more extensive selection of Greek fragments of *Quaes Gen* and *Quaes Ex*, with a superior manuscript base and a more accurate critical apparatus, including regular use of the Armenian itself. She also includes groups of unidentified fragments of *Quaes Gen* and of *Quaes Ex*. A few of these have since been located within the *Quaestiones*, along with a few fragments found elsewhere. Some of these are cited in my "Further Greek Fragments," 143–53, including one fragment (on *Quaes Gen* 1.49; see below, QE no. 33) which had been identified in the Früchtel MS, and which Petit identified in her review of Mercier, 404. I later learned that this text had been identified by Wendland, *Philos Schrift über die Vorsehung*, 55, n. 2 (although his reference is not completely precise). Also, *Quaes Ex* 2.110 had already been identified by Früchtel in "Neue Quellennachweise," 766. Finally, another fragment (Gessner 38 = *MPG* 136:881A8–9; Mangey 666.2; Harris 101.10) was located by Früchtel in his MS as the second half of *Quaes Ex* 1.6, and I have edited this text in a forthcoming article on that section.

214–28: Unidentified fragments of *Quaes Gen*:

| | | | |
|---|---|---|---|
| 1 | ὥσπερ κίονες — γένος | = | unidentified (Harris 69.5) |
| 2a | οὐ θέμις — ἀμυήτοις | = | unidentified (Harris 69.4a) |
| 2b | ἄχρις ἂν — ἀμώμητα | = | unidentified (Harris 69.4b) |
| 3 | τὸ οὖν — ἐγχειρήσεως | = | unidentified (Harris 71.7) |
| 4 | μελέτη τροφός ἐστιν ἐπιστήμης | = | unidentified (Harris 69.3) |
| 5 | εἰώθασιν — καιροί | = | unidentified (Harris 70.6) |
| 6 | τρεπτοὶ — ὑπολαμβάνομεν | = | unidentified (Harris 71.2) |
| 7 | συγκρύπτεται — δοκιμώτατον | = | *Quaes Gen* 3.3 (b) (†) (Harris 71.3) |
| 8 | τοὺς ἄρξαντας — πέρας | = | unidentified (Harris 71.4) |
| 9 | ὁ εὐλαβέστερος — κακοπαθῇ | = | unidentified (Harris 71.6) |
| 10 | οἱ ἑαυτῶν — θεοφιλής | = | unidentified (Harris 71.1) |
| 11 | τῶν φαύλων — πένητες | = | unidentified (Harris 69.1) |
| 12 | τὸ ἐπαισθάνεσθαι — ἀνδρός | = | unidentified (Harris 70.1) |
| 13 | φησὶ Μωυσῆς — βούλεται | = | unidentified (Lewy 83.31) |

| 29 | οἱ ὑπηρέται — θεοῦ | = unidentified (Harris 100.10) |
| 30 | ἄσπονδος — ἀπειλεῖν | = unidentified (Harris 100.11) |
| 31 | ἡ φορὰ — τυφλουμένην | = unidentified (Harris 73.1) |
| 32 | ἐντὸς φέρει — ψυχῇ | = unidentified (Harris 73.6) |
| 33 | τοῦ φαύλου — ἀνακέκραται | = *Quaes Gen* 1.49 (†) (Harris 73.7) |

# BIBLIOGRAPHY

Adler, Maximilian. "Das philonische Fragment De deo." *MGWJ* 80 (1936): 163–70.

————. *Studien zu Philon von Alexandreia*. Breslau: M. & H. Marcus, 1929.

Aland, Kurt. "Eine neue Schrift Philos?" *TLZ* 68 (1943): 169–70.

Alfonsi, Luigi. "Sul περὶ θεοῦ del P. 17027 di Berlino." *Aeg* 23 (1943): 262–69.

Arevšatyan, Sen. "Platoni erkeri Hayeren t'argmanowt'yan žamanakə" [On the Time of the Translation of Plato's Dialogues into Armenian]. *Banber Matenadarani* 10 (1971): 7–20.

Aristotle. *Aristotelis opera*. Vol. 2. Venice: Aldus Manutius, 1497.

Aucher, Joannes Baptista, ed. and trans. *Philonis Judaei paralipomena Armena: libri videlicet quatuor [sic] in Genesin, libri duo in Exodum, sermo unus de Sampsone, alter de Jona, tertius de tribus angelis Abraamo apparentibus, opera hactenus inedita, ex Armena versione antiquissima ab ipso originali textu Graeco ad verbum stricte exequuta saeculo V. nunc primum in Latium [sic] fideliter translata*. Venice: Typis coenobii PP. Armenorum in insula S. Lazari, 1826.

————, ed. and trans. *Philonis Judaei sermones tres hactenus inediti: I. et II. de providentia et III. de animalibus, ex Armena versione antiquissima ab ipso originali textu Graeco ad verbum stricte exequuta, nunc primum in Latium [sic] fideliter translati*. Venice: Typis coenobii PP. Armenorum in insula S. Lazari, 1822.

Awetik'ean, Gabriêl, Xač'atowr Siwrmêlean, and Mkrtič' Awgerean [Baptista Aucher]. "Nor baŕgirk' Haykazean lezowi" [New Dictionary of the Armenian Language]. 2 vols. Venice: I tparani

Srboyn Łazarow [Press of St. Lazarus], 1836–37. Reprinted: Erevan: Erevani hamalsarani hratarakč'owt'yawn [Erevan University Press], 1979–81.

Bernardakis, Gregorius N., ed. *Plutarchi Chaeronensis moralia*. Vol. 7: *Plutarchi fragmenta vera et spuria multis accessionibus locupletata*. Leipzig: B. G. Teubner, 1896.

Bernays, Jacob. "Herennius' Metaphysik und Longinos." *Monatsberichte der königlichen Akademie der Wissenschaften zu Berlin* (1876): 55–63. Reprinted in *Gesammelte Abhandlungen*, edited by H. Usener, 1:347–56. Berlin: Wilhelm Hertz, 1885.

————. *Phokion und seine neueren Beurtheiler: Ein Beitrag zur Geschichte der griechischen Philosophie und Politik*. Berlin: Wilhelm Hertz, 1881.

————. *Über das Phokylideische Gedicht*. Berlin: Wilhelm Hertz, 1856. Reprinted in *Gesammelte Abhandlungen*, edited by H. Usener, 1:192–261. Berlin: Wilhelm Hertz, 1885.

Boissonade, Jean François, ed. *Anecdota Graeca e codicibus regiis*. 5 vols. Paris: in Regio Typographeo, 1829–33. Reprinted: Hildesheim: Georg Olms, 1962.

Bonwetsch, G. Nath., and Hans Achelis, eds. *Hippolytus Werke*. Vol. 1. GCS, vol. 1, pt. 1. Leipzig: J. C. Hinrichs, 1897.

Bousset, Wilhelm. *Jüdisch-Christlicher Schulbetrieb in Alexandria und Rom: Literarische Untersuchungen zu Philo und Clemens von Alexandria, Justin und Irenäus*. Göttingen: Vandenhoeck & Ruprecht, 1915.

Bréhier, Émile. *Les idées philosophiques et religieuses de Philon d'Alexandrie*. Paris: Picard, 1908. 2d ed., Paris: J. Vrin, 1925. 3d ed., Paris: J. Vrin, 1950.

Bruns, J. Edgar. "The *Altercatio Jasonis et Papisci*, Philo, and Anastasius the Sinaite." *Theological Studies* 34 (1973): 287–94.

————. "Philo Christianus: The Debris of a Legend." *HTR* 66 (1973): 141–45.

Ceresa-Gastaldo, Aldo. "Philon de Carpasia (saint)." In *DSpir* 12.1:1374–77. 1984.

Chadwick, Henry. "Florilegium." Trans. by Josef Engemann. In *RAC* 7: 1131–60. 1969.

Cohn, Leopold. "Die Philo-Handschriften in Oxford und Paris." *Phlgs* 51 [N.F. 5] (1892): 266–75.

―――. "Einteilung und Chronologie der Schriften Philos." *Phlgs, Supplementband* 7 (1899): 387–435. Separately published (with original pagination): Leipzig: Dieterich, 1899.

―――. Review of Karl Holl, *Die Sacra Parallela des Johannes Damascenus*. *PhWoch* 17 (1897): 456–63, 484–93.

Cohn, Leopold, Paul Wendland, and (for vol. 6) Siegfried Reiter, eds. *PCW*.

Colson, F. H., ed. and trans. *PLCL*, vol. 9. 1941.

Combefis, Francis, ed. and trans. *S. Maximi Confessoris, Graecorum theologi eximiique philosophi, operum tomus secundus*. Paris: Cramoisy, 1675.

Conybeare, Frederic C. Review of Paul Wendland, *Neu entdeckte Fragmente Philos*. *The Academy* 40 (July–December 1891): 482–83.

Cramer, John Anthony, ed. *Anecdota Graeca e codd. manuscriptis bibliothecarum Oxoniensium*. Vol. 4. Oxford: University Press, 1837.

―――, ed. *Catenae Graecorum patrum in Novum Testamentum*. Vol. 2: *Catenae in Evangelia S. Lucae et S. Joannis ad fidem codd. mss.* Vol. 7: *Catenae in Sancti Pauli epistolas ad Timotheum, Titum, Philemona et ad Hebraeos*. Oxford: University Press, 1841 and 1843. Reprinted: Hildesheim: Georg Olms, 1967.

Dain, A. "Le codex Hauniensis NKS 182." *REG* 71 (1958): 61–86 (résumé on 511 [unnumbered]).

Delling, Gerhard, and Malwine Maser. *Bibliographie zur jüdisch-*

*hellenistischen und intertestamentarischen Literatur 1900–*
*1970.* TU, vol. 106. 2d ed. Berlin: Akademie-Verlag, 1975.

Devreesse, Robert, ed. "Anciens commentateurs grecs de l'Octateuque."
*RB* 44 (1935): 166–91; 45 (1936): 201–20, 364–84.

————. "Chaînes exégétiques grecques." In *DBS* 1:1084–1233. 1928.

————, ed. *Les anciens commentateurs grecs de l'Octateuque et des Rois*
*(fragments tirés des chaînes).* Studi e testi, vol. 201. Vatican
City: Biblioteca Apostolica Vaticana, 1959.

Diels, Hermann, and Walther Kranz, eds. *Die Fragmente der Vorsokratiker.* 2
vols. 6th ed. Dublin and Zurich: Weidmann, 1951–52.

Dölger, Franz. *Der griechische Barlaam-Roman: Ein Werk des H. Johannes*
*von Damaskos.* Studia Patristica et Byzantina, vol. 1. Ettal:
Buch-Kunstverlag, 1953.

————. Reply to reviews. *ByzZ* 48 (1955): 215.

Ehrhard, Albert. "Zu den 'Sacra Parallela' des Johannes Damascenus und
dem Florilegium des 'Maximos.' " *ByzZ* 10 (1901): 394–415.

Elter, Anton. *Gnomica I: Sexti Pythagorici, Clitarchi, Evagrii Pontici senten-*
*tiae.* Leipzig: B. G. Teubner, 1892.

————. *Gnomica homoeomata.* 5 vols. Bonn: Carl Georgi, 1900–1904.

Elorduy, Eleuterio. *Ammonio Sakkas.* Vol. 1: *La doctrina de la creación y*
*del mal en Proclo y el Ps. Areopagita.* Estudios Onienses,
series 1, vol. 7. Burgos: Sociedad Internacional Francisco
Suarez, n.d. (1959).

Fabricius, Ioannes Albertus, and Gottlieb Christophorus Harles. *Bibliotheca*
*Graeca.* 12 vols. Hamburg: Carolus Ernestus Bohn, 1790–
1809.

Faulhaber, Michael. *Hohelied-, Proverbien- und Prediger-Catenen.* Theologische Studien der Leo-Gesellschaft, vol. 4. Vienna: Mayer,
1902.

————. "Katenen und Katenenforschung." *ByzZ* 18 (1909): 383–95.

Fedwick, Paul J. "The Citations of Basil of Caesarea in the Florilegium of the Pseudo-Antony Melissa." *OCP* 45 (1979): 32–44.

Feldman, Louis H. *Josephus and Modern Scholarship (1937–1980).* Berlin and New York: Walter de Gruyter, 1984.

Fischer, Hans, Georges Petit, Joachim Staedtke, Rudolf Steiger, and Heinrich Zoller. *Conrad Gessner 1516–1565: Universalgelehrter, Naturforscher, Arzt.* Zurich: Art. Institut Orell Füssli, 1967.

Fraser, P. M. *Ptolemaic Alexandria.* 3 vols. Oxford, 1972.

Frey, Jean-Baptiste, ed. *Corpus Inscriptionum Iudaicarum.* Vol. 2: *Asie–Afrique.* Vatican City: Pontificio Istituto di Archeologia Cristiana, 1952.

Früchtel, Ludwig. "Griechische Fragmente zu Philons Quaestiones in Genesin et in Exodum." *ZAW* 55 [N.F. 14] (1937): 108–15.

————. "Nachweisungen zu Fragmentsammlungen." *PhWoch* 56 (1936): 1439.

————. "Neue Quellennachweise zu Isidoros von Pelusion." *PhWoch* 58 (1938): 764–68.

————, ed. "Philonis Alexandrini fragmenta Graece servata." 1963. Manuscript.

————, trans. "Über die Vorsehung." In *Philon von Alexandria, Die Werke in deutscher Übersetzung*, vol. 7, edited by Willy Theiler, 267–382. Berlin: Walter de Gruyter, 1964.

————. "Zum Oxyrhynchos-Papyrus des Philon (Ox.-Pap. XI 1356)." *PhWoch* 58 (1938): 1437–39.

Gärtner, Hans. "Aphthonius." In *KP* 1:431. 1964.

Garitte, Gérard. Review of G. R. Woodward and H. Mattingly, eds. and trans., *St. John Damascene, Barlaam and Ioasaph.* *Mus* 81 (1968): 277.

Geffcken, Johannes, ed. *Die Oracula Sibyllina*. GCS, vol. 8. Leipzig: J. C. Hinrichs, 1902.

Gessner, Conrad, ed. *Ioannis Stobaei sententiae, ex thesauris Graecorum delectae . . . .* Zurich: Christopher Froschauer, 1543.

[———, ed.] *Ioannis Stobaei sententiae, ex thesauris Graecorum delectae . . . , Huic editioni accesserunt eiusdem Ioannis Stobaei eclogarum physicarum et ethicarum libri duo, Item loci communes sententiarum, collecti per Antonium & Maximum Monachos, atque ad Stobaei locos relati.* Orleans: Franciscus Fabrus, 1609.

[———, ed.] *Loci communes sacri et profani sententiarum omnis generis ex authoribus Graecis plus quam trecentis congestarum per Ioannem Stobaeum, et veteres in Graecia monachos Antonium & Maximum: à Conrado Gesnero Tigurino Latinitate donati, & nunc primùm in unum volumen Graecis ac Latinis è regione positis coniuncti.* Frankfurt: Andreas Wechel, 1581.

———, ed. *Sententiarum sive capitum, theologicorum praecipue, ex sacris & profanis libris, Tomi tres, per Antonium & Maximum monachos olim collecti . . . .* Zurich: Christopher Froschauer, 1546.

Ginguené, Pierre Louis. "Annius de Viterbe." In *Biographie universelle, ancienne et moderne* 2:223–26. Paris: Michaud Frères, 1811.

Goodenough, Erwin R. *The Politics of Philo Judaeus: Practice and Theory.* New Haven: Yale University Press, 1938.

Goodhart, Howard L., and Erwin R. Goodenough. *A General Bibliography of Philo Judaeus.* In *The Politics of Philo Judaeus: Practice and Theory*, by Erwin R. Goodenough, 124–321, 329–48 (indexes). New Haven: Yale University Press, 1938.

Graetz, H. *Geschichte der Juden von den ältesten Zeiten bis auf die Gegenwart.* 4th ed. Vol. 3: *Geschichte der Judäer von dem Tode Juda Makkabi's bis zum Untergange des judäischen Staates.* 2 pts. Leipzig: Oskar Leiner, 1888.

Grossmann, C. G. L. *De Iudaeorum disciplina arcani*. 2 pts. Leipzig: University of Leipzig, 1833–34.

————, ed. *Philonis Iudaei anecdoton Graecum de cherubinis ad Exod. 25, 18*. Leipzig: Friedrich Fleischer, 1856.

Guillaumont, Antoine and Claire. "Evagrius Ponticus." In *RAC* 6:1088–1107. 1966.

Hadas-Lebel, Mireille, ed. and trans. *De providentia I et II*. *PM*, vol. 35. 1973.

Hadot, Pierre. "Fürstenspiegel." Translated by Josef Engemann. In *RAC* 8:555–632. 1972.

Haelst, Joseph van. *Catalogue des papyrus littéraires juifs et chrétiens*. Paris: Publications de la Sorbonne, 1976.

Haidacher, Sebastian. "Chrysostomos-Fragmente im Maximos-Florilegium und in den Sacra Parallela." *ByzZ* 16 (1907): 168–201.

Harnack, Adolf. *Geschichte der altchristlichen Litteratur bis Eusebius*. Pt. 1: *Die Überlieferung und der Bestand*. 2 vols. Leipzig: J. C. Hinrichs, 1893.

Harris, J. Rendel, ed. *Fragments of Philo Judaeus*. Cambridge: University Press, 1886.

Hausrath, August, ed. *Corpus fabularum Aesopicarum*. Vol. 1, fasc. 1. Leipzig: B. G. Teubner, 1940.

————, ed. *Corpus fabularum Aesopicarum*. Vol. 1, fasc. 2. 2d ed. Edited by Herbert Hunger. Leipzig: B. G. Teubner, 1959.

————. "Phaedrus." In *PW* 19.2:1475–1505. 1938.

Heinrici, Georg. Review of Leopold Cohn and Paul Wendland, eds., *PCW*, vol. 1. *TLZ* 22 (1897): 211–15.

Henry, Patrick, III. "A Mirror for Justinian: The *Ekthesis* of Agapetus Diaconus." *GRBS* 8 (1967): 281–308.

Hense, Otto. "Bion bei Philon." *RhMus*, N.F. 47 (1892): 219–40.

Hercher, Rudolf, ed. *Epistolographi Graeci*. Paris: A. F. Didot, 1873.

Holl, Karl. *Die Sacra Parallela des Johannes Damascenus*. TU, vol. 16, pt. 1. Leipzig: J. C. Hinrichs, 1897.

————, ed. *Fragmente vornicänischer Kirchenväter aus den Sacra Parallela*. TU, vol. 20, pt. 2. Leipzig: J. C. Hinrichs, 1899.

Hombert, Marcel. "Bulletin papyrologique XXI (1943 à 1946)." *REG* 61 (1948): 213–90.

————. Review of Klara Stahlschmidt, "Eine unbekannte Schrift Philons von Alexandrien (oder eines ihm nahestehenden Verfassers)." *CE* 18 (1943): 306.

Junod, Eric. "Les fragments grecs transmis et édités sous le nom de Philon." In *Biblia patristica, Supplément: Philon d'Alexandrie*, edited by Jean Allenbach, André Benoit, Daniel A. Bertrand, Annie Hanriot-Coustet, Eric Junod, Pierre Maraval, André Pautler, and Pierre Prigent, 9–15. Paris: Éditions du Centre National de la Recherche Scientifique, 1982.

Kantorowicz, Ernst H. "Deus per naturam, Deus per gratiam." *HTR* 45 (1952): 253–77.

Karo, Georg, and Johannes Lietzmann. "Catenarum Graecarum catalogus." *Nachrichten von der Königlichen Gesellschaft der Wissenschaften zu Göttingen*, Philologisch-historische Klasse (1902): 1–66, 299–350, 559–620.

Krumbacher, Karl. *Geschichte der byzantinischen Litteratur*. 2d ed. Munich: C. H. Beck, 1897. (Pp. 37–218 by Albert Ehrhard; pp. 911–1067 by H. Gelzer.)

Lequien, Michael, ed. and trans. *Sancti Patris nostri Joannis Damasceni . . . opera omnia quae exstant . . . .* Vol. 2. Paris: Delespine, 1712.

Lewy, Hans. "Neue Philontexte in der Überarbeitung des Ambrosius, Mit einem Anhang: Neu gefundene griechische Philonfragmente." *Sitzungsberichte der Preussischen Akademie der Wissenschaften*, Philosophisch-historische Klasse (1932): 23–84. Separately published (with original pagination): Berlin: Verlag der Akademie der Wissenschaften, 1932.

—, ed. *The Pseudo-Philonic "De Jona."* Pt. 1: *The Armenian Text with a Critical Introduction.* Studies and Documents, vol. 7. London: Christophers, 1936.

Loofs, Friedrich. *Studien über die dem Johannes von Damaskus zugeschriebenen Parallelen.* Halle: Max Niemeyer, 1892.

Mai, Angelo, ed. *Classicorum auctorum e Vaticanis codicibus editorum.* Vol. 4. Rome: Typis Vaticanis, 1831.

—, ed. *Philo et Virgilii interpretes.* Milan: Regiis Typis, 1818.

—, ed. Φίλωνος τοῦ Ἰουδαίου περὶ ἀρετῆς καὶ τῶν ταύτης μορίων, *Philonis Iudaei de virtute eiusque partibus.* Milan: Regiis Typis, 1816. (This is the initial edition of this work.)

—, ed. Πορφυρίου φιλοσόφου πρὸς Μαρκέλλαν, *Porphyrii philosophi ad Marcellam.* Milan: Regiis Typis, 1816. (This is the subsequent edition of this work.)

—, ed. *Scriptorum veterum nova collectio e Vaticanis codicibus edita.* Vol. 7. Rome: Typis Vaticanis, 1833.

Mangey, Thomas, ed. and trans. Φίλωνος τοῦ Ἰουδαίου τὰ εὑρισκόμενα ἄπαντα, *Philonis Judaei opera quae reperiri potuerunt omnia.* 2 vols. London: William Bowyer, 1742.

Marcus, Ralph. "An Armenian-Greek Index to Philo's *Quaestiones* and *De Vita Contemplativa*." *JAOS* 53 (1933): 251–82.

—, ed. and trans. *Philo, Supplement.* Vol. 1: *Questions and Answers on Genesis.* Vol. 2: *Questions and Answers on Exodus.* PLCL. 1953.

Marouzeau, J., and Juliette Ernst. *L'Année Philologique* 29 (1959): 138, 291.

Martini, Aemidius, and Dominicus Bassi. *Catalogus codicum Graecorum bibliothecae Ambrosianae*. 2 vols. Milan: U. Hoepli, 1906.

Massebieau, L. "Le classement des oeuvres de Philon." *Bibliothèque de l'École des Hautes Études*, Section des Sciences religieuses 1 (1889): 1–91. Separately published (with original pagination): Paris: Ernest Leroux, 1889.

Mayer, Günter. *Index Philoneus*. Berlin and New York: Walter de Gruyter, 1974.

Mercier, Charles, and Françoise Petit, eds. and trans. *Quaestiones et solutiones in Genesim III–IV–V–VI e versione Armeniaca, Complément de l'ancienne version latine*. PM, vol. 34B. 1984.

Metzger, Bruce M. *The Text of the New Testament: Its Transmission, Corruption, and Restoration*. 2d ed. New York and Oxford: Oxford University Press, 1968.

Meursius, Ioannes, ed. *Eusebii, Polychronii, Pselli, in Canticum Canticorum Expositiones Graecè [sic]*. Leiden: Ex Officinâ Elzeviriana, 1617.

Montefiore, C. G. "Florilegium Philonis." *JQR* 7 (1894): 481–545.

Mras, Karl, ed. *Eusebius Werke*. Vol. 8: *Praeparatio Evangelica*. 2 pts. GCS, vol. 43, pts. 1–2. Berlin: Akademie-Verlag, 1954–56.

Murphy, Frederick J. "God in Pseudo-Philo." *JSJ* 19 (1988): 1–18.

Nanni, Giovanni [Ioannes Annius]. *Commentaria fratris Ioannis Annii Viterbensis ordinis praedicatorum Theologiae professoris super opera diuersorum auctorum de Antiquitatibus loquentium*. Rome: Eucharius Silber, 1498.

Nautin, Pierre, with the collaboration of Louis Doutreleau, eds. and trans. *Didyme l'Aveugle, Sur la Genèse*. Vol. 1. SC, vol. 233. 1976.

Néroutsos-Bey, Tassos Demetrios. *L'ancienne Alexandrie*. Paris: Ernest Leroux, 1888.

Nicephorus Hieromonachos Theotokes, ed. Σειρὰ ἑνὸς καὶ πεντήκοντα ὑπομνηματιστῶν εἰς τὴν ᾽Οκτάτευχον καὶ τὰ τῶν Βασιλείων . . . . (= *Catena Lipsiensis.*) 2 vols. Leipzig: Breitkopf, 1772–73.

Norden, Eduard. *Das Genesiszitat in der Schrift vom Erhabenen. Abhandlungen der Deutschen Akademie der Wissenschaften zu Berlin*, Klasse für Sprachen, Literatur und Kunst, Jahrgang 1954, no. 1 (published 1955). Reprinted in *Kleine Schriften zum klassischen Altertum*, 286–313. Berlin: Walter de Gruyter, 1966.

Pack, Roger A. *The Greek and Latin Literary Texts from Greco-Roman Egypt.* 2d ed. Ann Arbor: The University of Michigan Press, 1965.

Paramelle, Joseph, with the collaboration of Enzo Lucchesi, eds. and trans. *Philon d'Alexandrie, Questions sur la Genèse II 1–7.* With an arithmological interpretation by Jacques Sesiano. Cahiers d'Orientalisme, vol. 3. Geneva: Patrick Cramer, 1984.

Perrot, Charles, and Pierre-Maurice Bogaert, with the collaboration of Daniel J. Harrington, eds. and trans. *Pseudo-Philon, Les Antiquités Bibliques.* Vol. 2: *Introduction littéraire, commentaire et index.* SC, vol. 230. 1976.

Petit, Françoise, ed. *Catenae Graecae in Genesim et in Exodum.* Vol. 1: *Catena Sinaitica.* Corpus Christianorum, Series Graeca, vol. 2. Turnhout: Brepols, Leuven University Press, 1977.

————. "En marge de l'édition des fragments de Philon (Questions sur la Genèse et l'Exode): Les florilèges damascéniens." In *Studia Patristica*, vol. 15, pt. 1, edited by Elizabeth A. Livingstone, 20–25. TU, vol. 128. Berlin: Akademie-Verlag, 1984.

————, ed. *L'ancienne version latine des Questions sur la Genèse de Philon d'Alexandrie.* Vol. 1: *Édition critique.* Vol. 2: *Commentaire.* TU, vols. 113–14. Berlin: Akademie-Verlag, 1973.

————, ed. "Les fragments grecs du livre VI des Questions sur la Genèse de Philon d'Alexandrie." *Mus* 84 (1971): 93–150.

————, ed. *Quaestiones in Genesim et in Exodum: Fragmenta Graeca*. PM, vol. 33. 1978.

————. Review of Charles Mercier, ed. and trans., *Quaestiones in Genesim I et II e versione Armeniaca*. *Mus* 92 (1979): 403–4.

Petrosean, Matat'ia [Bedrossian, Matthias]. *New Dictionary Armenian-English*. Venice: S. Lazarus Armenian Academy, 1875–79. Reprinted: Beirut: Librairie du Liban, n.d.

Pitra, Jean-Baptiste, ed. *Analecta sacra spicilegio Solesmensi parata*. Vol. 2: *Patres antenicaeni*. Typis Tusculanis, 1884.

Powitz, Gerhardt. "Textus cum commento." *Codices manuscripti* 5 (1979): 80–89.

Praechter, Karl. "Der Roman Barlaam und Joasaph in seinem Verhältnis zu Agapets Königsspiegel." *ByzZ* 2 (1893): 444–60.

————. Review of Antonio Bellomo, *Agapeto diacono e la sua scheda regia*. *ByzZ* 17 (1908): 152–64.

Preuschen, Erwin, ed. *Origenes Werke*. Vol. 4: *Der Johanneskommentar*. GCS, vol. 10. Leipzig: J. C. Hinrichs, 1903.

Radice, Roberto. *Filone di Alessandria: Bibliografia generale 1937–1982*. Elenchos, vol. 8. Naples: Bibliopolis, 1983.

Raoul-Rochette, Désiré. Review of Angelo Mai, ed., Φίλωνος τοῦ Ἰουδαίου περὶ ἀρετῆς καὶ τῶν ταύτης μορίων, *Philonis Iudaei de virtute eiusque partibus*. *Journal des Savans [sic]* (1817): 227–38.

Review of Angelo Mai, ed., *Philonis Judaei de Cophini festo et de colendis parentibus cum brevi scripto de Jona*. *Leipziger Literatur-Zeitung [sic]*, no. 276 (November 3, 1818): 2201–4.

Richard, Marcel. "Florilèges spirituels, III. Florilèges grecs." In *DSpir* 5: 475–512. 1964.

————. "Hippolyte de Rome (saint)." In *DSpir* 7.1:531–71. 1969.

————. "Les »Parallela« de saint Jean Damascène." In *Actes du XIIe Congrès International d'Études byzantines (Ochride, 10–16 septembre 1961)* 2:485–89. Belgrade: Comité Yougoslave des Études byzantines, 1963.

————. *Opera minora*. Edited by E. Dekkers, M. Geerard, A. van Roey, and G. Verbeke. 3 vols. Turnhout: Brepols, Leuven University Press, 1976–77.

Richter, C. E., ed. *Philonis Iudaei opera omnia*. 8 vols. Leipzig: E. B. Schwickert, 1828–30.

————, ed. *Philonis Iudaei opera omnia*. 8 vols. Leipzig: Carl Tauchnitz, 1851–53.

————, ed. *Philonis Iudaei opera omnia*. 8 vols. Leipzig: Otto Holtze, 1880–93.

Rose, Valentin, ed. *Aristoteles pseudepigraphus*. Leipzig: B. G. Teubner, 1863.

Rostagni, Augusto, ed. and trans. *Anonimo, Del sublime*. Milan: Istituto Editoriale Italiano, 1947.

Royse, James R. "Further Greek Fragments of Philo's *Quaestiones*." In *Nourished with Peace: Studies in Hellenistic Judaism in Memory of Samuel Sandmel*, edited by Frederick E. Greenspahn, Earle Hilgert, and Burton L. Mack, 143–53. Chico: Scholars Press, 1984.

————. "Philo and the Immortality of the Race." *JSJ* 11 (1980): 33–37.

————. "The Original Structure of Philo's *Quaestiones*." *SP* 4 (1976–77): 41–78.

————. "The Oxyrhynchus Papyrus of Philo." *BASP* 17 (1980): 155–65.

————. "Two Problems in Philo's *Quaestiones*." *REA*, n.s. 16 (1982): 81–85.

Runia, David T. "Philo's *De aeternitate mundi*: The Problem of its Interpretation." *VC* 35 (1981): 105–51.

Sandbach, F. H., ed. *Plutarchi moralia.* Vol. 7. Leipzig: B. G. Teubner, 1967.

————, ed. and trans. *Plutarch's Moralia.* Vol. 15: *Fragments.* LCL, 1969.

Sbordone, Francesco. "Recensioni retoriche delle favole esopiane." *Rivista indo-greco-italica* 16 (1932), fasc. iii–iv, pp. 35–68 (= pp. 141–74 of the entire volume).

Schmidt, Ernst A., trans. *Aristoteles, Über die Tugend. Aristoteles Werke in deutscher Übersetzung,* edited by Ernst Grumach, vol. 18: *Opuscula,* pt. 1. Berlin: Akademie-Verlag, 1965.

Schmitt, Charles B. "Pseudo-Aristotle in the Latin Middle Ages." In *Pseudo-Aristotle in the Middle Ages: The "Theology" and other Texts,* edited by Jill Kraye, W. F. Ryan, and C. B. Schmitt, 3–14. Warburg Institute Surveys and Texts, edited by W. F. Ryan and C. B. Schmitt, vol. 11. London: The Warburg Institute, University of London, 1986.

Schmitt, Rüdiger. "Die Erforschung des Klassisch-Armenischen seit Meillet (1936)." *Kratylos* 17 (1972): 1–68.

Schürer, Emil. *Geschichte des jüdischen Volkes im Zeitalter Jesu Christi.* 4th ed. (Vol. 1 is 3d and 4th ed.) 3 vols. Leipzig: J. C. Hinrichs, 1901–9.

————. Review of J. Rendel Harris, ed., *Fragments of Philo Judaeus. TLZ* 11 (1886): 481–83.

————. *The History of the Jewish People in the Age of Jesus Christ (175 B.C.—A.D. 135).* A new English version, revised and edited by Geza Vermes, Fergus Millar, and (for vol. 3) Martin Goodman; literary editor, Pamela Vermes; organizing editor, Matthew Black. 3 vols. (Vol. 3 consists of 2 pts.) Edinburgh: T. & T. Clark, 1973–87. (Vol. 3, pt. 2, par. 34, pp. 809–89, "The Jewish Philosopher Philo," is by Jenny Morris.)

Semenov, V., ed. *Melissa.* Edited and with an introduction by Dmitrij Tschizhewskij. Slavische Propyläen, vol. 7. Munich: Wilhelm

Fink, 1968. (Reprint of the 1894 edition, which I have not seen.)

Ševčenko, Ihor. "A Neglected Byzantine Source of Muscovite Political Ideology." In *Harvard Slavic Studies* 2:141–79. Cambridge: Harvard University Press, 1954.

Siegert, Folker, trans. *Drei hellenistisch-jüdische Predigten, Ps.-Philon, "Über Jona", "Über Simson", und "Über die Gottesbezeichnung 'wohltätig verzehrendes Feuer' ", I: Übersetzung aus dem Armenischen und sprachliche Erläuterungen.* WUNT, vol. 20. 1980.

———, ed. and trans. *Philon von Alexandrien, Über die Gottesbezeichnung "wohltätig verzehrendes Feuer" ("De Deo"): Rückübersetzung des Fragments aus dem Armenischen, deutsche Übersetzung und Kommentar.* WUNT, vol. 46. 1988.

Sjöberg, Erik, and Gustav Stählin. "ὀργή D III." In *TWNT* 5 (1954): 418.

Speranskij, Mikhail, ed. *Serbische und bulgarische Florilegien (Pchele) aus dem 13.–15. Jahrhundert.* Edited and with an introduction by Dmitrij Tschizhewskij. Slavische Propyläen, vol. 28. Munich: Wilhelm Fink, 1970. (Partial reprint of the 1904 edition, which I have not seen.)

Speyer, Wolfgang. *Die literarische Fälschung im heidnischen und christlichen Altertum: Ein Versuch ihrer Deutung.* Handbuch der Altertumswissenschaft, Erste Abteilung, Zweiter Teil. Munich: C. H. Beck, 1971.

Stählin, Otto, and Ludwig Früchtel, eds. (prepared for publication by Ursula Treu). *Clemens Alexandrinus.* Vol. 3: *Stromata Buch VII und VIII, Excerpta ex Theodoto, Eclogae propheticae, Quis dives salvetur, Fragmente.* GCS, vol. 52, pt. 3. 2d ed. Berlin: Akademie-Verlag, 1970.

Stahlschmidt, Klara. "Eine unbekannte Schrift Philons von Alexandrien (oder eines ihm nahestehenden Verfassers)." *Aeg* 22 (1942): 161–76.

Stern, Menahem, ed. and trans. *Greek and Latin Authors on Jews and Juda-*

*ism*. Vol. 1: *From Herodotus to Plutarch*. Jerusalem: The Israel Academy of Sciences and Humanities, 1974.

Sternbach, Leo, ed. *Gnomologium Parisinum ineditum*. Cracow: Sumptibus Academiae Litterarum, 1893.

———, ed. *Gnomologium Vaticanum e codice Vaticano Graeco 743*. Foreword by Otto Luschnat. Texte und Kommentare, vol. 2. Berlin: Walter de Gruyter, 1963. (Reprint of articles in *WS* 9 [1887]: 175–206; 10 [1888]: 1–49, 211–60; 11 [1889]: 43–64, 192–242.)

———, ed. *Photii patriarchae opusculum paraeneticum, Appendix gnomica, Excerpta Parisina*. Cracow: Sumptibus Academiae Litterarum, 1893.

Susemihl, Franz, ed. *[Aristotelis Ethica Eudemia,] Eudemi Rhodii Ethica, adiecto de virtutibus et vitiis libello*. Leipzig: B. G. Teubner, 1884.

Tcherikover, Victor A., Alexander Fuks, and (for vol. 3) Menahem Stern, eds., (and vol. 3) with an epigraphical contribution by David M. Lewis. *Corpus papyrorum Judaicarum*. 3 vols. Cambridge: Harvard University Press for the Magnes Press, Hebrew University, 1957–64.

Terian, Abraham. "A Critical Introduction to Philo's Dialogues." In *Aufstieg und Niedergang der römischen Welt*, pt. 2: *Principat*, vol. 21, pt. 1, edited by Wolfgang Haase, 272–94. Berlin and New York: Walter de Gruyter, 1984.

———. "A Philonic Fragment on the Decad." In *Nourished with Peace: Studies in Hellenistic Judaism in Memory of Samuel Sandmel*, edited by Frederick E. Greenspahn, Earle Hilgert, and Burton L. Mack, 173–82. Chico: Scholars Press, 1984.

———, ed. and trans. *Philonis Alexandrini de animalibus: The Armenian Text with an Introduction, Translation, and Commentary*. Studies in Hellenistic Judaism, Supplements to *SP*, vol. 1. Chico: Scholars Press, 1981.

Tischendorf, Constantin, ed. *Anecdota sacra et profana*. Leipzig: Emilius
    Graul, 1855. 2d ed., Leipzig: Hermann Fries, 1861.

————, ed. *Philonea, inedita altera, altera nunc demum recte ex vetere scrip-
    tura eruta*. Leipzig: Giesecke et Devrient, 1868.

Uthemann, Karl-Heinz, ed. *Anastasii Sinaitae opera: Viae dux*. Corpus
    Christianorum, Series Graeca, vol. 8. Turnhout: Brepols,
    Leuven University Press, 1981.

Wachsmuth, Curt, ed. "De gnomologio Palatino inedito." In *Satura philo-
    loga Hermanno Sauppio obtulit amicorum conlegarum decas*,
    7–42. Berlin: Weidmann, 1879.

————. *Studien zu den griechischen Florilegien*. Berlin: Weidmann, 1882.

Wendland, Paul. *Neu entdeckte Fragmente Philos: Nebst einer Untersuchung
    über die ursprüngliche Gestalt der Schrift De sacrificiis Abelis
    et Caini*. Berlin: Georg Reimer, 1891.

————. *Philos Schrift über die Vorsehung: Ein Beitrag zur Geschichte der
    nacharistotelischen Philosophie*. Berlin: R. Gaertner, 1892.

————. Review of Karl Holl, *Die Sacra Parallela des Johannes Damascenus*.
    *TLZ* 22 (1897): 9–14.

————. "Zu Krumbachers Geschichte der Byzantinischen Litteratur[2] S.
    600." *ByzZ* 7 (1898): 166–68.

Winston, David, trans. *The Wisdom of Solomon*. Anchor Bible, vol. 43.
    Garden City, New York: Doubleday, 1979.

Woodward, G. R., and H. Mattingly, eds. and trans. *St. John Damascene,
    Barlaam and Ioasaph*. LCL, 1967. (Reprint of the 1914
    edition with an introduction by D. M. Lang.)

Wyttenbach, Daniel, ed. Πλουτάρχου τοῦ Χαιρωνέως τὰ ἠθικά, *Plutarchi
    Chaeronensis moralia*. Vol. 5, pt. 2. Oxford: Clarendon
    Press, 1800.

Zahn, Theodor, ed. *Acta Joannis*. Erlangen: Andreas Deichert, 1880.

————. *Forschungen zur Geschichte des neutestamentlichen Kanons und der altkirchlichen Literatur*. Pt. 2: *Der Evangeliencommentar des Theophilus von Antiochien*. Pt. 3: *Supplementum Clementinum*. Erlangen: Andreas Deichert, 1883–84.

Ziegler, Konrat. "Das Genesiscitat in der Schrift ΠΕΡΙ ΥΨΟΥΣ." *He* 50 (1915): 572–603.

# INDEX OF REFERENCES

Citations which occur on a page only within the footnotes are noted with an 'n.' Apart from section E below, citations in the Index locorum are not included here.

## A. Bible

## D.  Fragmenta spuria

## E. Other Ancient Writers

## F. Manuscripts

Included are descriptions or general comments, but not mere citations.

# ARBEITEN ZUR LITERATUR UND GESCHICHTE DES HELLENISTISCHEN JUDENTUMS

## HERAUSGEGEBEN VON
## K.H. RENGSTORF

1. SCHRECKENBERG, H. *Bibliographie zu Flavius Josephus.* 1968. ISBN 90 04 00115 8
3. BAER, R.A. *Philo's Use of the Categories Male and Female.* 1970. ISBN 90 04 00117 4
4. WILLIAMSON, R. *Philo and the Epistle to the Herbrews.* 1970. ISBN 90 04 00118 2
5. SCHRECKENBERG, H. *Die Flavius-Josephus-Tradition in Antike und Mittelalter.* 1972. ISBN 90 04 03418 8
6. BROCK, S.P.; FRITSCH, C.T.; JELLICOE, S. (eds.). *A Classified Bibliography of the Septuagint.* 1973. ISBN 90 04 03596 6
7. SCHÜPPHAUS, J. *Die Psalmen Salomos.* Ein Zeugnis Jerusalemer Theologie und Frömmigkeit in der Mitte des vorchristlichen Jahrhunderts. 1977. ISBN 90 04 04813 8
8. OPPENHEIMER, A. *The Hellenistic-Roman Period.* Transl. from the Hebrew by I.H. Levine 1977. ISBN 90 04 04764 6
9. LUCCHESI, E. *L'usage de Philon dans l'Œuvre exégétique de Saint Ambroise.* Une ,,Quellenforschung" relative aux Commentaires d'Ambroise sur la Genèse. 1977. ISBN 90 04 04898 7
10. SCHRECKENBERG, H. *Rezeptionsgeschichtliche und textkritische Untersuchungen zu Flavius Josephus.* 1977. ISBN 90 04 05263 1
11. NIKIPROWETZKY, V. *Le commentaire de l'écriture chez Philon d'Alexandrie.* Son caractère et sa portée. Observations philologiques. 1977. ISBN 90 04 04797 2
12. DEUTSCH, G.N. *Iconographie de l'illustration de Flavius Josèphe au temps de Jean Fouquet.* 1986. ISBN 90 04 07121 0
13. NORDHEIM, E. VON. *Die Lehre der Alten.* I. Das Testament als Literaturgattung im Judentum der hellenistisch-römischen Zeit. 1980. ISBN 90 04 06053 7
14. SCHRECKENBERG, H. *Bibliographie zu Flavius Josephus.* Supplementband mit Gesamtregister. 1979. ISBN 90 04 05968 7
15. CAZEAUX, J. *La trame et la chaîne.* (I) Ou les structures littéraires et l'exégèse dans cinq des traités de Philon d'Alexandrie. 1983. ISBN 90 04 06582 2
16. MONTES PERAL, L.A. *Akataleptos Theos.* Der unfassbare Gott. 1987. ISBN 90 04 06928 3
17. SCHALIT, A. *Untersuchungen zur Assumptio Mosis.* 1989. ISBN 90 04 08120 8
18. NORDHEIM, E. VON. *Die Lehre der Altern.* II. Das Testament als Literaturgattung im Alten Testament und im Alten Vorderen Orient. 1985. ISBN 90 04 07313 2
19. VILLALBA I VARNEDA, P. *The Historical Method of Flavius Josephus.* 1986. ISBN 90 04 07616 6
20. CAZEAUX, J. *La trame et la chaîne.* (II). Le cycle de Noé dans Philon d'Alexandrie. 1989. ISBN 90 04 09179 3
21. AALEN, S. *Heilsverlangen und Heilsverwirklichung.* Studien zur Erwartung des Heils in der apokalyptischen Literatur des antiken Judentums und im ältesten Christentum. Mit einem Geleitwort von E. Baasland, Hrsg. von K.H. Rengstorf. 1990. ISBN 90 04 09257 9
22. ROYSE, J.R. *The Spurious Texts of Philo of Alexandria.* A Study of Textual Transmission and Corruption with Indexes to the Major Collections of Greek Fragments. ISBN 90 04 09511 X